Grant Writing in Higher Education

Related Titles of Interest

Successful College Teaching: Problem-Solving Strategies of Distinguished Professors
Sharon A. Baiocco and Jamie N. DeWaters
ISBN: 0-205-26654-1

Faculty Work and Public Trust: Restoring the Value of Teaching and Public Service in American Academic Life
James S. Fairweather
ISBN: 0-205-17948-7

Emblems of Quality in Higher Education: Developing and Sustaining High-Quality Programs
Jennifer Grant Haworth and Clifton F. Conrad
ISBN: 0-205-19546-6

Writing for Professional Publication: Keys to Academic and Business Success
Kenneth T. Henson
ISBN: 0-205-28313-6

Learner-Centered Assessment on College Campuses: Shifting the Focus from Teaching to Learning
Mary E. Huba and Jann E. Freed
ISBN: 0-205-28738-7

Revitalizing General Education in a Time of Scarcity: A Navigational Chart for Administrators and Faculty
Sandra L. Kanter, Zelda F. Gamson, and Howard B. London
ISBN: 0-205-26257-0

The Adjunct Professor's Guide to Success: Surviving and Thriving in the College Classroom
Richard E. Lyons, Marcella L. Kysilka, and George E. Pawlas
ISBN: 0-205-28774-3

Teaching College in an Age of Accountability
Richard E. Lyons, Meggin McIntosh, and Marcella L. Kysilka
ISBN: 0-205-35315-0

An Introduction to Interactive Multimedia
Stephen J. Misovich, Jerome Katrichis, David Demers, and William B. Sanders
ISBN: 0-205-34373-2

Teaching Tips for College and University Instructors: A Practical Guide
David Royse
ISBN: 0-205-29839-7

Creating Learning-Centered Courses for the World Wide Web
William B. Sanders
ISBN: 0-205-31513-5

Designing and Teaching an On-Line Course: Spinning Your Web Classroom
Heidi Schweizer
ISBN: 0-205-30321-8

Leadership in Continuing and Distance Education in Higher Education
Cynthia C. Jones Shoemaker
ISBN: 0-205-26823-4

Shaping the College Curriculum: Academic Plans in Action
Joan S. Stark and Lisa R. Lattuca
ISBN: 0-205-16706-3

The Effective, Efficient Professor: Teaching Scholarship and Service
Phillip C. Wankat
ISBN: 0-205-33711-2

For further information on these and other related titles, contact:
College Division
ALLYN AND BACON
75 Arlington Street, Suite 300
Boston, MA 02116
www.ablongman.com

Grant Writing in Higher Education

A Step-by-Step Guide

Kenneth T. Henson

The Citadel

Boston • New York • San Francisco
Mexico City • Montreal • Toronto • London • Madrid • Munich • Paris
Hong Kong • Singapore • Tokyo • Cape Town • Sydney

This book is dedicated to my wife, Sharon,
the recipient of my most important proposal.

Executive Editor and Publisher: *Steve Dragin*
Senior Editorial Assistant: *Barbara Strickland*
Marketing Manager: *Tara Whorf*
Editorial-Production Administrator: *Annette Joseph*
Editorial-Production Service: *Holly Crawford*
Composition Buyer: *Linda Cox*
Electronic Composition: *Publishers' Design and Production Services, Inc.*
Manufacturing Buyer: *Andrew Turso*
Cover Administrator: *Kristina Mose-Libon*
Cover Designer: *Joel Gendron*

For related titles and support materials, visit our online catalog at
www.ablongman.com

Between the time Website information is gathered and then published, it is not
unusual for some sites to have closed. Also, the transcription of URLs can result in
typographical errors. The publisher would appreciate notification where these
errors occur so that they may be corrected in subsequent editions.

Library of Congress Cataloging-in-Publication Data

Henson, Kenneth T.
    Grant writing in higher education: a step-by-step guide / Kenneth T. Henson.
      p. cm.
    Includes bibliographical references and index.
    ISBN 0-205-38919-8
    1. Proposal writing in education—Handbooks, manuals, etc. 2. Proposal
writing for grants—Handbooks, manuals, etc. 3. Education—Research grants—
Handbooks, manuals, etc. I. Title.

LC241 .H46 2004
379.1'2—dc21
        2002038392

Printed in the United States of America

10 9 8 7 6 5 4 3 2 1   08 07 06 05 04 03

Contents

Preface

Grant Writing in Higher Education: A Step-by-Step Guide is written as a practical guide to help novice and experienced grant writers develop grant proposals that will be funded. Because the focus is narrow and clear, this book uses a straightforward writing style, avoiding unnecessary jargon and complex sentences and paragraphs—structures that uninformed and misinformed writers sometimes mistakenly consider to be reflections of scholarship.

Because attitudes invariably shape behavior, this book begins by identifying several attitudes that prevent grant writers from producing highly desirable and fundable proposals. Because these attitudes are commonly held misconceptions, they are labeled "the myths of grant writing." Each myth has been identified and addressed because it is a major barrier to serious grant writers. While some attitudes prevent the production of successful proposals, other attitudes clearly impact positively, moving proposals toward acceptance. These positive attitudes will also be identified.

Many, perhaps even the vast majority of books and workshops given to help grant writers, are delivered at an abstract level. At best, such books and workshops leave the participants and readers with some general ability to talk intelligently about grant writing but unable to actually prepare a fundable grant proposal. At worst, the all-too-familiar general approach leaves would-be successful grant writers bewildered and confused. To make sure that you finish this book with a clear idea of how to prepare a successful proposal, this book has a section that describes the parts of a proposal. Because a leading cause of rejection is poorly prepared budgets, this section will contain a separate segment on preparing budgets. Here, you will learn how to prepare budgets that will impress the reviewer and also how to test your budget to ensure that it is reasonable and sound.

Grant opportunities exist because individuals, institutions, and agencies need help meeting their goals. This means that to be a successful grant writer you must first grasp a clear understanding of each potential funder's goals, get a clear understanding of your own unique abilities to deliver these goals, and convince the funder that you will do a better job of meeting these goals for the funder than any of the many other proposal writers would do.

Successful grant writing requires a major shift in perspective. This book has a section designed to help you match your own reasons for writing grant proposals with the expectations of the potential funder. Here, you will be guided to develop a list of your own unique strengths, the strengths of your company or institution, and the strengths of your particular geographic region. With these in hand, you will learn how to carefully craft a proposal that will effectively convince the funder that, indeed, you will deliver the best service for the particular job.

Most people find that words alone fall short of preparing them to write a superior grant proposal. For most struggling grant writers, the most helpful learning device is a well-written, sample proposal with a clear explanation of the proposal's strengths. Some grant-writing books offer theoretical grants as prototypes or blueprints. No doubt, these help clarify the readers' understanding of what pieces a good proposal should contain and how these pieces fit together, but this book goes a step further and provides several actual proposals that have been funded for a few thousand dollars to over a million dollars each. Because the author wrote each of these successful proposals, he is able to point to the unique strengths of each proposal and identify the reasons that the particular proposal was selected for funding above all of the competition.

Successful grant writers know that for a proposal to succeed, it must be submitted not as a stand-alone proposal but as a package. This book identifies the essentials in a proposal package and explains how to develop each segment.

Writing style is a strong quality affecting grant acceptance and rejection. This book explains how to develop a style that will facilitate acceptance of your proposals. Furthermore, the writing style used throughout this book models this style.

A few years ago, the editor of a leading journal was giving a workshop on writing for publication. When he arrived at the part of the workshop that dealt with topics, a participant asked, "How can I find a good topic?" In his own words, the presenter repeated his response to that question. "You don't need a lot of topics. All you need is just one good topic." With a worried look on her face, a small, quiet lady asked, "But what if you don't have one good idea for a topic?" Obviously, that participant understood that there is little comfort in knowing that only one good topical idea is required if you don't have even one good idea. This book has a section on selecting a topic. Here you will learn the qualities of a good topic, and you will be given guidance in finding good topics in your field.

Once you have found a good topic, crafted a good proposal, and developed an auxiliary package, it is time to find a funder. The technology chapter directs readers to the best sources available on the Internet for locating funding agencies.

Highly successful grant writers do not use a one-shot, piecemeal approach. Instead, they develop an ongoing, lifelong grant-writing program. When a proposal is funded, they immediately begin working to ensure that, if the opportunity to submit it for future refunding arises, they are standing ready with a state-of-the-art revision ready to submit. This is just one technique they use to ensure refunding; they also establish a track record of the success attained through this proposal. This book provides detailed help for building a personal writing program that will ensure refunding of current proposals and successful funding of future proposals.

Because of the unprecedented pressure on educators at all levels to improve their teaching, a section is included to help you learn how to use your publications and grants to improve your teaching.

I want to thank all of the dedicated middle-level teachers and those educators who told their stories through the case studies in this book.

1

A Matter of Attitude

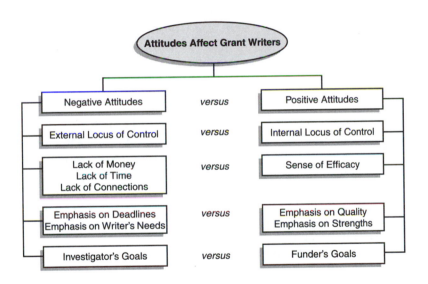

Grant writing is about power. We write grants because they empower us to do things we otherwise could not do. Some of us write grants to empower us to help others. Others of us write grants to get the power to travel; some of us write grants to further our expertise or our education, thus eventually empowering us to earn much more money.

A serious, mature student who was within weeks of receiving a final degree made an appointment with his advisor simply to ask the question, "How should I choose one job opportunity over another?" The wise professor replied, "Accept the position that will afford you the most opportunities to do the things you want to do."

Most of us have learned the hard way that money is important, especially if you don't have a lot of it. Grant writing is a surefire way to get money. Even more important, by planning and managing our grant writing, we can earn the power to do what we want to do, perhaps not all the time, but, for sure, much of the time.

Locus of Control

Becoming a highly successful grant writer is a multidimensional process that requires knowledge, skills, and hard work. The good news is that this goal is within everybody's reach, and the knowledge required to achieve the level of success that *you* wish to achieve is within the covers of this book. But the recipe for success is under lock and key. The key to the mastery of the necessary knowledge and skills is in your head. Put simply, it is your determination and willingness, *not* your ability but your *willingness* to cast away certain attitudes and reel in other attitudes.

Psychologists call this *locus of control*. The most basic and yet most important attitude to success in any endeavor is your belief in yourself. You either have the belief that you can control most of the events in your life *(internal locus of control)* or you believe that most of the events in your life are controlled by external forces that are beyond your control *(external locus of control)*. Success in any field requires an internal locus of control, which includes a sense of efficacy ("I am in charge, I can learn to do anything as well as anyone can, and I can achieve at any level that I am willing to strive for"). With this attitude, becoming a highly successful grant writer is a piece of cake. If, however, you have some reservations about your ability to do this, it is time to get a grip on it. The following attitudes can and in all likelihood will make the difference between a would-be successful grant writer and a highly successful grant writer. You must first cast away the myths that defeat many otherwise capable grant writers.

Now check your own locus of control. Is it external? Do you spend most of your life reacting to the actions of others or blaming others for the conditions that be-

fall you? Or is your locus of control internal? Are you a proactive, take-charge sort of person? Do you believe you can succeed at grant writing at the level you choose to succeed?

Grant-Writing Myths

Myths are superstitions, and like all superstitions, they have their roots in ignorance. Myths have the power to misguide and limit the success of otherwise intelligent, professional people. Following are some commonly held myths about grant writing that limit and inhibit the success of many professionals. Know these myths and steer clear of them and those who espouse them.

Availability of Money

Myth Number One: There is no money available.   At any time in history, there are events to which one can point and say that grant writing just isn't what it used to be. Skeptics will tell you that because of this event or that event there just isn't money available, and therefore writing grant proposals at this time is a waste of time and energy. They may point to a pot of gold that once was available and no longer exists. This is wrong; not only is money available but also great sums of it, just waiting for someone to claim it. Furthermore, there are individuals, institutions, and agencies that are as desperate to find the right person or organization to give this money to as you and others are desperate to receive it.

Through two decades of giving workshops on college campuses from coast to coast, I have learned that such myths are created by people who haven't taken time to learn how to write competitive grant proposals, who do not plan to develop such skills, and who, either consciously or subconsciously, would prefer that their colleagues not learn these skills. By spreading these myths, their strategy is to discourage others from successfully developing proposals that will be funded, thereby proving their claim that grant writing is really a hopeless endeavor. I advise my workshop participants not to talk about grant writing to colleagues who do not write grants; indeed, when overhearing such comments, the best response is to say nothing and just walk away.

This does not suggest that you should avoid discussing your grant writing. On the contrary, at the end of my grant-writing workshops, I am frequently asked, "What further advice would you give us?" When asked this question, I always respond similarly. I advise my participants to identify coworkers or colleagues who are writing grants and form a support group. This group would meet once or twice monthly, perhaps over a brown-bag lunch, to share their experiences. Each meeting would feature a discussion led by one or two of the members, perhaps sharing their ideas for proposals or their progress on proposals that are already under way, asking for reactions and suggestions from their coworkers. As proposals reach completion, members could ask the other members to read them against their proposed budgets and give feedback.

Myth Number Two: The money that is available goes to big, prestigious institutions and agencies, not to individuals, small institutions, and small agencies. Wrong again. While it is true that each year hundreds of millions of dollars go to large institutions, hundreds of millions of dollars also go to individuals and small institutions, such as small businesses, schools, hospitals, and governments.

As a matter of fact, many grant-funding agencies purposely seek out individuals, small institutions, or small agencies to help because they believe in and want to promote entrepreneurship. Many industries with funding foundations also favor proposals that come from local residents; therefore, by responding to local requests for proposals (RFPs), you will actually have an advantage over the giants with reputations for getting the big bucks.

When funding agencies do prefer directing their resources toward larger institutions, it is often because of the credibility of the particular institution. You can develop the same high level of credibility by crafting credible proposals with responsible budgets and, when you do receive approval for a proposal, by managing your funded proposal in a responsible fashion. If you are to build this much-needed credibility, you must also learn how to effectively document your positive track record in grant writing and grant management.

This topic will be discussed further in Chapter Six, "Keeping Your Grant." Remember that regardless of how rich a funding agency may be, those individuals who manage the funding of proposals are held accountable for investing their monies wisely and for getting a high rate of return for their investment. This means that you should never waste funds or allow others in your organization to do so. On the contrary, you should design a system that prevents overspending. Furthermore, you must develop a system for clearly documenting your return for each dollar spent.

For those who design an effective system that shows prudent management of resources, getting the second grant and future grants funded becomes much easier. Success (not size) begets success, but only when you carefully document your success.

> *If you are, indeed, a proactive individual and you believe in your own ability to set and achieve your own goals, this is the perfect time to set two or three grant-writing goals. What are your major professional and personal goals? Use grant writing to meet these goals. Jot down two or three such goals, and design your future grant proposals accordingly.*

The Importance of Connections

Myth Number Three: Successful grant writing requires connections, and I don't have any. To be sure, when used effectively, knowing people in the funding agency can be a valuable asset. If you have colleagues or friends in the office, or even have friends who know people in the funding agency, you should use these contacts; let them know about your application. But the old saw, "It's who you know, not what you know that matters," is dull from overuse. All you have to do to dispel this myth in your own mind is to step back and think, "If I were charged with the responsibility of giving away someone else's money, would I look to friends or would I ask what the owner wanted to get from this money and try to find the proposal that would get the most return for the dollar?"

In Chapter Eight, you will see advice taken from the Internet, and some of that advice distinctly suggests an effective way for grant-writers to develop both the grant-writing expertise and the connections that many believe are essential. One of the most effective means of achieving both of these goals is to volunteer to be a proposal reader for a major funding agency, such as the National Institutes of Health or the National Science Foundation. Often these agencies have all the readers they need at the moment, but if you continue to offer your services, sooner or later, you will be granted this opportunity.

Becoming an evaluator enables you to get inside the evaluators' heads. By reviewing many proposals, you can notice and record in your grant-writing notebook those characteristics that impressed you and also those traits that caused you to downgrade some proposals. This gives you a foundation for designing strong proposals.

Most funders have wealth, and whether individuals or institutional representatives, most are wise enough to know what they or their employers want. They are capable of hiring evaluators who will ensure that they get their money's worth out of every dollar spent. So, to be a successful grant writer, all you have to do is be able to prepare a proposal that will convince the evaluators that, if given the opportunity, you will outperform all of the competition in delivering the desired services.

Instead of requiring connections, successful grant proposal writing requires following guidelines and crafting an excellent proposal that meets all of the expectations of the potential funder. Indeed, most grant proposals are evaluated by a team of readers, who are provided with a rating form. See the sample rating form in Appendix A. Notice that this sample form is weighted; that is, each criterion for evaluating the proposals is assigned a relative number of points. Notice, too, that there is a space for totaling the points for each proposal. After all proposals have been evaluated, the grant is awarded to the proposal having the most points. Often, by checking the RFP or by contacting the prospective funder, you can obtain a copy of the rating form.

Having a copy of the rating form can put you in the driver's seat, for now you know the relative values the funders expect the evaluators to place on the different proposal parts. By looking closer, you can extend the advantage that the rating form is capable of giving you over those less fortunate competitors who do not have this tool. For example, notice that this particular rating form begins with a set of instructions to the evaluators.

First, this form tells the evaluators to "Study entire proposal before beginning the rating process because information relevant to a single rating criterion may be found in several sections of the proposal." This tells us that the reviewers will be looking for overall strengths and overall weaknesses. This suggests that we should highlight the major strengths—never assuming that the readers will automatically notice and appreciate these strengths—to help them understand the significance of each strength.

Second, although the reviewers are given these explicit instructions, there is no guarantee that they will follow them. We know that, faced with a big job of evaluating many proposals, some evaluators will be tempted to jump right in and begin assigning points to the various parts. To ensure that those evaluators will notice all of the strengths in our proposals, we can make certain that each strength is included in an appropriate proposal part.

This rating form continues to talk to those who know how to listen. "On page 4 suggest any revisions that would better meet the overall objective of improving statewide teacher qualification in mathematics, chemistry, and physics." This particular proposal rating form was designed to be used to evaluate proposals written to improve statewide teacher qualifications in math, chemistry, and physics. It reminds the evaluators to keep their eyes focused on the proposal's mission and to reward those investigators who have convinced them that they would do the best job of reaching this main mission. We can strengthen our proposals by responding to the advice given to the evaluators and by keeping the overall purpose or mission of the funder in mind when developing each and every part of the proposal.

Getting Time to Write Grants

Myth Number Four: I don't have time to write grants. Today's pace is such that all of us are scurrying to get through the tasks that face us each day, get into our cars, and hit the freeways, where almost everyone finds seventy miles an hour uncomfortably slow. To accommodate this lightening-fast lifestyle, yield signs have been replaced by merge signs, where disaster awaits because many people don't take the time required to look for oncoming vehicles. If we do take the time to watch the behavior of others, we realize that it is, indeed, a mad world; no wonder we conclude that we don't have time to write grants. Yet, the truth is that we have the same number of hours in the week that everyone else has. We must spend much of this time sleeping and working. Incidentally, we may not need quite the number of hours of sleep nightly as we think we do. When Thomas Edison was working on his light bulb theory, two other teams of scientists in other countries were working on the same theory. For many months, all three of these teams knew that the light bulb was about to be invented and, furthermore, they knew that the prize would go to the first team to construct a workable product. How right they were! Today, few people know that this race even happened.

During the final months before the discovery, Thomas Edison seldom went home at the end of the day; instead, he curled up on his lab tables and took short power naps. For months, these teams worked around the clock, testing every kind of filament imaginable, trying to discover a material that would light up without immediately burning out. Some of the advice taken from the Web and shown in Chapter Eight is that grant writers must have a passion if, indeed, they are to become successful at this skill. Consider the passion required to drive an individual such as Thomas Edison and the other team members to such extremes, then consider the rewards!

The good news for aspiring grant writers is that such extreme sacrifices are not required. All that is required to find the time needed to become a highly successful grant writer is to put yourself in the position of the motorist who is approaching a merge sign, slow down for just a moment, and monitor your own lifestyle. Most of us will be surprised at how many hours we waste daily, engaged in nonproductive activities. For example, consider the time you spend watching poor entertainment on your television. Let's face it; the vast majority of sitcoms are so silly that people with maturity levels above adolescence find most of the shows embarrassingly juvenile and boring. Furthermore, the reason we are willing to tolerate the mediocrity is that after a hard day's work, we are so desperate to escape the daily frustrations, rushing, and tension, and just relax that we will tolerate almost anything. Ironically, this type of entertainment is not relaxing. Those who grab a bite of dinner and either wolf it down before turning on the television or, even worse, take it to the television to eat without even attempting to taste it totally miss the point. We tell ourselves we are too tired to go another moment, but the truth is that we are not tired, at least not physically. The majority of today's jobs don't require enough physical labor to rest us, let alone to make us tired. Unfortunately, today's lifestyle leaves most of us emotionally drained. We turn on the television to relax, yet we discover that watching television doesn't work. Five or six hours later, when it is time for bed, we realize that we are just as tired as ever.

At this point, I hope you will permit me to add one professional experience to illustrate the fallacy that is hidden in this "lack of time" myth. It was Saturday morning. Three colleges and universities in Cincinnati had pooled their resources to offer a writing-for-publication workshop. The morning began with a delicious on-site breakfast. Now it was time to get down to work. The large room was completely filled with professors who had come to sharpen their writing and publishing skills, although from the outset at least one person, who sat up front, was skeptical about whether the workshop could work for him. I had delivered the workshop so many times to so many audiences that, not only did I anticipate the question that followed the raised arm, but also I knew when this question would come. The skeptic was careful to phrase his question just right.

"I hear that you write a lot of articles and grants."

"A couple or so a year," I replied.

"I also hear that you are a college dean."

"That's correct."

"How large is your college?"

"We have one-hundred ten full-time faculty and about ninety part-time faculty, and we serve just over three thousand students."

"Then, when do you find time to write?"

Realizing that this was a legitimate question, and, furthermore, a very good question, I welcomed it and responded calmly and kindly.

"This is an excellent question, and it deserves an honest and complete answer, but first let me tell all of you when I do *not* engage in grant writing or writing for publication. I do not write between the hours of 7 A.M. and 7 P.M. on Monday through Friday. During these times, I am either driving to or from work or I am at work, usually sitting in a meeting worrying about the enormous amount of incoming mail, both hard copies and email, and worrying about the number of phone calls that are collecting on my answering machine and the number of people who will be waiting at my door the moment I return to my office. I also do not write on Sunday morning because I am usually in church. I never write on Saturday night, because I am somewhere on a dance floor highly engaged in American and Latin ballroom dancing. Because I graduated from three major universities and I love sports, I don't get much grant writing done on Saturday afternoons in the fall or at night during the winter months. I have shared these details to assure you that even the busiest people have time to write grants.

But, I have told you when I do *not* write, and, if I remember correctly, that was not your question. You asked when *do* I find time to write grants. I usually find that I can get in at least six hours of writing grants, books, and articles on Saturday morning."

I explained that I have a routine. Being an early riser, I enjoy getting up early on Saturday morning, walking two miles over some steep hills, and driving to my favorite fast food restaurant for a quick breakfast, where I sit, sip my coffee, and write for the next five or six hours.

So, my first advice is that you examine your own routines. Do not give up those activities that you enjoy most, and this includes golfing, tennis, running, and watching sports and other shows that you really enjoy. Unlike watching third-rate television, these activities are relaxing, and we need them.

Many participants in my workshops have young families. I always advise them to take care of their families before settling down to write. While raising my own family, I cannot think of a time that I ever put my writing ahead of the children's homework. My kids are grown now and they still avoid dining room tables because we spent so many evenings there working on math and chemistry assignments. That may speak to the quality of the help I gave them; I hope not. I know that my responsibility for helping with their homework was more important than my responsibility for writing, and I also know that I always found time to write after they went to bed.

Giving writing-for-publication workshops and grant-writing workshops helps me analyze my own routines. Recently, in a workshop in Texas, a participant raised an unexpected question, and I responded with an equally unanticipated answer.

"You said that to be productive, you need large blocks of time to write. During these long writing periods, when do you take breaks?"

I was slightly stunned by this question, for I realized that not only had I never thought about that question, but also that I never consciously take breaks. While I will admit that often I enjoy activities such as dancing and watching my own schools play ball even more than I enjoy writing on grants and articles, I do, nevertheless, enjoy writing. In fact, there have been many times when I have gotten so intense and so excited over a piece of research I was doing or a grant proposal or article I was writing that I stayed up all night working on it, knowing that I had to be at work at 8 A.M. More than once, this excitement was so obvious that my children would look into my eyes and say, "Dad, you are really wired, aren't you?" So, I answered the workshop participant's question about when I take breaks, "I suppose when I am writing I never think of taking breaks because I cherish the time that I allocate to write, and I enjoy writing so much that when I am writing, I consider myself to already be on break."

If you do not find writing so exhilarating, check your topic. I write about topics in which I am profoundly interested and topics that I continuously research and read about. I enjoy it because, unlike when I am at work and always doing what others tell me to do, writing gives me great freedom. I am free to choose my own preferred topic. I can write what I choose to write. I can even choose my audiences. Unlike most other times in my life, when I write, I am totally in charge. Finally, I work to meet the mission of my institution and the goals of my employers. I write grants to make my own life better. I am happier at work when I know I am doing a good job, so many of my grants are directed toward improving my job performance; my grants give me programs that I want to pursue, equipment to use to pursue them, and time. By spending time writing a grant, I can actually buy much larger blocks of released time to do more of the things that I enjoy doing. Sometimes I wonder how people can have time not to write articles and grants.

Here is one final tip for managing your grant-writing time. When you notice that an RFP has an uncomfortably short deadline, yet this is a topic that you desperately want to pursue, go ahead and draft your proposal. Take all the time you need, with the idea that you will willingly miss the forthcoming deadline, but that you won't let that stop you. You will take all the time you need to craft this proposal to meet the funder's goals, and you will submit it at a later time—perhaps a year from now if the same agency issues this or a similar RFP.

Often the same agencies will reissue proposals from year to year. I use this time to refine the proposal to make it better meet increased expectations of the evaluators. These revisions are usually important, yet they are minor adjustments. This means that your having the basic outline and parts of the proposal in place before the RFP is issued will give you time to polish the program during the year as you discover and collect important data to support your proposal. It will also give you time to prepare charts, tables, and graphs, which will be needed to persuade the evaluators that your proposal is superior to the others they receive.

Now, I have shared my own strategies for finding time to write, but how about your own schedule? In a seven-day week how many uninterrupted hours during the day and night can you find that you could use for the sole purpose of writing grants? You might want to jot down these times and develop a routine that takes advantage of these interruption-free times.

> *Realizing that finding all the time needed to write grant proposals is just a matter of setting priorities and then allocating the necessary time to get this job done, take a moment to focus on your own schedule, the professional demands at work, and your responsibilities at home. Protecting the time needed for exercising, entertainment, and responsibilities to family, find a couple of hours (day or night) that will be uninterrupted and let others know that this is your grant-writing time. Like dieting, success at grant writing requires an ongoing commitment—a change in lifestyle—but it need not and should not seriously disrupt those activities that are most important to you.*

Need for Quality

Myth Number Five: Getting published just requires preparing a grant proposal, and luck does the rest.   Uh oh! Now we have slipped back into our external locus of control syndrome, blaming outside forces, such as luck, for our success and failure. The truth is that just writing a lot of grant proposals is highly unlikely to lead to a high level of success. Successful grant writing requires writing *top quality* grant proposals. A few excellently crafted grant proposals, targeted to the appropriate markets, are likely to succeed at a level far beyond the success that comes from writing many mediocre proposals.

Sometimes our vision is clarified when we put ourselves in someone else's place. When I give writing workshops, I assign editing work to my writers. In fact, I even ask them to play the role of editors and tell me how to prepare a manuscript that would be publishable in their journals. When they do this, they immediately begin selecting better topics and improving their writing styles. They examine their journals and discover some of the permanent features of these journals for the first time. When I teach my graduate course on writing for publication, we spend over 80 percent of the class time editing each others' manuscripts, because I know that good writing is good editing, and there is no better way than editing to become a good writer.

When giving grant-writing workshops, I take every opportunity to put the participants in the role of grant proposal evaluators. What would impress you most if you were responsible for selecting one grant over another? First, you would consider your agency's mission. What kinds of jobs does the agency want to get done? What evidence is there that Proposal A will do a better job than Proposal B, or vice versa? So, the first thing that you would look for in the proposal is assurance that this proposal writer would do a better job than the competitors would do.

Next, if you were hired to evaluate proposals, you would want to get your money's worth, a high rate of return on each dollar. So, when developing your budget, you would want to be economically responsible. Suppose you have three or four proposals that appear to do high-quality work. Then, you probably would select a proposal with one of the lower budgets, but only if you believed the budget was realistic and did, indeed, provide for a quality job. In summary, luck plays a major role in determining the grant writer's success only when the grant writer depends on it. Effective grant writing shadows and diminishes the role that luck plays in determining success.

> *What do you think? How would you evaluate your own chances of getting a proposal funded if you had taken time to develop a very high-quality proposal and had developed a responsible budget?*
>
> *So, my suggestion is that you put quality over quantity. Write a few very good proposals and target each to an appropriate potential funding source.*

Meeting Deadlines

Myth Number Six: Meeting the deadline is everything.　　Wrong again. By itself, meeting the deadline is nothing. The only times when meeting the deadline is important are those times when you submit a high-quality proposal on time.

Consider the following example, which I call the *Eleventh Hour Syndrome*. During those eleven years that I was heading a large organization, I coined the term *Eleventh Hour Proposal*.

Precisely as the second hand joined the other hands in a perfectly vertical position, I began closing my office door to have my brown-bag, working lunch. Then, I heard a familiar voice excitedly address my secretary, who was exiting the door on the opposite side of the office,

> "Wait, wait, wait. Before you close the door, please, I need the dean's signature on this grant proposal. It must be delivered to the state capitol building before closing time today."

Because of the enormous level of business we conducted daily, I had a rule that all papers that required my signature had to be left overnight to provide the time required to read and reflect on them. Yet, because this was one of our outstanding faculty members—indeed, she held the university's most prestigious research, teaching, and service award—and because she had earned the college much money from her previous grants, I made an exception and agreed to examine the proposal over the noon hour. Big mistake! I scanned the thick proposal, whipped my pocket calculator out of my top desk drawer, and checked all of the figures in the budget. At 1 P.M., I signed and returned the proposal, only to learn later that I had overlooked a date in the proposal. Among its many parts, the proposed project included a new course to be taught for the first time the following semester. But this was impossible; at our university, getting a new course proposal through all the necessary channels took months. Policy requiring new courses to be stated in the catalog before the courses are actually offered could take up to another two years. Later, when I was questioned about my having approved this proposal, I was so embarrassed that I refused to make further exceptions to my overnight reading policy.

Others who give grant-writing workshops may not use the term *Eleventh Hour Proposals*, but they are aware of the damage that rushing to meet a short deadline often causes. Dr. Donald Orlich, a grant-writing expert in the state of Washington said he considered this habit of rushing to meet deadlines one of the greatest weaknesses of grant writers. He set a minimum time of twenty working days for writers to have available before a proposal is due, warning that the writing of proposals for complex projects or for projects to which writers have not already given considerable thought will require more than twenty days.

In summary, there is no prize for meeting deadlines, only penalties for missing them. These penalties can easily be avoided by submitting your proposal to an alternative funder or to the same funder during the following funding cycle.

Collaborative Writing

Myth Number Seven: Collaboration will reduce the workload and time required to succeed.   At some point in every workshop, a participant will ask whether collaborating with colleagues is a good practice and whether it will reduce the workload and the time required to craft a quality proposal. Collaboration has both advantages and disadvantages. When the right people collaborate, the quality of the proposal and the quality of the experience can be enriched, making the decision to collaborate a good choice. But do not base your decision to collaborate on the hopes that it will reduce the workload or the writing time. On the contrary, working with others requires meetings to iron out a clear understanding about the purpose and nature of the project and the procedures to be followed during the data-gathering and writing processes.

I always follow this response by telling the participants that a better question is, If I decide to collaborate, how many partners should I have and how should I choose them? Unless the project is a multimillion dollar proposal with many varied facets, I would recommend a maximum team size of no more than four, and preferably three, because the larger the team, the greater the time that will be needed to complete the project.

When participants ask for help in choosing the right partners, usually they are referring to expertise: How can I ensure that I choose colleagues with the right combination of content expertise? I can tell by the way the question is worded that the participant is using the word *expertise* to mean the colleagues' subject matter expertise. The only expertise that I believe is important to consider is not content expertise at all, but rather the skills needed to collect and treat the data and the skills required to draft and refine the proposal.

For example, three colleagues, who happened to be good friends, decided to write a massive grant proposal. One was a seasoned author, one an editor of a national journal, and the other the head of the educational research department in their college. They made a good team. The fact that one was a writer, one an editor, and the other a researcher and statistician was a definite plus, but only because of the process they used. From the outset, they decided what jobs were to be done and which team member(s) would perform each job. They had informally discussed the topic they would pursue, and they decided to begin by developing a huge questionnaire to gather the data they needed to write the grant. They decided that the development of the questionnaire would be the only part of the work that all three partners would do together. Then, their assignments began to get very specialized. The writer was a proactive thinker who volunteered to sequence the questions and formulate an outline because he envisioned the articles that would eventually emerge from the findings of the study. In other words, he wanted each section of the proposal to concentrate on related information that would be meaningful to certain people. He also wanted a similar, separate section of related questions to gather data for each of several additional audiences. In essence, his plan was to write several articles from the data gathered by this single questionnaire. The editor accepted responsibility for physically mailing the questionnaires and communicating with the respondents to ensure a high rate of return. When the data arrived, the researcher fed the data into the computer and interpreted the results. With the results in hand, the author drafted the articles. A large project can provide the substance for several articles, and articles are needed to establish a successful track record that the collaborators can use as fodder for sequential or related future grant proposals. The author and editor edited and rewrote each article several times.

A key to the success of these collaborators was their willingness to begin by dividing the responsibilities equally among the participants. An even greater factor in producing a successful project was the fact that all of these three collaborators were self-motivated. When people ask how they should select their grant-writing partners, I always tell them to use people's work habits. Select partners whose work habits are similar to your own. Don't mix personality types. When a Type A personality collaborates with a Type B personality, the Type A, self-driven personality has to wait for the laid-back Type B partner to start the job and then wait for the partner to complete it because the Type B partner appears to think a deadline is the time that has been set to begin, not finish, the project. Likewise, the laid-back Type B person, who joined the team to enjoy the process, can't enjoy it because his uptight partner is always pushing him to work faster.

> How about your own preferences? Are you willing to risk your success to a colleague? Whom do you know who, you are confident, will get the job done and be an asset more than a liability? What parts of the job would you want to do yourself, and what parts would you want your collaborator(s) to do?
>
> Should you collaborate? That's a very personal question and one that you alone must answer. Refer to your major professional goal and to your personal goals, and then make a list of the advantages you might gain from collaborating on grant proposals. Make a similar list of disadvantages. These might include the facts that it takes more time and should you choose partners who are not proactive, take-charge Type A personalities, you are entrusting the future of your grant writing to others.
>
> If you decide not to collaborate, good. Your grant-writing program has reached an important milestone. If your decision is to collaborate, make a list of colleagues whom you know to be self-starting, task-oriented professionals. You might also wish to identify the roles you want to play in collaboration so you will have this information available each time you collaborate.

Effect of Needs on Acceptance

Myth Number Eight: The grants are awarded to those applicants who have the greatest needs.   Because they believe that grants are awarded to those who have the greatest needs, many novice grant writers put their attention and energy into convincing funders that their needs exceed the needs of all other applicants. This thought needs to be examined. Most grants are awarded not for the purpose of helping the investigators but to help the investigators meet the funder's needs; therefore, attention should be focused on convincing funders how you can do a better job than your competition.

Matching Your Strengths with the Funder's Goals

Some proposal writers use a shotgun approach; writing their proposal first and then seeking a funder to support it. Others use a rifle approach, first selecting an RFP and then carefully crafting their proposal to meet the specifications in the RFP. Both approaches require the writer to understand the nature of the funder, the proposal writer's own strengths, the strengths and needs of the writer's company or institution, and the strengths and needs of the writer's community.

Is it possible that you might present such a strong need for money that the funder might take pity and fund your grant just because you need help so badly? Yes, this is a possibility, but it is much more probable that the funder will be motivated by your skills and strengths. People like to invest their money not on losers but on winners. Emphasize your strengths and those of your institution and local community and use them to convince the funder that you will do a better job than the other applicants of meeting the funder's goals.

Whether you choose to use the shotgun approach and write your grant proposal and then look for a funder or you use the rifle approach and begin by locating a possible funder and craft your proposal accordingly is your choice. Some grant writers are successful using the first approach; others are successful using the latter approach. Both approaches require the grant writer to be highly familiar with the funder's goals. Incidentally, the shotgun approach is usually more successful for getting small grants, and the rifle approach is usually more successful in garnering very large grants. Decide how much money your grant will require, and before sending it to a funder, make certain that the funder supports projects in this cost range. Also, check to see if there are any major funders in your area. Remember the adage that most grants that are funded by corporations are funded in the shadow of the corporation's smokestack.

As indicated earlier, grant writing is as much artwork as it is science, and there is no one right way to write grant proposals. However, many workshop participants are looking for more than just a set of guidelines or suggestions; they want a model. This book presents several such models. One highly successful model, known as the Triangular Model for Writing Grants, is shown in Figure 1.1, The Triangular Model for Matching Strengths with the Funder's Goals and Practices.

Using this model, the writers keep one eye on the funder's goals and the other on their areas of expertise. The model includes their personal strengths, the strengths of their organization or institution, and the strengths of the community.

Using the Triangular Model in Figure 1.1, select a topic that is of particular interest to you, and list your personal strengths, the strengths of your employing institution, and the strengths of your community to convince a potential funder that you would be the best person for the job. List a few of your personal and professional goals.

The Funding Source
- What types of projects has it funded?
- What is the range of dollars given to projects?
- What types of subjects does it avoid?

Yourself
- What type(s) of experience do you have?
- What limitations do you have?
- What personal characterisitcs make you especially well suited for this project?

Your Institution and Community
- What special resources (including human resources) are available to support this project?
- What special needs does your institution/community have?

FIGURE 1.1   The Triangular Model for Matching Strengths with the Funder's Goals and Practices

Further Reflection

This chapter has been about attitudes that generally affect people's levels of success when they write grant proposals. It has been written according to my own experiences writing proposals and giving workshops. But what about you? It is not the attitudes of others or what others think that will determine your success; it is *your* attitudes. So, take a moment to assess your own thinking.

> *On a scale of zero to ten, what score would you give your self-confidence? Like many of us, did you grow up being taught to be modest? Not to evaluate yourself generously? Do you associate a high level of self-confidence with bragging or vanity? After all, nobody likes a bragger. But we need to build on our strengths, and to do this we must first acknowledge them. You have the ability to succeed at grant writing at the level you choose to succeed and to the degree that you are willing to work to make it happen.*

Summary

Because people's attitudes inevitably shape their behavior, the single most important factor that determines the degree of success that people experience when writing grant proposals is their attitudes. Many individuals who desire to write grants and who otherwise have the talents to become outstanding grant writers are prevented from reaching their goals by several misconceptions about the process. The most important attitude a grant writer can have is a sense of efficacy: "I *can* and I *will* become a highly successful grant writer. I will learn what I need to know, I will develop the necessary skills, and I will succeed at the level that I choose to succeed."

The attitude just described reflects an internal locus of control: "I am in charge of my world." Most people who don't have this take-charge attitude don't succeed, and they live lives of failure built on excuses. Because they don't succeed, they don't want others to succeed, especially their own coworkers or colleagues; it makes them look bad. So, they initiate and promote false beliefs about grant writing, myths that they use to dissuade others from succeeding. For example, they may say that the grant money sources have been emptied by the slow economy, that the grant money always goes to large, well-known organizations, that it takes connections to be successful, or that there just isn't time to write grants. These are simply wrong; millions of dollars are waiting to be distributed. Connections are great, if you have them, but they are not at all necessary. All that is required to get this money is to produce a better proposal than the competition. We all have twenty-four hours in a day and seven days in a week; within this amount of time, there are always enough periods of wasted time, which, if scheduled, will be enough time to become a highly successful grant writer. In fact, you don't need to give up the activities you enjoy.

Success in grant writing does not come from rushing to produce a lot of proposals and meet deadlines. Success comes from learning how to produce an excellent proposal, targeted to a specific RFP, and from taking the time required to make a proposal that is better than the other submitted proposals.

Recap of Major Ideas

- Attitudes shape behavior; therefore, your grant-writing skills cannot exceed your belief in your own abilities.
- A strong internal locus of control is a prerequisite to successful grant writing.
- Money is always available for well-written proposals that focus on an RFP.
- The major goal for grant writers is to produce proposals that convince readers that the writer will do a better job of meeting the funder's goals than all the competitors would do.
- Plenty of time is available for those who assign grant writing a high priority.
- Meeting the deadlines has no rewards unless coupled with very well written proposals.
- Compared to writing alone, collaboration forces the writer to lose some control and requires additional time and work.

Reference

Henson, K. T., & Eller, B. F. (1999). *Educational psychology for effective teaching.* Belmont, CA: Wadsworth.

2

Parts of a Proposal

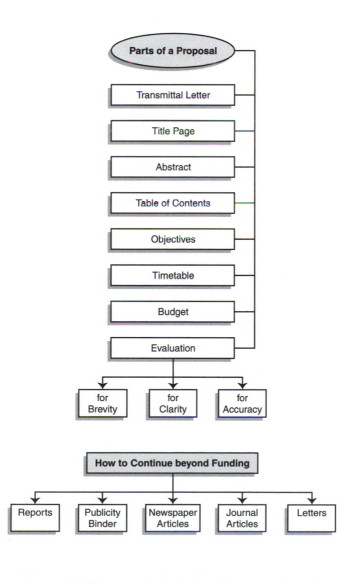

Novice grant writers often find the task of writing grant proposals daunting because, although it can play an important part in the lives of today's professionals, few college programs prepare their students for this responsibility. Through the years, grant writing has mysteriously remained a major responsibility in many professions; yet it has not managed to become part of college curricula, and new professionals are expected to develop the necessary grant-writing skills on their own. With the absence of any leadership, most novice professionals don't even know what parts to include in their proposals. It is little wonder that without any grant-writing training in most programs, students can earn the highest degrees in their disciplines, graduate, and begin their careers totally bewildered over the grant-writing process. But it doesn't have to be that way, and it shouldn't be. This chapter is written to help you decide what parts to put in your proposals and to provide guidance in the writing of each part.

Some RFPs specify the parts to be included in the proposals their evaluators expect to find in the proposals they read. For those grants that do specify certain parts, these specifications, like all requirements stated in RFPs, should be adhered to rigorously. Each chapter of this book contains some important guidelines, and by following each to a "t" you can increase the chances that your proposals will be funded. None of these guidelines is more important than this: Always address each part of the proposal as directly, clearly, and convincingly as you can.

Unfortunately, most RFPs do not specify the exact parts their proposals should have, and for those RFPs, the decision as to exactly which parts to include is somewhat subjective. For example, while one might argue that all proposals should require a budget or transmittal page, it is less certain that all should contain an abstract or a title page. When written correctly, each of the proposal parts can become an opportunity to sell your proposal to the readers; therefore, when you are in doubt as to whether to include one of the parts, include it.

This chapter introduces those parts of a proposal that have proven successful in applying for more than thirty grants; therefore, while some of these parts are not offered as prescriptions, each has proved to be important and should be given close consideration. You can think of the parts as tools that you can use to enhance the acceptance of your proposals. These parts include a (1) transmittal letter, (2) title page, (3) abstract, (4) table of contents, (5) purposes, goals, and objectives, (6) timetable, (7) evaluation, and (8) budget.

Transmittal Letter

The transmittal letter is a short one- or two-page letter written by the senior officer at a company or institution. Its purposes are to introduce the proposal and to assure the potential funders that the institution supports the proposal.

By signing the transmittal letter, the senior officer agrees to stand behind the promises and commitments made by those who wrote the proposal.

The importance of keeping the transmittal letter short can be appreciated by remembering the last time you saw a guest speaker or keynote speaker being introduced by a windy introduction that turned out to be as long as the anticipated speech. Perhaps you wanted one of the long hooks used in Vaudeville acts to bring the introduction to an abrupt close. The evaluators have that power; if your proposal's transmittal letter is too long, all they have to do is put it in the rejection file and go to another proposal. So, when you ask your senior officer for a transmittal letter, you might wish to ask for a short transmittal letter. An even better approach is to draft the letter and ask the senior officer to make the necessary adjustments in the letter and then put it on his or her letterhead. Like the rest of the proposal, the transmittal letter should be written in a clear, straightforward style.

At a minimum, the transmittal letter should contain the following:

- The president's phone number
- The president's fax number
- The president's address
- A statement of purpose

Notice that the sample transmittal letter shown in Figure 2.1 immediately defines the problem that the investigators plan to address. The letter also answers an important question, "Why us? Why should we be the ones to study this problem? What special skills or resources do we have that suggests that we would be more successful than others who are responding to this RFP?" Notice too, that this letter uses recent data from a credible source to substantiate its claim that the problem really is significant.

> *Using the sample transmittal letter shown in Figure 2.1, you can develop your own generic transmittal letter template. Your template letter should include some of your special needs and some of your unique strengths that you can use in all types of proposals.*

Title Page

A title page is a sparse page that resembles the top page of a business report or the top sheet on a college research assignment. See Figure 2.2. At a minimum, the title page should include the following:

- The project's title
- The name of the company or institution submitting the proposal
- The date

Mr. Robert P. Anderson, Executive Director
Southwest Foundations, Inc.
108 Holly Hill Drive
P.O. Box 55
Lubbock, TX 79493

Dear Mr. Anderson:

A recent study released by the U.S. Department of Health has reported obesity as the number one health problem of America's youths.

The Nurse Practitioner Program in the School of Allied Health and Nursing at Southwest University seeks support for the enclosed proposal, titled the Ashley Obesity Reduction Program for America's Youths. We have taken a holistic approach to this problem because we believe that most of today's weight problems result from a change in lifestyle. Our proposed program begins at the pre-elementary school level because this same report says that poor eating habits and sedentary lifestyle begin at this early age.

We have chosen to send this proposal to you because we know that your organization is committed to improving the health of individuals at all ages, especially teenagers and children.

Because our state has the highest rate of obesity in the nation, we believe that our need for addressing this issue is acute; however, your decision to attack this problem is based on an even greater factor: Our organization has studied health practices among youths and has experimented with developing health foods for over one hundred years. We have accumulated a knowledge base to build upon.

Please let us know if further information or explanation is needed. Thank you for considering this proposal.

Sincerely,

Jania K. Worley, President
Southwest University
301 University Avenue
Lubbock, TX 79493
Phone: (704) 822-5186
Fax: (704) 822-5102

FIGURE 2.1   Sample Transmittal Letter

A Proposed Method for Enhancing the Purity of Steel

Submitted to: The Vulcan Foundation

by
The Rocky Mountain Bureau of Mines

July 21, 2004

FIGURE 2.2   Sample Title Page

The title page may also include additional information, such as the amount of money requested or the names, phone numbers, and fax numbers of the investigators. But, since the title page serves as a graphic organizer, enabling easy and quick identification of your proposal, and because your proposal is likely to be one of many proposals being evaluated, brevity is essential.

If you are responding to an RFP, check the RFP to make sure that your title reflects the purpose(s) described. If you are not responding to an RFP, check the mission statement of your targeted funder. You might literally pull some key words from this statement to use in your title, giving your proposal a closer-than-average similarity to the major concerns and goals of the targeted funding agency.

Chapter Five will caution grant writers against the tendency to load their proposals with unnecessary jargon (unfamiliar words with unclear meaning, chosen to impress the reader). Using a few key words to give focus to the proposal is another matter, because it does keep the writer on target and it suggests to the reader that you understand and intend to serve the funder's mission.

Abstract

An abstract is a short description of the proposal. Some funders require an abstract; others do not. Check your RFP. If an abstract is required, follow the specifications precisely. Most RFPs that require abstracts specify required lengths (for example, *Include a 250 word abstract*). Other RFPs that require abstracts specify maximum lengths (for example, *Include an abstract, not to exceed 500 words*). These common restrictions reflect the purpose of abstracts, which is to enable the evaluators to make a quick assessment of all the proposals received. The evaluators may begin the evaluation process by conducting an initial screening, and to make this screening, they may read only the abstracts. As explained further in Chapter Three, many grant proposal evaluators receive so many proposals that they have to find a way to reduce the number of proposals they must deal with to a small fraction of all the proposals they receive. This makes the abstract extremely important.

Other RFPs do not require or, indeed, even mention an abstract, leaving the choice to you. If your proposal is longer than two or three pages, serious consideration should be given to preparing an abstract. Carefully written, the abstract will highlight your proposal's major features. To ensure that your proposal works to its maximum possible potential, examine the RFP to learn the most important purposes and goals of the funder. Extract a few of these key concepts for your abstract. Then, think about your own reasons for writing the proposal and the unique qualities of your proposal. Include some of these unique features. Think of the abstract not as a requirement but as an *opportunity* to sell your ideas to the evaluators, and construct it accordingly. Once you have drafted your abstract, edit it until it reads smoothly. A sample proposal abstract is seen in Figure 2.3.

Table of Contents

Some RFPs specify a table of contents as a requirement but most RFPs leave the decision to include or omit a table of contents to their writers. Like the title page and abstract, the table of contents is a visual tool that can work for you and, therefore, is too important to omit. Furthermore, the table of contents can be constructed easily and quickly. For example, see the table of contents shown in Figure 2.4.

Begin by titling your table of contents. Then, using Roman numerals, list the major parts of the proposal. On the right-hand side of the page, insert the page numbers. When you have completed filling in all of the parts, check your list and make certain that you have not overlooked any parts. A simple omission can be interpreted as carelessness and can lose the confidence of funders, who may generalize and conclude that you will be equally careless with the implementation of your proposal.

Responding to the critical shortage of high school physics teachers, the University of _____ proposes a 10-week summer institute which will better prepare secondary teachers who are now teaching physics or who anticipate teaching physics this fall but who lack certification in the area of physics. Each participant will be given a total of 266 contact hours of physics courses, laboratory experiences, tutorials, and seminars, providing students the opportunity to earn 12 semester credit hours.

During the fall semester, each participant will be visited at his or her own school and provided opportunity to ask further questions and share successes and criticisms of the materials developed in the institute.

FIGURE 2.3 Sample Proposal Abstract

Physics Teachers Summer Institute Proposal
Table of Contents

FIGURE 2.4 Sample Table of Contents

Purposes, Goals, and Objectives

Purposes are global statements used to explain the general expectations of the funder. For example, a purpose of a grant proposal might be to reduce the pollution in a particular part of the city. This is a little vague. It doesn't tell what types of pollution, how great the need is to reduce pollution, or how the forthcoming reduction of pollution is to be measured.

Goals are used to break the purposes down into parts. One goal might be to reduce the number of pollutants in the air; another one might concern the water. But neither of these goals answers the question, What types of air pollutants or water pollutants? Or, How much does the funder want these to be reduced? So, goals are broken down into objectives, which are much more specific. For example, one objective might be to reduce the amount of sulfur in the air to one part in each 10,000 parts. Each objective should be a short statement with an action verb written in present or future tense.

> *Get a copy of your company or institution's mission statement. Examine it for goals. For each goal, write one or two specific objectives telling how you can help reach each of these goals.*

Timetable

Funders always want to know the different stages in the project, when you can begin implementing the project, and how long each stage will take. If the project has several steps or phases, it is the investigator's responsibility to make a clear distinction between each phase and inform the funder as to when each phase will start and end. Because funders often have so many proposals to consider, failure to communicate the different phases and the time frame for each can be disastrous; unclear proposals simply get put aside and end up in the rejection pile.

The flow chart is an excellent tool to use to show your sequence of events and the times you expect to begin and end each event. As you assign the time for each phase, remember that funders give their support because they have a job that they want to get done. If there is an urgency to get the program into operation, the evaluators will be sensitive to the urgency and may be highly influenced by the ability of some investigators to complete the job sooner than others. This suggests that you should be ready to immediately begin putting the first implementation phase of your project into action as soon as you learn that your project has been funded. But remember also that the funders demand quality work; allow the time you believe will be required to do a good job. The goal here is to present a timetable that shows that you are ready to begin implementing your project and that, once you begin, you will move the project forward from one phase to another until it becomes operational. See Figure 2.5.

Notice that the flow chart shown in Figure 2.5 lists all of the steps in chronological order and also includes specific beginning and ending dates for all phases of the project.

In retrospect, it is easy to see that this timetable has a major omission. It fails to include plans to disseminate information. At the beginning of the first summer session (June 1), plans to have a news reporter on hand should have been included. Most funders like to have publicity on their programs showing their generosity and commitment to the causes they support. The publicity can also be filed and used in future years to strengthen applications for further grants.

Make a list of at least three or four strategies you can always use to publicize your grants. Write these strategies down, including the addresses and phone numbers of consultants and news reporters. You might also want to include the editors and addresses of journals to which you would like to target articles you write to help others use these new programs.

Another factor to consider is extending the timetable to show your plans to continue the program *after* the funder's support is withdrawn. Obviously, not all grant proposals are written to establish programs, so providing

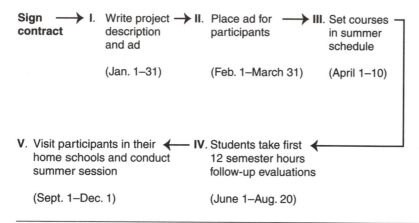

FIGURE 2.5   Sample Timetable

information on how you plan to sustain your program once the funds dry up was not listed as a proposal part on the checklist provided later in this chapter. If, however, your proposal does involve establishing a program or an ongoing service, having a clear statement explaining how you propose to keep your program alive could be one of the most influential parts of your proposal. Grant funders know that a very high percentage of funded programs immediately die once the funding ends.

> *As you know, hindsight offers opportunities to discover omissions that were not visible at an earlier time. Examine the sample timetable shown in Figure 2.5 and see if you can find other events and dates that could improve the project by adding them to the timetable.*

Evaluation

Most RFPs require the investigators to arrange for external evaluations to make comprehensive assessments of their programs. Others permit investigators to conduct the evaluations themselves. When given the choice between conducting the evaluation yourself and hiring an external evaluator, seriously consider the latter choice. Regardless of how objective and accurate your own evaluation might be, it is always subject to suspicion; therefore, it is usually far better to commission a third party to perform the evaluation. Always select a company or evaluation consultant who has no connections with your company or institution.

Although you decide to use an external evaluator, you should consider collecting your own data. These data can be quickly and easily gathered. The grant whose timetable is shown in Figure 2.5 won over the competition five years running. The continuing success can be attributed to a very simple annual evaluation. Each year, *after* the summer institute was over, the investigator drove to see the participants and ask them two questions: *"What did you get in last summer's institute that you have been able to implement?"* and *"What might we have done in the institute that would have helped you even more?"* Having the proposal win over the competition for five consecutive years was a great payoff for asking two simple questions. (Of course, each year we used the answers to these two questions to rewrite and improve the proposal.)

Budget

Be Reasonable

Virtually all RFPs require budgets to show how much money they will be asked to provide and how that money will be spent. Naturally, a major concern is always the need for the investigator to be a good steward of funds. Two principles should be remembered at the onset of constructing a budget. First, do not succumb to the common temptation to purchase a computer or other items that are not absolutely essential to perform the responsibilities of the grant. Even if a computer is essential, to avoid suspicion of the evaluators, consider renting one instead of purchasing it. Second, treat the grant money as though you were spending your own money. Ask for enough money to do a good job, but don't be overly generous with someone else's money.

Some grant writers argue that the budget should be the first part of the grant-writing process because by developing the budget first and then writing the body of the grant, they are able to stay within the limits specified in their budget. Others find this process too restrictive and prefer to spell out all other parts of the program and, then, as a final step, prepare the budget. The order is a personal choice. Regardless of when the budget is written, however, it must reflect the mission of the proposal. This means that the items that cost the most should be the most essential parts.

Begin by listing the most costly, tangible items. Then list the most costly intangibles. Salaries are often among this latter group. Don't forget to include overhead expenses. If you work at an institution of higher learning, check with your grants office for the exact amount to ask for overhead. If your institution, business, or organization is small and does not have a grants and contracts office, your administration can provide this information.

Make In-Kind Contributions

A part of the budget that has become increasingly important over the years is in-kind contributions. These are noncash contributions that your company or institution makes to the project. In-kind contributions have become increasingly more important because funders have expected investigators to make larger and larger contributions. Indeed, many grants of recent years require an even dollar-for-dollar match.

Again, the investigator can use in-kind contributions to make this match. These include such items as portions of salaries of employees who spend time working on the project. The investigators themselves may offer to spend a portion of their time codirecting the program and therefore should list the percent of their salary that is reflected in the percent of their working time spent on the project. Don't forget to also count the time that secretaries and other clerical employees might spend on the project. The cost of building space required to house the project can be calculated and counted as an in-kind contribution. The space includes buildings and rooms rented especially for the project, and it also includes buildings and space that your employer already owns. Don't forget to include the cost of utilities and photocopying.

Once your budget is drafted, review it for missing items and to see that it mirrors the body of your proposal. For example, the most expensive items should not include expendable items.

Remember that once the program is in operation, you may not be able to adjust the budget for at least a year. Furthermore, it is conceivable that the funder may wish to negotiate for a smaller budget. Desperate to have their proposal funded, some investigators accept cuts in their budgets that are so severe that they cannot conduct the project effectively. This is a common mistake. One way to plan to cushion against possible forthcoming negotiations is to plan an extra dimension into the proposal, perhaps a service that would be a nice feature but not an indispensable one. So, when the funder says you must cut the budget by 10 percent or 20 percent, for example, this could be done by eliminating this expendable feature, without damaging the rest of the proposal. Most funders like this feature because it gives them an opportunity to exercise caution against padded or inflated budgets without sacrificing the quality of the overall project.

Checklist

To guard against omissions, some grant writers make a checklist of all the major parts in their grant proposals. They use this as a first *and* last step. This is an easy task if you list each part of the grant under a subheading. It is further simplified by putting each subheading in italics or bold letters. The checklist might contain the following parts:

- Transmittal letter
- Title page
- Abstract

- Table of contents
- Purposes, goals, and objectives
- Timetable
- Evaluation
- Budget

Summary

Grant writing can be made easier by knowing exactly what parts your proposal should include. Many RFPs list the parts the evaluators will expect to see when they examine and evaluate the proposals. Some evaluators are given evaluation guides or rating sheets with instruction to give each proposal part a numerical rating. When the scoring is complete, these evaluators simply add the scores and award the grant to the proposals with the highest scores. Therefore, it behooves the investigator to (1) follow the directions and include every part that is listed in the RFP and (2) ask whether a proposal evaluation score sheet is available for use in preparing the proposal.

For the many RFPs that do not specify the exact parts they wish to have in their proposals, remember that each part can be a tool to sell your proposal to the evaluators; therefore, you should seriously consider including all of the parts discussed in this chapter.

Because many evaluators receive an unmanageable number of long, poorly written proposals, brevity and clarity should be the goal when writing each part. Include just enough in each part to do the job, and the job, of course, is to communicate clearly and persuasively. Putting quality above everything else is an equally important principle to use as a guideline when preparing proposals. While it is to your advantage to be both economical and expedient, promising to deliver too much too soon can be disastrous. Common sense and good judgment should temper your temptation to overcommit.

Credibility is an indispensable quality for all grant writers. Experienced grant writers who have written previous grants and have successfully implemented them have an advantage over novice grant writers, but only if they have collected data and maintained records to substantiate their success. Novice grant writers can offset this advantage by keeping careful records and by using their first grant and each succeeding grant to establish their own record of credibility.

While this may appear as a Catch-22 situation for novice writers, it is possible to put credibility into that first proposal by citing the literature. Funders expect to see evidence of need for the proposed program or product, and they expect to see data to support any claims that the investigators make, including their claims to have expertise or other resources such as the facilities and human power needed to support their proposal. Locating and citing studies that support your generalizations can be tantamount to taking that extra step to ensure acceptance of your proposal. Chapter Six suggests that all grant writers develop a system for collecting data and storing it systematically and orderly, so that it can be retrieved easily and quickly. Chapter Six also presents an easy, yet highly functional system for achieving this goal.

When your proposal is complete, check it against your parts checklist to see that no part was inadvertently omitted. As incredible as it may sound, sometimes investigators become so wrapped up in the writing of their proposals that they leave out some of the most important parts, including the budget, when they are mailing; therefore, you should use this checklist again when you are literally putting the budget in an envelope to mail.

A final check is also needed to remove any grammatical or mathematical errors. Simple errors give the impression that the investigator is careless, leaving the evaluators to believe that anyone who makes errors in the proposal will be equally careless in overseeing the grant, if, somehow, the flawed proposal is eventually funded.

Recap of Major Ideas

- Some RFPs specify the parts the evaluators expect to see in all proposals. Evaluators frequently assign points to each part of the proposal and total the scores to determine which proposals will be funded.
- Clarity and brevity should be the goals for preparing each part of each proposal.
- Each part of each proposal can be used as a tool to garner support for the proposal.
- Most funders value the ability to deliver a quality program or product over the needs of the investigators; therefore, do not emphasize need over ability.
- Investigators should avoid including extra equipment purchases, such as computers.
- Investigators should be prudent but realistic when preparing their budgets.
- RFPs should always be followed meticulously.
- Investigators can strengthen their proposals by citing reports and articles.
- Each proposal should include a method for publicizing the program.
- Investigators should explain how their proposals will be continued after support from the funder is discontinued.

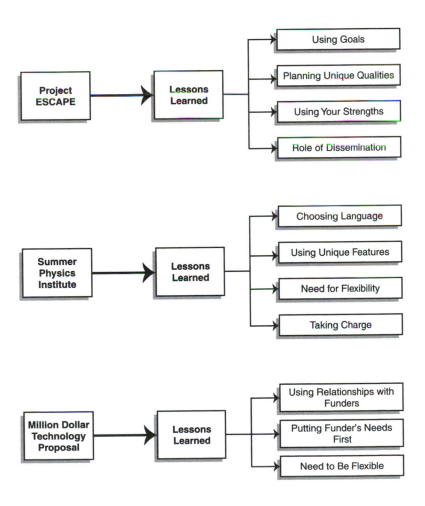

3

Three Winning Proposals

Project ESCAPE	Lessons Learned	Using Goals
		Planning Unique Qualities
		Using Your Strengths
		Role of Dissemination
Summer Physics Institute	Lessons Learned	Choosing Language
		Using Unique Features
		Need for Flexibility
		Taking Charge
Million Dollar Technology Proposal	Lessons Learned	Using Relationships with Funders
		Putting Funder's Needs First
		Need to Be Flexible

Prelude

Grant writing is a slippery business. The nature of grant writing is such that you can write about it or talk about it at great lengths without causing the audience to understand how to do it successfully. Sometimes what is needed is a good example of a real grant proposal, one that was carefully crafted, submitted for evaluation, and chosen above its competitors for funding. Each of the following three sections focuses on a separate grant proposal that has met all of these conditions. Each section will point specifically to the strengths of each of the proposals—unique features that are responsible for that proposal's having been selected above its competition. Each of these unique strengths is a quality that you can include in your proposals. To make these experiences more realistic, each of these sections is written in the first person.

Many grant-writing workshop participants say that they need to see some proposals that have been funded. While this is clearly helpful, participant's often need explanations for particular features in the proposals and the writer's techniques for getting the proposals funded. Put another way, participants find it helpful to have someone walk them through the process, explaining the reasons for particular features in the proposals and pointing out the steps followed in getting the proposals funded. This chapter will introduce three different proposals and will explain the features of each and the steps followed in getting each funded.

Proposal One: Project ESCAPE

It was early December and I was barely out of my doctoral program. I had moved 500 miles to take my first higher education teaching position at a Midwestern university, choosing this position over several others because it provided ready access to a mainframe computer, a half-time editor for the faculty's use, and the opportunity to work with a nationally known professor in the department, a prolific writer who enjoyed sharing his expertise by teaching a course to the faculty titled "Writing for Professional Publication."

Purpose of the Proposal

Having received a doctoral degree in curriculum and research, and having the level of optimism that characterizes most recent graduates, I was determined to create a better teacher education program than anyone had ever seen before. I wanted a very different program, and if my wants were granted, this program would be totally field based; all of the pedagogy would occur not on the university campuses but in elementary and secondary classrooms. A second major condition for this new program is that it would be totally performance based.

I checked with the university's office of grants and contracts to locate a potential funder for a performance-based, school-based, teacher education program. The news was disappointing; no known source was currently funding program designs for higher education programs. So, I talked to my colleagues, who found my idea interesting but who also knew of no possible funding source for such a program.

Our school had a nice teachers' lounge where we often retreated between classes for a quick cup of coffee to prime ourselves for the next class. As I sat quietly, enjoying a moment of silence and a good cup of coffee, two colleagues entered the room, barely acknowledging my presence because they were engrossed in their own conversation. One was telling the other about a new teacher burnout program that he had heard was coming to the local schools. As this colleague talked, I sipped my coffee and listened. The purpose of some forthcoming grant money was to design programs to rejuvenate teachers who were experiencing emotional burnout.

As the discussion continued, I thought about my desire to create a performance-based, school-based teacher education program, wondering whether the new teacher burnout program and my personal dream for a model teacher education program might, in some way, be connected. Being an early riser, I was fortunate to have my teaching load in the mornings, freeing my afternoons for conducting research, preparing lessons, and handling other professional responsibilities, including grant writing. So, the next morning I taught my classes, went directly to my car, and drove to the state capital where I began asking about the proposed teacher burnout program. I wasn't professionally mature enough to solicit the help of my legislators, but I had one force on my side: persistence. I was determined to have my model teacher education program.

The State Department of Education office had both good news and bad news. The good news was that the rumor I had heard was true; money had been appropriated to support teacher burnout research. The bad news was that the money was earmarked, not for universities, but for elementary and secondary schools. The further less-than-good news was that the request for proposals (RFP) had already been issued and it had a short deadline. The job was too big for one individual to do alone in the short time available. In retrospect, for an inexperienced group of writers, quickly creating a proposal wasn't very realistic. But, fortunately, I was too inexperienced to realize the odds, and even had I known of the slim chances for success, I was probably too determined and self-assured to respect these odds. All I knew for sure was that if I didn't try, I was certain not to have my dreams become a reality. Even with an outside chance, the only way to meet this challenge was to locate some interested partners who were willing to work through part of their Christmas break. Still determined, I located three equally inexperienced colleagues who agreed to spend part of their holidays preparing a grant proposal. Following is a description of that proposal.

Examine your own workplace. Do you have a coffee or a lunch group; a golf, rac-quet ball, or other exercise group; or a civic club where you can gather ideas for research project topics? Or as in this case, do you have a place where you might learn of funding opportunities? Choose one of these group gatherings to routinely discuss your creative ideas and keep an ongoing record of the positive or negative reactions of your colleagues. Should you choose to collaborate on a proposal, this record will help you identify colleagues who share your commitments.

Putting the Funder's Goals First

Our program was not created to replace the existing, traditional teacher education program; rather it was aimed at a small cohort of exceptionally bright students who sought to escape the traditional route to teacher education, students who would prefer to develop their pedagogical skills in elementary and secondary classrooms. As with all successful grant proposals, our own professional and personal goals had to become secondary to the potential funder's goal. According to this RFP, the funder's goal was to reduce the level of teacher burnout in elementary and secondary schools throughout the state. So, to be competitive, our proposal had to proclaim reducing teacher burnout as its paramount goal, and we had to devise a method to convince the evaluators that our proposed program would meet this goal.

Unique Features

Our program would not purport to erase all teacher burnout in the state; rather, we proposed to identify a manageable number of highly competent teachers who just happened to be experiencing burnout. We decided that a manageable number of participants would be fifty teachers, so we settled on twenty-five elementary school teachers and twenty-five secondary school teachers.

We wanted to believe that the best proposals are always the ones that are selected for funding, but we knew that this is not always true. Although we did not know why this happened, we knew that often some of the best proposals are overlooked. The most important thing we knew was that each proposal that is accepted for funding is selected because it is different from the other proposals; it has one or more qualities that make it stand out above the many other competing proposals. We knew that we had better use this knowledge well to enhance the chances that our proposal would be accepted. All we had to do was to make certain that our proposed program had some unique features that the evaluators would consider strengths.

In a sense, our program would be unique because it was performance based. This was a uniqueness, and we knew that the evaluators would proba-bly consider it desirable because performance-based programs were becoming popular and performance-based assessment was being proposed for all schools. But we knew that this uniqueness might not be enough; after all, some of the other proposals might be performance based.

> *Just as it is important that grant writers remain willing to put the goals of the potential funders ahead of their own goals, it is equally important that grant writers have their own professional and personal goals identified and in mind at all times. Take a few moments and jot down some of your professional and personal goals. Make each of these goals time specific by giving it a deadline. By this time next year, I will have done such and such.*

When choosing unique qualities for your own proposals, it is important that you *keep your attention on the purpose of the program, as it is stated in the RFP*. My own personal purpose for this proposal was to develop a superior, performance-based model for a teacher education program, one that our college and other colleges could use to prepare future teachers. But, to my knowledge, the evaluators for this program weren't interested in my goal; they wanted a program that would eliminate some of the teacher burnout pervasive in elementary and secondary schools throughout the state. They wanted to jump start those teachers who had emotionally burned out.

Using the Literature

We researched the literature that related to the funder's goal—teacher burnout—and discovered that there was agreement—we found at least two supporting articles—that the point at which most teachers experience the most burnout is during their sixth or seventh year. We said so, citing these articles. Citing current journal articles, books, and research has value in itself; it earns the evaluators' confidence, reassuring them that they are entrusting their money to individuals who are knowledgeable and current in their field, individuals who are willing to put forth the energy required to substantiate their work. Citing references also suggests that the proposal writers are thorough, reassuring the evaluators that if their proposal is chosen for funding that these writers will make the extra effort needed to ensure that their project succeeds.

> *Check a few of the journals in your field, some that you may choose to target some of your own articles and note the referencing style used in these journals. Most disciplines have a preferred referencing style. By examining a few of these journals, you can determine the preferred or most frequently used style in your discipline. Get a copy of the style manual—the latest edition—and add it to your grant-writing library. (For further instruction in establishing a grant-writing library, see Chapter Six.) Reading this manual from time to time should become routine behavior in your ongoing grant-writing program.*

Keeping the potential funder's central purpose in mind, we decided to design a program that would rejuvenate teachers who were experiencing high levels of burnout. We were careful to specify that the teachers chosen would be exceptionally talented teachers. This served our grant proposal well because while many of our competitors were building a case based on their *needs* (a common mistake among grant writers), we were basing our program, not on our needs, but on our strengths. Some investigators (grant writers) believe that the prize goes to the institution or individuals with the greatest needs. I don't. People like to identify with winners, and people like to invest in winners; so we wanted our proposal to have the markings of a winner throughout.

Dealing with Disagreement

So far, it sounds as though we collaborators were in perfect agreement on all issues. Actually, nothing could be further from the truth, we were the clumsiest collection of individual thinkers imaginable, and this will be revealed later; but, we were a congenial collection of individuals, and we used our disagreements to strengthen our program.

Too often, teams fall apart when they learn that they do not agree on all issues. Actually, disagreement can be helpful if it is managed appropriately. Once a decision to collaborate has been reached, the leader should immediately call a meeting to plan and organize the strategy for this group. During this first meeting, all members should agree to express their feelings and beliefs and then *go with the majority;* unanimity is not necessary. If the group has a member who is known for being argumentative, or a member who has a record of writing minority reports, eliminate that member. Remember that regardless of how excited that member may be over the proposed grant topic, the best predictor for future behavior is prior behavior; get rid of that member or get out of the group yourself. From the onset, we agreed to let all members express their preferences on every issue but to let no member impede the progress of the proposal.

Using Modules

Through surveying the literature, we learned that other performance-based programs used modules to develop the desired skills. We knew that modules were an effective way to develop teaching skills, so we, too, chose to use modules in our program. Modules provide a way to ensure that the program has clear objectives and that it has activities to cover all objectives. To teach our teachers and students about modules, we even wrote a module on modules. See Appendix C: "A Module on Modules." We also knew the value in shared ownership; people work harder when they perceive the project as their own, not a job to be done for somebody else. Because we had chosen to use the best teachers, it seemed to make sense to give them a lot of leadership. These were the brightest of the bright and the best of the best, so we wanted to use their talents and, at the same time, give them ownership in the program.

Unlike other performance-based programs, which were written by professors and research and development (R and D) experts, we decided to entrust our teachers to write the modules. We went a step further. Unlike all other performance-based programs that we found in our review of the literature, whose objectives and topics were chosen by professors and R and D teams, we decided to let our teachers choose the topics for their modules. In a sense, this plan was flawed because most of the teachers had far less writing skill than we had envisioned, yet, putting teachers in charge of writing their own modules was one of the best decisions we made because it gave them ownership and commitment. We simply began by telling the teachers that they had been chosen for this program because their respective principals had identified them as being among the best of the best teachers in their respective schools. We asked them to reflect individually on their teaching and tell us what one or two areas they might choose if they could improve even more. Would they improve their classroom management? Testing skills? Motivational skills? For their module topics, teachers could choose an area of individual weakness or they could choose to develop a model that focused on and taught future teachers their greatest strengths.

To avoid duplication, we made a comprehensive list of all areas identified and matched individual teachers with one of their top preferences. Each topic would become a learning module, which would immediately improve the skills of the teacher who developed it and we would develop a dissemination plan to ensure that these models would eventually impact teachers throughout the state.

If it is, indeed, true that people like to be associated with winners, it will behoove any serious grant writers to assess their own strengths. In his 1994 inaugural address, Nelson Mandela wrote,

Our deepest fear is not that we are inadequate. Our deepest fear is that we are powerful beyond measure. It is our light, not our darkness that most frightens us. We ask ourselves who am I to be brilliant, gorgeous, talented, and fabulous? Actually, who am I not to be! Your playing small doesn't serve the world.

There is nothing enlightened about shrinking so that other people won't feel insecure around you. We were born to manifest the glory that is within us. It is not just in some of us; it's in everyone. As we let our own light shine, we unconsciously give other people permission to do the same. As we are liberated from our own fear, our presence automatically liberates others.

Without being overly modest, take a few minutes to make a list of your own strengths. Consider both your personal and professional qualities.

Any doubt that teaching is an art will quickly be dispelled by looking at the list of modules these teachers chose (see Appendix B).

After some six months had passed, news that our proposal had been selected for funding arrived. Unfortunately, I was teaching a three-week-long comparative education course in London, England. I returned on a Saturday, checked my mail, and found both good and bad news. The good news was that our proposal had been selected above all the competition for funding; the bad news was that the program was to start full-time at 8 A.M. Monday, leaving us only one day to prepare. Naturally, we panicked. Our naysayer voices spoke: "There's no way we can do this on such a short notice." "We don't even have a room to meet in." "Half of these teachers are probably on vacation; how will we reach them?" "We don't even have a program to follow."

An important and often overlooked advantage of grants is that they provide opportunities to do things differently, things that otherwise would be impossible. Another overlooked advantage is that every funded grant is loaded with learning opportunities. The common expression "Every grant you write is easier than the one before" is true, at least for alert participants who note and record their successes and failures.

Each graduate of our program was promised teacher certification. The summer would be spent writing modules. Each teacher would carefully compute an estimate of the number of hours required to complete the module. The module would then be assigned a number of credits. For example, modules that require forty-five or more hours to complete would earn three credit hours of coursework.

Some modules were required of all students who participated in this program because they were based on content that was either required for graduation or for teacher certification. For example, all students in this program had to successfully complete the module on classroom management and the module on testing. The state also required a minimum number of credits in pedagogy; so our students had to complete enough modules to earn the minimum number of credits. Having completed these required modules, the student could then choose the modules preferred to earn the remaining credits. This enabled the students to ESCAPE the normal routine on campus, thus the acronym ESCAPE (Elementary and Secondary Competency Approach to Performance Education).

Disseminating the Grant

When grant money is appropriated by federal, state, or local governments the *evaluators look for assurance that the funded programs will serve the largest number of individuals possible.* Knowing this, you can give your proposal a boost by explaining how large numbers of people will benefit from your proposed program. We wanted our project to benefit more teachers than the fifty who were directly involved in writing the modules, so we put stipulations on each module they produced. Because we knew that many teachers would be bored by a lot of reading assignments, we limited the amount of reading and required each module to have a corresponding videotape. These videotapes were eventually made available to all teachers throughout the state. So that other teachers would be tempted to use these modules, we required each module to have a flowchart, providing easy-to-follow steps for its application. Notice that the sample flowchart in Figure 3.1 guides each student, step-by-step through the program.

This flow chart was designed for the module titled, "A Module on Modules." This particular flow chart provides its unsuccessful users an opportunity to recycle again and again until they succeed. This is a strong quality that can be planned into any module.

As mentioned earlier, one of the favorite modules, "A Module on Modules," was created to help these teachers develop the other modules. Now this same module would be the first module required of all students who would participate in the ESCAPE Program. It served as a guide to prepare them to follow and use the other modules.

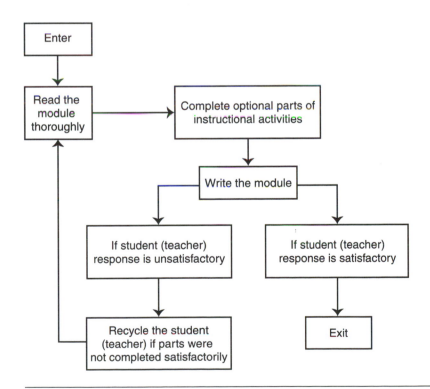

FIGURE 3.1   Sample Flowchart

Lessons Learned from Project ESCAPE

Although a good proposal can never be guaranteed funding, the grant writer who uses the tips set forth in this book can significantly improve the probability of acceptance and can learn from the successes and failures associated with each proposal. Following is a list of lessons learned through writing the Project ESCAPE grant:

- Flexibility is essential.
- The desires of the funder must take precedence over the proposal writer's needs.
- Grant writers should remain alert at all times, listening for new funding opportunities.
- The probability of a proposal's acceptance can be increased by including unique features.
- Persistence can turn road blocks into highways of success.
- The roles of collaborators should be spelled out clearly before the project begins.
- To be competitive, each proposal must have unique features.
- Citations from recent books and journals can and will strengthen proposals.
- Demonstration of exactly how the product will be disseminated for the use of others enhances the chances of a proposal's success.
- Disagreement among collaborators can improve a proposal *if* the partners can express their differences and move onward.

Proposal Two: The Summer Physics Institute

As discussed in Chapter One, grant writing has many benefits, and these benefits differ from one grant writer to another, depending on the professional and personal goals of each grant writer. Successful grant writing requires knowing what benefits you most want to derive from each grant. A major benefit, perhaps even the most important of all, is the self-satisfaction grants can provide by helping you to help others.

The Role of Passion

Having grown up in a rural area, I attended a small, two-room elementary school with three grades in each room. Since then, having worked in hundreds of schools in this country and abroad, I am convinced that my elementary schooling was second to none. The smallness of the classes, the integrated program, and the outstanding teachers made a perfect combination.

By today's standards, the school I attended for my next six years of schooling was also small, with only forty-six students in my graduating class.

Unlike my elementary school years, the smallness of my high school had a serious disadvantage: the curriculum was extremely limited. As a lover of both sports and music, I found the absence of a football team and the absence of a band a major handicap. Later, in college, I would discover that for a student who preferred science and mathematics over other subjects, the absence of a foreign language, particularly Latin, was a major disadvantage. The proverbial straw was broken when, in my senior year, I was told that the limited curriculum offerings in my small high school would not enable me to take both advanced science and advanced mathematics. At the beginning of my senior year, I refused to choose between taking advanced science and advanced math, and, instead, transferred to a larger school with a more diversified curriculum.

After becoming a teacher of science and mathematics, and later returning to my home state to work as a teacher educator, I began writing grants to help improve the educational opportunities of others. A rumor was heard that our state, like all other states, was passing legislation that would provide block grants for universities to improve the knowledge and teaching skills of the state's high school teachers of mathematics, chemistry, and physics. I quickly contacted our dean of arts and sciences. Because he was a chemist, I proposed that we collaborate on two grant proposals; he would take lead and be the principal investigator on a chemistry grant proposal and I would do the same on a physics proposal. Because each state was limited to one grant in each discipline, winning either grant would require writing the best proposal in the state. Our chemistry proposal was rejected, but our physics proposal was accepted.

Knowing that we could not directly improve the knowledge and skills of all physics teachers in the state, we focused on those teachers who had little or no background in physics. We proposed to identify ten very bright teachers with little or no coursework in physics and bring them to campus for sequential summer institutes in physics. Our goal was to improve their knowledge of physics and their pedagogical knowledge and skills.

> *Many individuals are so discouraged by their limitations that they are permanently dissuaded from writing grants. This chapter says that by looking at our limitations, often we can turn these limitations into strengths and then bring substantial strengths to our grant proposals. Reflect on your own background and identify some of your major limitations. Can you think of a way to use these limitations to strengthen your future grant proposals?*

Choosing Language

The fact that money was being provided to improve science and math teaching skills at a time when the nation's math and science teachers were being criticized for students' low standardized test scores in science and math was no coincidence. The most common adjective found in the many education reform reports and articles was *rigor*. The writers were saying that our teacher education programs that prepared science and mathematics teachers lacked rigor. I used this knowledge and made our proposed program very *rigorous*. Each summer, each participant would take a full twelve-semester hours of physics. This would be a heavy load, indeed, but these were especially gifted teachers. Instead of just "talking the talk" about rigor, this project turned the talk into real program improvements.

Unique Features

Through having had previous proposals funded, I knew that to be seriously considered for funding, a proposal has to get the attention of the evaluators, and gaining the evaluators' attention required a proposal to have one or more unique features. So, I reasoned that if one unique feature would help our proposal get funded, several unique features would almost make it a shoe-in. This proposal would definitely have several unique features including the following:

1. It would be highly rigorous.
2. It would have a special course taught by a special teacher.
3. It would have a weekly seminar that would be very nontraditional and motivating.
4. It would be loaded with laboratory experiences that required no expensive materials or equipment.
5. It would have a special evaluation system that occurred at a unique time.

A Special Course.   Most of the coursework in this program would be standard physics courses, but the program would also have a very unique course on pedagogy for physics teachers. Instead of the common course on generic teaching methods or the common course on science methods, this course would be a special treat for teachers who were faced daily with challenging physics problems at the end of each chapter in their high school physics textbook. Even the textbook for this course would be special; unlike the books used in other college classes, it would not be a college text at all but would be the state-adopted textbook for high school physics classes. Once each week, the participants in this summer institute would have the unusual opportunity of seeing an expert work the end-of-chapter problems.

Our physics department had seventeen full-time faculty members and any could have worked these problems with little effort, but we decided to use none of them. The current literature had many articles on *master teachers*. To the layperson, and consequently to legislators, this term had a good ring. Of course, everyone should want all of our elementary and secondary classrooms staffed with master teachers. We took advantage of this knowledge and hired a local high school physics teacher who had earned the title, *master teacher*. Each week this teacher would leave her school for three hours to come over to the university and work the problems at the ends of the chapters in her high school physics text. What a treat for inadequately prepared teachers who were struggling with many of these problems. What a boost for a proposal!

As a sidebar, it is interesting that although the evaluators really liked the idea of our using a master teacher, and although this unique feature undoubtedly played a major role in their decision to fund this proposal, after one summer we decided to replace this highly competent master teacher because the program participants refused to give her the respect and cooperation that they gave to college professors. If we were starting all over from the beginning, would we include the high school master teacher? Indeed, we would. Another group of teachers might have responded differently. Anyhow, the first objective of grant writers must be to have a good idea and the second objective is always to sell this idea to the evaluators. We believe that the master teacher component was a major factor in getting this proposal accepted.

Chapter Five "Developing an Appropriate Writing Style" advises that too much ill advice is given to grant writers regarding the need to use jargon and other unfamiliar language, yet, like the previously discussed teacher burnout proposal, this proposal was aimed at getting funds that were established by legislators, and legislators pay an inordinate amount of attention to the language their constituents use. What we did that was different is that we didn't just use the language *master teacher*; we actually used a master teacher, and instead of just using the term *rigorous* to describe our program, we required each student to take a very heavy set of demanding courses.

A Weekly Seminar.   As discussed in Chapter Two, effective grant writers learn to keep one eye on the RFP, being careful to respond to every part, while keeping the other eye on their own resources (what they have to offer that the competitors do not have or do not think about offering). Because our university was large and diverse, it was rich with resources, especially human resources. We wanted to bring all of these resources to the bargaining table, so we developed a weekly seminar.

Each Friday, the participants and the codirectors of the institute had lunch together in a dormitory cafeteria. After a leisurely hour-long period of eating and socializing, we would walk together to meet a special member of the university faculty who had volunteered to give us a special seminar. We were careful to invite professors who had topics that we knew would be of high interest to high school physics teachers. Among the many excellent speakers was a physics professor whose specialty was robotics. He brought a robot that he had designed and built and had it perform tasks at our commands. His presentation was unique in that through his work, the university had made the cover of *Time Magazine* twice by intervening to save a local multimillion dollar company that was scheduled for closing.

Another seminar was conducted by a member of the physics department whose specialty was quasars. That seminar had a segment that involved our going to the observatory at night to examine quasars. Since only a few physicists specialize in quasars, these teachers had an interesting story to share with their students the following fall.

Another fascinating seminar was conducted by a former member of the faculty who had been retired for seventeen years and who remained physically fit by working out at the university health center and by walking five miles a day, three days a week. This retired professor had spent his professional career teaching physics and researching the personal lives of famous physicists. He talked at ease for two hours, keeping us mesmerized with his fascinating stories, using a catalog drawer of 3" × 5" cards. Each card told a story about a particular physicist, and included personal information that was unknown to most people. Imagine the high school students' reactions to their teachers' personal encounters with robots, quasars, and stories on the personal lives of the physicists in their textbook. Imagine the influence that such a variety of unusual experiences would have on the proposal evaluators' ultimate decision.

> *Every grant proposal needs a unique feature to separate it from all of its competing proposals; and, as with this proposal, all grant writers bring this uniqueness to their projects by using their colleagues in the workplace or elsewhere and using their expertise. Make a list of professional colleagues and their respective areas of expertise. Include those colleagues who have unusual expertise and those who have unusually high levels of expertise.*

Other Unique Features.   Other unique features included an abundance of inexpensive laboratory experiences and a special evaluation system. I asked my university to provide an automobile and gas so I could personally visit each participant *after* the summer ended and the participants returned to their schools. I wanted to see what they had found useful and what we might have done that would have helped even more. These evaluations showed an unexpected level of commitment and provided feedback, which I used to strengthen each subsequent proposal.

Lessons Learned from the Summer Physics Institute Grant

- Grant writers can garner support by studying the mission and goals of potential funders simply by closely examining the goals set forth in the RFP.

- All proposals can be strengthened by adding one or more unique features.
- Grant writers can strengthen their grant-writing programs by making a list of colleagues with unique expertise and colleagues with exceptionally high levels of expertise.
- Flexibility is an indispensable trait for all grant writing.
- Serious writers must never trust others to write their grants.

Proposal Three: A Million-Dollar Technology Proposal

Apart from providing the means of improving programs and initiating new programs, perhaps the next greatest advantage to having a grant proposal funded is the opportunity it provides the authors to improve their grant-writing skills. Never has this been more obvious to me than the experience of writing a million-dollar technology proposal.

When I assumed responsibility for providing leadership at a very large college, I was shocked to learn that the college had no policy to ensure that the students left their program equipped with the technology skills that they would need throughout their careers. I was equally shocked to learn that this large college had only one computer lab and that that lab was woefully ill-equipped with dated computers. For years, the university, itself, had been slow to embrace technology. The president was unwilling to commit to any innovations that would require recurring expenses; he knew that technology is money and energy hungry. The more you spend on technology, the more you discover that you must spend to keep your investments from becoming dated.

I assembled a team of faculty members who indicated that they shared my concern, placed the director of our research and evaluation office in charge, and gave the team its assignment, which was to write a grant proposal that would correct our technology shortage. The team began meeting once a week to discuss this assignment. After a few weeks, the intervals between the meetings began to grow. I became concerned with the lack of progress and began nudging the team leader. My nudging turned to prodding. A year passed. It became clear to me that if a proposal was going to be written, I would have to write it.

Using Relationships with Potential Funders

I began by investigating possible funding sources, learning that in recent years, in order to avoid investing in equipment that required recurring expenditures, our university had resisted purchasing computers for its faculty and offices. It had, nevertheless, hired a major computer company to wire all of the dormitories to make computers available for students. With some 7,000 students living on campus, the running of cables to each room was an expensive project, so I wondered if the company who had gotten this large bid would be a good place to submit a proposal to meet our needs.

I asked my administrators if they might arrange for me to meet with one of this company's funding officers and was told that two officers would give me thirty minutes of their time in one joint session. I had only one shot, and I was determined to make the best of this unusual opportunity. I quickly researched the company's funding history and learned that it was a leader in funding distance education. So, I drafted a proposal that focused on distance education. We served some schools that were located in mountainous terrain. Each day, some of our students commuted over three hours each way to attend classes and another three hours to get back home, often after one A.M., only to have to get up and arrive at their schools by 7:30 the same morning. If anyone could benefit from a distance education grant, it was surely our institution. Distance education would enable us to take our classes to teachers who were having to teach all day, attend evening classes, and then drive home past midnight in time to get a few hours sleep before leaving for work the next morning. Clearly, nobody's need for distance education exceeded ours, and the company was a proven leader in distance education. It seemed a perfect match.

But here is where I believe many grant writers fail, and that is by putting all of their energy into one proposal and going for all or nothing. I was far too committed to improving our college to take that risk, so after drafting a distance education proposal, I drafted a second, very different proposal, then another and another until I had five rough drafts for five distinctly different proposals. I made two or three good color transparencies with graphs, charts, and tables for each proposal, enabling me to communicate my ideas clearly and quickly. After all, I had an average of only five minutes to present each proposal; that would leave five minutes, and I had special plans for those remaining five minutes.

I arrived early, set up the projector, and tested it. I ordered my transparencies so that I could give my presentations without notes and could stay within the allotted time for each. Twenty-five minutes had passed and I had given all five proposals. Now, it was time for a showdown, so I played my final trump card. I put one final transparency on the screen showing the title and a one-sentence description of all proposals and asked the officers to rate them. A zero would be given to any proposal that completely missed the target, one point to any that sparked an interest, and two points to any that the officers found especially intriguing.

Frankly, I believe that the evaluators considered my strategy a little excessive. They were reluctant to assign written numerical ratings to my proposals, but they were willing to discuss their reactions verbally, and the strategy paid off. I was shocked to learn that my favorite proposal, the distance learning proposal had sparked no interest. The officers' position was one of "We've done distance education, so let's move on to something new." Only one proposal aroused the interest of both of these evaluators. I was shocked to learn that it was the one proposal that focused on the topic that they knew nothing about, laboratory schools. But neither of these issues concerned me, for now I had my direction and I knew exactly what I had to do. I would target all of my energy in one direction.

As I carefully crafted this proposal, I proposed to replace our one, severely dated computer lab with twenty of the latest personal computers available and one server. Because our large special education department was located across campus, I proposed an identically equipped computer lab for that building. Since I had worked with the English department to establish university-wide writing requirements, I proposed a similar lab for the English department. Our large laboratory had separate wings for the elementary, middle, and high school; so I proposed the same type lab for each of these wings.

Using Your Strengths

Our laboratory school was an outstanding school in its own right. Although its students came from all socioeconomic levels of the community and two-thirds of the students had no other connection with the university, these students consistently scored among the highest of any in the state. The laboratory school was an intricate part of every education student's program. I proposed that all of these computer labs and all of the individual computers would be connected into one large network. This enabled our methods professors to introduce a piece of software and then take their students over to the lab school to see that same piece of software being applied in a classroom of students the same age as those the students planned to teach. This was a long-time dream of mine, and I knew of no college anywhere that had such an ideal system.

> *The success of this grant proposal can be attributed, at least in part, to the customer-client relationship of our university to the funder. Put frankly, we were a good customer. Think about your own workplace. Can you identify a company for which your company or institution has been a good customer? Now, try to identify a project that would benefit both you and this company.*

Using the Literature

When the proposal draft was completed, I researched the literature to find support for this program and to find data that would convince the potential funders that, although my ideas were without precedence, they were pedagogically sound. First, I defined *laboratory school* and then I reported research from the literature that showed the effectiveness of lab schools, and that, in spite of their effectiveness, all but one hundred lab schools in the country had been eliminated to save money. I then showed that the nation had only six lab schools that included all grades from nursery through high school and, of these, ours was the largest.

I made one point perfectly clear: by funding this proposal, the company would become an active partner with this great institution called *laboratory schools*. Even the father of the laboratory school, John Dewey, would have applauded this proposal.

In all, I had asked for a package of hardware and connections that cost $1.1 million. To my absolute astonishment, the company funded it in full; not one cent was negotiated. This, in itself was a victory, for it was the only proposal I had ever written that didn't require negotiation. With the letter of acceptance in hand, I asked my university to provide nice furniture for each of the 110 computers. This, too, was granted at a cost of $85,000.

Lessons Learned from the Technology Grant

The technology project taught me that successful grant writing requires serious commitment, determination, and tenacity. It reinforced my belief that if you have a good idea, you have the fortitude to investigate the market and carefully craft your proposal to make it fit the goals of a potential funder, and you are persistent, you can get your proposal funded. Our college had a number of good grant writers, and in fact each year our faculty consistently took second place among the nine colleges on our campus in the number of dollars generated through grant writing. As the senior officer in the college, I read, edited, and approved dozens of proposals each year. I already had learned that most fly-by-night proposals—that is, proposals that are quickly written to meet short deadlines—are rejected and, in contrast, proposals that are carefully written, and rewritten again and again are usually funded, if not on their first submission, then on a resubmission.

This proposal also taught me that if you are really serious about grant writing, never trust someone else to do your work. I was the one who felt this burning need to update our college's technology. My colleagues had gone along for years, comfortable without new equipment. They had adjusted well in the university's culture, which had no serious commitment to technology. Would I ever again collaborate on a proposal? Absolutely! But, from that time forward, I would make certain that each partner shared my level of commitment and passion for the proposal. Would I ever entrust the leadership for the writing of a proposal that I dreamed up to someone else? Absolutely not!

The proposal reinforced my belief that successful grant writers must remain flexible, acknowledging that the first and most important goal is to carefully design a proposal that will meet the funder's goals at a level promised by none of the competing proposals. It also reinforced my belief that while establishing need is an important factor in persuading funding agencies to support your proposal, it pales in comparison to the ability to convince the funder that you and your institution are winners. You must use your own unique strengths and the strengths of your institution and community to persuade your funder that you will do a better job than others would do at reaching the funder's goals.

Summary

Grant writing is a highly competitive activity and a high level of success demands a well-structured approach. Yet, by choosing potential funders that have goals that parallel their own goals and by carefully crafting their proposals to make them meet the funder's goals, grant writers can succeed at the level that they are willing to work to achieve.

Serious grant writers have their own personal grant-writing programs. These programs are ongoing, as they continuously listen and look for opportunities and as they continue to build their grant-writing resources through staying current with the literature in their field, maintaining ongoing lists of data, including their own strengths and weaknesses. Although they may carefully select colleagues to collaborate with them, these grant writers do not trust their grant-writing programs to others; so when they do choose to collaborate, they select partners who are self-motivated self-starters—individuals who do not require prodding.

Excellent grant writers are flexible—so flexible that they always put the funder's goals ahead of their own, sometimes even changing the major thrust of their proposals.

Grant writers can give all of their proposals an advantage over competitors by including unique features in each proposal. Two additional advantages can be gained by (1) making lists of strengths and weaknesses and learning to use both their strengths and their weaknesses to strengthen their proposals and (2) seeking out grant proposal topics that can be advantageous to the potential funder in ways external to the goals stated in the RFPs.

Recap of Major Ideas

The following guidelines can be used to strengthen grant writers' proposals:

- Always put the funder's needs first.
- Follow the RFP to a "t".
- Stay alert for new grant ideas and for new funding opportunities.
- Know your strengths and limitations.

- Don't be discouraged to learn that sometimes the best proposals are rejected.
- Always be flexible in both your thinking and your practices.
- Include unique features in each proposal.
- Disassociate yourself with those who would discourage you from writing grants.
- Never completely trust others to write your proposals.
- Keep up with current trends and developments in your field.
- Know your own professional and personal goals and use grant writing to reach them.
- Be persistent.

4

Using Action Research to Write Grants

Grant writing has a quality that requires taking risks. Like investing in the stock market, there's no guarantee that you will get a fair return for your time and energy. On the contrary, there's no guarantee that you will get anything at all; it could be a total loss. Furthermore, you could get an ugly rejection, which could damage your self-confidence and perhaps even your professional reputation among your immediate peers.

Different people react differently to those activities that involve risks. Some run away. Looking over their shoulders, they seem to scream out, "I'm not afraid to do it. I don't fear rejections. I would like to write grants, but I just don't have time to write grants!" Or, "I'm not a researcher or a grant writer; I'm a teacher. I want to spend my time preparing for my classes." Such comments as these imply that grant writing and good teaching are somehow mutually exclusive, and the people who choose teaching over research don't explain how they are able to stay current in their field while remaining so detached from research and grant writing. Other people react just the opposite. Like moths drawn to a flame, they find the risk and the challenge irresistible.

Of course, grant writing is not the only behavior that scares some and stimulates others. Research has the same effects on people. But, like grant writing, research is just a paper tiger—if you master a few basic skills and select the right type of research.

Action Research

Because there is one type of research that is quick, easy, and nonthreatening and yet is a valuable tool to those grant writers who learn how to use it, I encourage all grant writers, including beginners, to use this type of research. Of course, the chapter title is a dead give-away as to which type of research this is: *action research*. Action research is easy to conduct—in contrast to the dissertations and other major research challenges that many of us faced in college. Action research does not require the investigators to master complex research methodology or complicated statistical designs. Rather, it enables researchers to use skills they already possess.

In a sense, everybody is a researcher. Anyone who ever prepares food and experiments with spices, measuring, and tasting is a researcher, and, in fact, our home kitchens are perfect examples of research laboratories. Every time we go shopping, if we try even one new product or brand for our first time, we are conducting research. When the vacuum cleaner stops picking up debris and we check to see whether the bag is full, we are performing action research. When golfers select a new club or adjust their swings or when an angler selects a new lure or a new casting method, these athletes are using action research.

While these examples of action research may appear trite, they deliver an important message; we all conduct research. Conducting action research at work is just as easy as conducting it at home. We might be a little more formal and write down our problems, our predictions, and our results, but that, too, is very elementary and poses no serious challenge to anyone.

Using Questionnaires

Sometimes aspiring grant writers say that they want to write grants but they don't know how to begin. Others say that they would write grants, but they don't believe they know enough about the current developments in their field. They know that if their proposal is to be successful, they must first convince the evaluators that they are on the cutting edge of the research and practices in their profession.

The solutions to all of these concerns can be found in the use of surveys, and each survey requires only one short, well-constructed questionnaire. At this point, I would like to share with you a short, simple, one-page questionnaire that I have used for two decades. See Figure 4.1. By revising this questionnaire each time it is used, this simple, one-page questionnaire has enabled me to share the results of these surveys with more than one million readers.

I encourage grant writers to reflect on their professional goals and also on their personal goals and to select topics that can help them reach these goals. My purpose for using this questionnaire was to stay current in the field of publishing so I can help others become more successful, published authors. I wanted to help them avoid the common mistakes that frequently lead to rejection.

As noted in Chapter One, the success of grant writing for all grant writers depends on their knowing their own goals. Some participants bring ideas or dreams to my workshops and quickly use the workshops to learn how to fulfill those dreams. Others bog down at the beginning because they don't believe they have the knowledge or skills they would need to really help others. The questionnaire is a tool that quickly fulfills this need for these reluctant participants. You, too, can develop a questionnaire that will quickly gather all the data you will need to write a convincing grant to support and fulfill your desire to help others or to reach other professional goals.

For example, I used my questionnaire to editors to help individuals write and publish journal articles. Perhaps you, too, would enjoy using your expertise to help others. Reexamine the professional and personal goals you identified and listed in Chapter One as important to you. Now, examine your professional work and identify a topic that you can research to move you nearer to one or more of these goals.

EDITOR'S INFORMATION FORM

Name of Editor _____

Name of Journal _____

Address _____

1. a.   _____ Approximate number of subscribers.
    b.   Your primary audience is _____.

2. _____ % of the contributors are university personnel.
    _____ % are graduate students, and _____ % are K–12 classroom teachers;
    _____ % are K–12 administrators; _____ % specialists; _____ % other:

3. Refereed 10 yrs ago? _____ Refereed now? _____ If yes, nationally?
    _____ , or in the office? (by the editor and/or the editorial staff) _____ If
    refereed, is it anonymous? _____ Other? _____
    Please explain _____.
    Do you provide the referees with a rating instrument? _____

4. _____ % of the articles in your journal report research data, i.e., what per-
    cent of the articles report the results of a study conducted by the author(s)?

5. _____ % of the total number of articles published in one year relate to a
    particular theme or issue.

6. _____ % of all manuscripts received are accepted for publication.

7. _____ days lapse before we answer query letters. (please estimate)

8. _____ days lapse before we acknowledge receipt of a manuscript.

9. _____ weeks lapse before we make the publishing decision.

10. _____ months lapse between acceptance and actual publication.

11. _____ manuscript pages is our preferred article length. Our max. length is
    _____ pp. Our min. length is _____ pp.

12. In addition to the original, how many photocopies do you require? _____

13. Required style: APA ____ , MLA ____ , Chicago ____ , Other ____ .

14. Accept dot matrix? _____ Letter quality? _____ Photocopies? _____ .

15. Good black & white photos would enhance acceptance in this journal?
    none _____ , possibly _____ , likely _____ .

16. To inquiries about possibly submitting a manuscript, do you welcome
    query letters? _____ , phone calls? _____ Which do you prefer? _____ .

17. Some common mistakes made by contributors.

18. Recommendations to contributors:

FIGURE 4.1   Sample One-Page Questionnaire to Editors

I chose to include this chapter on action research because of its practicality; put simply, action research works. Actually, this is an understatement; not only does action research work, but also it is efficient in that it has a high rate of return for the modest amount of energy and time required to use it. To illustrate the effectiveness of action research, I want to return to the one-page questionnaire, which I have used for twenty years. Collectively, this simple questionnaire has enabled me to communicate with more than a million people. But I need to emphasize that I added one thing to this questionnaire that made it effective, and that is hard work; hard, not in the sense of being difficult, but in the sense of being carefully designed and carefully conducted.

As a result, this questionnaire has provided the data required to write many manuscripts, no fewer than ten in a single journal, the *Phi Delta Kappan,* a premiere journal that rejects about 95 percent of the manuscripts it receives. The same one-page questionnaire has provided data to write several book chapters and the data needed to conduct some 300 workshops on grant writing and writing for publication. I have also used these same data to teach a course on writing for publication and to convince grant proposal evaluators to accept several grants.

But, if I might reiterate an earlier statement, I believe this success is a joint product of the survey and hard work. The acts of developing a questionnaire and mailing it out to potential funders, by themselves, are totally inadequate and are likely to produce little success. Let me explain how my ethic of hard work made the difference.

Individuals who have worked with questionnaires are likely to know that an important prerequisite to their success is getting an acceptable return rate. This could mean anywhere from 20 percent to 40 percent. Over the years, the return rate for this questionnaire has averaged just over 90 percent. (The exact return rate for each mailing is clearly documented in each article.) I believe that the quality of the data reported is equally high. By using the following advice, you can experience this same level of success.

Suggestions for Developing Questionnaires

Developing an effective questionnaire is a multistep process. Omitting any of these steps will likely diminish both the rate of return and the quality of the responses.

Selecting a Topic.   Begin developing your questionnaire by selecting a topic that you believe the respondents will consider important. People will be much more likely to take the time to respond to your questionnaire if they consider it important. Better yet, try to find a topic that meets the needs of the respondents. By completing such questionnaires, the respondents are helping themselves. Notice that the questionnaire to editors, shown in Figure 4.1, is designed to help writers prepare better manuscripts and target those manuscripts to appropriate editors. I knew that poorly prepared manuscripts and manuscripts submitted to the wrong journal are major problems at publishing houses.

Because you are using this questionnaire to gather data to use in your grant proposal, you might also consider the needs of the potential funders. This means that before choosing a survey topic, you might want to survey the current funding opportunities. Finding an RFP on a topic that fits your interests is an important step in your grant-writing program.

> *Now that you have begun thinking about your own professional goals, list two or three of your professional goals and two or three personal goals. As you continue to explore grant opportunities, try to tie some of the funders' goals you see in RFPs to some of your own goals.*

Length of Questionnaire.   Because the rate of return of questionnaires drops dramatically when they are longer than one page, I strongly recommend that you limit each questionnaire to one page. This can be difficult when you have a lot of questions that you need to ask. I have found two or three ways to squeeze in additional questions.

Thanks to the availability of computers, you are no longer limited to finite number of words on each page. By selecting a slightly smaller typeface, you can ask a few additional questions. You can add even more questions by using a legal-size page. One final suggestion for getting in more questions: Keep each question short.

Types of Questions.   Those who develop questionnaires can choose from two types of questions: open-ended and closed. Alternatively, they can choose to use both. I recommend the latter choice—several closed questions and only two or three open-ended questions. The reason for limiting the number of open-ended questions is that they require more space and threaten to expand the overall length of your questionnaire beyond one page. The reason for including open-ended questions is that they have the power to reveal insights of the respondents, often important insights that cannot be gained through the use of closed questions.

Arranging the Questions.   Once you have determined how many items to use, the next job is to decide their sequence. My advice is that you look ahead and try to picture your grant proposal in your mind. Will it begin by showing a need? Most proposals do. If so, seek out those questions that will gather data that will convince the funder that you are familiar with that need.

Next, your proposal must convince the funder that you are the best prepared of all the grant writers to meet this need. At this point, you may wish to refer to Chapter One and the discussion of the Triangular Model. First, review your strengths. Try to think of a few questions that will turn any weaknesses into strengths.

In conclusion, arrange your questions in the same sequence as the one you envision for your proposal. Having them in this order will make the data more accessible as you proceed with developing your grant.

Now return to your research topic and write a few quick-answer questions to gather the data you need to convince a funder to sponsor your project.

Suggestions for Administering Questionnaires

Testing the Questionnaire. Once the draft copy of your questionnaire is complete, it is time to test it. First, put yourself in the role of a recipient and test the questionnaire. When you find ambiguity, rewrite the question. One thing you cannot afford to have in your questionnaire is ambiguity. If the question isn't totally clear to you, rewrite it.

Next, ask a colleague to complete the questionnaire in your absence and without your explanations. If the colleague finds any question to be less than crystal clear, you need to know it. If the respondent suggests ways to improve either the questionnaire as a whole or an individual question, listen and thank your colleague. The pointing out of the ambiguity alone is priceless because you can be certain that others will see this ambiguity. Some grant writers are reluctant to share their unfinished work with others. If you don't have a colleague with whom you feel comfortable sharing your questionnaire, put it aside for a few days. This will enable you to see duplications, omissions, and ambiguities that you were unable to see while working closely with the instrument.

Sending the Questionnaires. Prior to actually sending the questionnaire, I write a short letter to alert the recipients that they will soon will receive the questionnaire. See Figure 4.2.

I always enclose a self-addressed, stamped envelope with this letter.

Whether or not you will choose to use all, some, or none of these suggested steps is your decision, but remember that grant writing is a probability game, and each of these steps can actually raise the probability that your questionnaire will be completed and returned. The same is true for using questionnaires.

Preparing a Cover Letter. When I mail the questionnaire, I always enclose a cover letter. See Figure 4.3.

Now draft a short preliminary questionnaire cover letter for your project. Your two main goals in this letter should be clarity and brevity.

Dear

Within the next few days, you will be receiving a short, one-page questionnaire about _____. The purpose of this survey is to _____ . I have kept the questions short and easy to make the job easy and fast. I hope you will take a few minutes to complete and return this short questionnaire. Thank you.

Sincerely,

Kenneth T. Henson
[title]

FIGURE 4.2   Preliminary Questionnaire Letter

Dear

Enclosed is the short questionnaire that I promised to send. By completing this form, you will [here I make a promise statement telling the respondents how their completing this form will actually serve them].

Please check the box below if you wish to receive a copy of the results of this survey.

Thank you very much for your assistance.

Sincerely,

Kenneth T. Henson
[title]   __ Yes, I would like to receive a
                                         copy of the results of this
                                         survey.

FIGURE 4.3   Sample Questionnaire Cover Letter

So far, I have explained that I begin each action research project by

- Selecting a topic of importance to my recipients
- Devising a short, one-page questionnaire
- Completing the questionnaire myself, as though I were a recipient
- Correcting any ambiguous items
- Asking a colleague to complete the questionnaire
- Correcting any ambiguous items
- Devising a short cover letter
- Mailing the cover letter, questionnaire, and a self-addressed, stamped envelope

I allow about ten working days and check my return rate. From all this work, I don't expect a return of more than 40 to 50 percent of the questionnaires, but I *want* an even higher return rate, so I don't stop yet. Instead, I continue by preparing and mailing a follow-up letter such as the one shown in Figure 4.4.

Now write a short follow-up letter for your questionnaire. Remember that the purpose is to persuade the recipients to complete their questionnaires because doing so will help others, which will result in their helping themselves.

Notice that the follow-up letter does not blame the respondent. It also emphasizes the brief nature of the questionnaire. (Only a few minutes are required to complete this form.) Finally, it expresses gratitude and is accompanied by a self-addressed, stamped envelope.

I wait another ten working days. By now, if I am lucky, my total return rate has reached 60 to 70 percent; so, I make my final play. With a stack of blank questionnaires before me, each with the name of one of my missing recipients, I begin phoning. My conversation follows this path:

"Hello Mr./Ms./Dr._____."

"This is Ken Henson in Charleston, South Carolina."

"Recently I attempted to send you a short questionnaire. You may not have received it."

At this point, I pause just briefly. Often the recipient openly acknowledges having received the questionnaire and apologizes for failing to complete it. My intent here is to remain positive and enthusiastic, so I quickly explain that I understand and that it doesn't matter because I have a copy of the form in front of me, and if I might have just five minutes of his or her time, I can jot down the answers. I have never been refused this request. The results usually take the total return rate into the low ninety percentile. I know that I will never reach all of the remaining ten percent because people today are active and

Dear

Recently, I mailed a short, one-page questionnaire to you [here, I insert the purpose of the questionnaire to show how completion of the questionnaire will benefit the recipient]. Because that letter may have been lost in the mail, I am enclosing a copy of the questionnaire. By taking a few minutes to respond to these quick questions, you will help [here, I restate the benefits].

Thank you for your time.

Sincerely,

Kenneth T. Henson
[title]

FIGURE 4.4   Sample Questionnaire Follow-Up Letter

mobile. I know that the people I reach on the phone are busy, so I respond to their cooperation by moving through the questionnaire very quickly.

For studies such as this, which return to the same respondents year after year, I do one other thing; I return their completed questionnaire from the year before, along with the letter shown in Figure 4.5. Each year, several respondents report no changes. Some mark only one or two changes. Occasionally, a respondent will change the majority of the answers.

Summary

This concludes the process that I use to handle questionnaires. Many colleagues consider my efforts excessive because they assume that the whole purpose in them is to get a return rate that they also consider excessive. In addition to a higher return rate, I believe the extra attention results in more accurate data.

Using Action Research and Grant Writing to Improve Teaching

Because improvement of teaching in all disciplines and at all levels, from kindergarten through graduate school, has become a major goal, either real

Dear

Thank you for participating in my biennial survey last [date]. I am repeating that survey and again would like to invite you to participate.

To make this job easier and faster, I am returning a copy of your previous responses. Please use a colored pen and cross out any responses that have changed and enter the new data. If no changes have occurred, just mark NO CHANGES across the top of the form.

Thank you again for your assistance.

Sincerely,

Kenneth T. Henson
[title]

enc: Last year's returned questionnaire
         S.A.S.E.

FIGURE 4.5   Revised Questionnaire Cover Letter

or political, of every governor and every legislature, the following section is included to show how this goal can be achieved.

A young graduate student who had worked incredibly hard putting herself through graduate school wanted to get the most return possible from her investment of time, energy, and money; so upon receiving her doctorate, she asked her major professor for advice, "Should I pursue opportunities that take me elsewhere or should I remain in the area where I grew up?" Her professor didn't give her a yes or no but instead offered her a much wiser response, "Pursue those job opportunities that will enable you to do what you want most to do," making no reference at all to either salaries or geographic location. At first, his suggestion didn't seem to help at all because she was weighing the benefits of staying near her relatives and the benefits of relocating to earn more money, and he had said nothing about either. Instead, this sage professor focused on the nature of the job itself: "Take the job that will let you do those things you most wish to do."

Participants in my grant-writing workshops often seem to be at the same stage as the young graduate student. Perhaps they are asking the wrong questions, without first facing their doubts about writing grants at all. The first question that a would-be grant writer should ask is, "Do I really want to do this?" "If so, why?" "Is it the best way I can spend my professional time?"

"What do I want to gain from grant writing?" After all, there are better ways to spend time if it's only for entertainment; also, there's a down side. If the proposal is rejected, that's not a great feeling. "Do I really want to take that risk?"

> *Consider the wise professor's advice. Focus on your job. What do you find most satisfying about your chosen profession? After all, you did choose this profession. Was it your lust for more knowledge? Did you fall in love with the content in your field? Perhaps, you chose higher education because you knew that it could lead to teaching, and you really enjoy sharing your expertise with others.*

This part of this chapter is included because colleges and universities, even large, flagship, research universities are putting an unprecedented emphasis on quality teaching. College presidents are politically wise to push research and service to the side, at least publicly, and proclaim their institutions as *teaching* colleges. Although they know that research, service, and teaching are a trilogy of indispensable parts and to remove either and proclaim it over the others is tantamount to proclaiming one leg of a three-legged stool as more important than the others, the current emphasis on teaching offers faculty an opportunity to cash in on the part of the job that many professors enjoy most, and that is teaching.

Hopefully, you have chosen to write grants and conduct research because you realize that, correctly planned and designed, these can enrich your teaching. If you desire to become a superb teacher, why not use research and grant writing to achieve this goal?

Action research offers many advantages over other types of research. First, unlike major, empirical research projects that use mainframe computers, action research can be done using personal computers or no computers at all. Furthermore, if your goal is to improve your teaching, action research can lead to success with this goal even if you never succeed in getting a grant proposal accepted. Put boldly, action research offers something that no grant proposal could ever offer: guaranteed success. It has other advantages. Unlike the old dissertation-type research, which can, and often does, leave permanent scars on researchers, action research is totally safe. I often joke in my workshops, telling my participants that one dissertation is enough for a lifetime and is, indeed, one too many for some of us, who are left with permanent jerks and twitches. But action research is totally painless; it is quick and incredibly simple and easy to conduct. Yet, it offers an opportunity to improve your teaching immensely.

In the 1950s, a professor at the University of Florida designed a simple and easy, yet elegant and productive series of studies to improve her teaching. Fifty years later, these studies are still improving teaching on college campuses and in elementary and secondary school classrooms throughout the country. As Dr. Mary Budd Rowe watched others teach, she noticed that when posing questions, teachers seemed to give students an inadequate amount of time to respond. Indeed, unless the student immediately produced the answer that the teacher was seeking, the teacher promptly turned to another student, to whom the teacher directed the same question. At least this seemed to be the habit of the local teachers. She wondered if this was just a local practice or if perhaps it were a national practice or malpractice. Then, too, maybe this was just her perception; maybe these teachers were giving students more time than she thought. So, she set up some very simple studies.

What a simple question she asked: "When teachers direct questions to particular students, how long do they usually give the student to respond?" Her methodology was equally simple and easy: while watching teachers teach, she merely used her watch to measure the time that lapsed following each question before the teacher redirected the question to another student. Fifty years later, Dr. Rowe's findings from these simple studies still shock teachers at all levels. Put simply, she found that, on the average, teachers give their students only one second to begin responding to each question.

Dr. Rowe had suspected that teachers were failing to give students adequate time to answer their questions, but even she was surprised to learn that the average wait-time for a response was only one second. She wondered whether this tendency to move on so quickly to the next student made any difference. After all, if teachers do this routinely, maybe students are so accustomed to it that it doesn't affect their responses. But she wasn't willing to assume this, so she returned to the drawing board and devised a study to answer this question. She simply videotaped several teachers teaching several lessons. Then she played back the tapes, and each time a teacher gave students only one second to answer, she noted the quality and length of the response. Occasionally, when teachers gave students a couple of extra seconds to respond, she noted the quality and length of these responses. The differences were monumental! When teachers increased the wait-time from one second to three seconds, their teaching became more effective.

Following are just a few of her findings:

- The length of students' responses increases.
- The number of unsolicited but appropriate responses increases.
- Failure to respond decreases.
- Students' confidence increases.
- The incidence of speculative creative thinking increases.
- Teacher-centered teaching decreases.
- Pupils give more evidence before and after inference statements.
- The number of questions pupils ask increases.
- The number of activities students propose increases.

- Slow students contribute more.
- The variety of types of responses increases.
- Students react more to each other.

The Power of Action Research

The power of action research to improve teaching is clearly illustrated in this simple little study. All of the listed advantages occur just for knowing to do nothing but wait two additional seconds following each question directed to a student. By itself, any one of these advantages would make the simple study worthwhile. This doesn't mean that they are of equal value, however. On the contrary, perhaps the most important of all is that teacher-centered teaching decreases. As you will see, this is a product of teachers getting involved in action research.

Twenty years after Dr. Rowe's wait-time studies, a similar set of studies was conducted. A young man pursuing his doctorate was assigned the task of supervising ten student teachers. While observing these student teachers' classes, he thought he noticed a difference in what students considered important qualities for their teachers to have and what teachers, themselves, considered the most important qualities for a teacher to have. So, he handed each of his student teachers a 3″ × 5″ card and instructed each student teacher to write in order of descending importance the ten qualities they believed most valuable in their teachers. Giving the student teachers a few minutes to jot down these qualities and get them in their proper order, he then collected the lists and gave each student teacher another blank 3″ × 5″ card to be given to each student teacher's cooperating teacher with the same instructions. When the ten cooperating teachers' cards were returned, the two lists were compared, he found the following:

Student Teacher List	*Cooperating Teacher List*
Interest in students as individuals	Knowledge of subject matter
Patience, willingness to repeat	Ability to discipline
Fairness	Formality, sophistication
Explains things clearly	Interest in subject
Humorous	Intelligence quotient

Notice the big difference in these lists. None of the top five qualities that the students considered most important showed up on the teachers' list, and vice versa! Consider the implications this simple little study has for teachers at all levels. Doesn't it stand to reason that any teacher could improve his or her teaching by knowing what the students consider the most valuable teacher qualities? Incidentally, the best teachers do know what their students consider important. During the 1950s, news correspondent William Jeremiah Burke spent several weeks traveling throughout the country interviewing teachers of the year. His goal was to identify those qualities that had led to these teachers having been selected the top teacher in their respective states. Burke discovered only one quality that all of these teachers of the year reported to have attributed to their successes; all teachers said they were successful because they had a mutually respectful relationship with each of their students. Former Minnesota teacher of the year Duane Obermeier said that he teaches respect by being respectful to his students and by treating them as he would like to be treated.

How few teachers at any level realize that the key to their success is not more knowledge in their content areas, more highly structured lesson plans, or the ability to maintain a well-disciplined classroom; rather, the key is simply to learn how to show respect for the academic and personal needs and feelings of each student. Notice the simplicity of these two little studies. Each could be replicated easily. The data from replicating either of them could be used to write a grant to study other ways of improving teaching. For example, you might consider designing a grant to compare the lecture method with the case study method or the inquiry method with the simulation method. Or the Socratic method with the discovery method, or journal keeping with story telling.

The possibilities are endless. You could compare the attitudes of students toward various methods, or you could measure the initial learning that resulted using two different methods. Or you could measure the amount of retention say two weeks or so after the lessons were taught. You could even vary your approaches with each of these methods. For example, you could measure the amount of content learned when using visual aids with lectures against the amount learned when giving lectures with no visual aids. A second powerful effect of conducting such action research studies was hinted at earlier in this chapter and that is the impact that involvement with action research has on teachers. Some of these include the following:

- Teachers become lifelong learners.
- Teachers' classes become less teacher-centered.
- Teachers become more open to change.
- Teachers become problem solvers.
- Teachers become more analytical and critical of their own behaviors.
- Teachers become daily readers in their discipline and in pedagogy.
- Teachers become more aware.
- Teachers become more collaborative.

So, by choosing the right type and topic for research, teachers can gather data to support grant proposals and simultaneously use the data to improve their teaching. For more information on the benefits of action research to teachers see Appendix D.

If you are a teacher at any level, kindergarten through graduate school, take a moment to list two or three topics that you could study to improve teaching or to improve your curriculum.

Using Reviews of the Literature

Some skeptics might question whether the previous report on the effects of action research on teachers might be considered research at all. They might say that the discussion was only a *review of the literature* on research. This introduces an important, though often overlooked, point: Using research to enhance one's grant writing and teaching does not require the teacher or grant writer to conduct research at all. By simply reviewing the literature and reporting the research conducted by others, grant-proposal writers can build convincing support for their grants. An examination of the proposal shown in Appendix E shows that the principal investigator used a review of the literature to build a need for his grant. In other words, he didn't survey physics teachers to learn that over 85 percent of the nation's high school physics teachers are teaching out of field; he only read this and cited the source.

Why then is it necessary to cite this source? Because it tells the reader (and potentially future proposal evaluators) that this grant writer is in touch with this issue, that he has carefully investigated the problem, leaving clear impressions that this investigator has already developed some expertise on this topic and, if given the opportunity (i.e., if his proposal is funded), he will conduct his investigation with equal diligence. Although most requests for proposals may make no mention of an expectation that the recipient must show evidence of credibility, all funders will be favorably predisposed to support those proposals that present the authors as being knowledgeable and credible in the field.

Using Qualitative Research

As noted earlier, the examples discussed so far (wait-time and teacher versus student perception of important teacher qualities) are simple, easy, and fast to research. Yet, all of these studies are examples of *quantitative* research. Grant writers should not limit their use of research in support of their grants to quantitative studies. Following is a discussion of several types of non-quantitative or *qualitative* research that can be used to strengthen research proposals and also teaching. Among others, these include journal reading, case studies, journal keeping, and story telling.

Journal Reading.   Some educators may find the idea of considering journal reading as research a little strange while others may totally reject the suggestion that journal reading is, or ever should be, considered a type of research. Yet, the literature is convincing: when teachers systematically read current journals in their content field and articles on the teaching of their content field (pedagogical articles), the quality of their teaching is significantly enhanced.

At this point, one could even argue whether reading is a legitimate type of research at all. But any concerns that grant funders might have about semantics are likely to be overshadowed by their concern about the results. By reporting on professional literature that says that journal reading improves teaching, skilled grant writers can use this information to request funds to support proposed reading programs.

Case Studies.   Case studies, whether contrived or real, offer teachers an opportunity to involve students in meaningful decision making. The Harvard School of Business not only uses the case study method, but also has used the case study method as the main teaching and learning vehicle in that school for three-quarters of a century.

Case studies put students in the center of the teaching/learning process. Through using case studies, students learn how to sift through a body of information, identify the most relevant information, and then use it to solve problems and make decisions. Because case studies involve students and permit them to use their own judgment, they are highly motivating. Because students usually work in teams, the case study method builds socialization skills and teaming skills.

Journal Keeping.   Journal keeping is a powerful teaching method because it forces students to express their ideas in writing. Former Pennsylvania teacher of the year Howard Selekman requires his students to write daily at the beginning of each period, at the middle of the period, and at the end of the period. While his students are writing, he, too, is writing. "We write about things we understand and we write about things we don't understand." Journal keeping informs students about their own knowledge. Only when they begin writing it down do they know what they understand, what they think, how they perceive, and how they feel.

Problem Solving.   Swiss psychologist Jean Piaget, Italian educator Maria Montessori, and Russian psychologist/sociologist Lev Vygotsky had one thing in common; they knew that when conditions permit children to solve problems, they have a natural inclination to do just that. Piaget saw it in his own children as he quietly observed them while they played. Vygotsky watched children as they interacted with each other, often talking their way through a problem. He called this process *negotiating meaning*. Whether alone or with peers, children are challenged by problems, and when they discover a solution, they find it satisfying.

Many teachers are unable to use this natural curiosity to enhance learning because they cannot resist the temptation to get involved and solve the problems themselves or at least give unnecessary hints. At the other extreme are those teachers who simply distribute worksheets or put problems on the board and let the students do the rest. Neither extreme is helpful; when using problem solving, teachers should first make sure that the students understand the problem and then ensure that they know how to solve it. An occasional question can tell the teacher whether the students are on track.

Using Story Telling

One of the most powerful routes to improving instruction while producing substance for grant proposals is story telling. (For more information about story telling and constructivism, see Appendix F.) Story telling is enjoyed equally by students of all ages.

Constructivism is a term that is so new that it has not found its way into most dictionaries, not even computer dictionaries; yet, with the beginning of the new millennium, no other form of teaching is as popular. At its simplest, constructivism is a way of teaching that realizes that individual students have to create their own understanding or knowledge by connecting new information to their prior experiences.

Story telling is a perfect method for introducing new information, but how do you get students to tie it to their prior experiences? One way is to use *concept mapping,* which is a system for identifying and tracking major ideas and then showing relationships among the major ideas. For example, a teacher may tell a story to illustrate a concept being studied. Constructivism depends heavily on problem solving; students are given problems and then are led to discover their solutions. Students simply write down major ideas found in a story and then draw lines to show which concepts are related to which other concepts.

Students, too, can be invited to tell stories. An effective approach to inviting students to tell their own stories is to begin a story and have each student write an ending. By sharing their endings with classmates, students may draw connections that would never have been made by the teacher.

Summary

Colleges and universities, big and small, are emphasizing quality teaching throughout their campuses. Never before have teachers, nursery school through graduate school, been held so accountable for their teaching. Wise educators know that some research is necessary to establish and sustain quality teaching. This chapter focuses on action research and its use to enhance teaching while getting teaching grants funded.

This chapter has given examples of action research that show that to be highly effective in getting funded and in improving teaching, grants need not be complex or sophisticated. On the contrary, the simplest and most straightforward surveys can provide data that teachers can use to significantly improve the quality of their future teaching. A sample survey questionnaire is shown in Appendix G. Interestingly enough, in the act of getting involved with action research—that is, research conducted to solve practical problems, such as improving classroom learning—several benefits accrue. The teachers become lifelong learners—more analytical and critical of their own teaching— better collaborators with their colleagues, and their lessons become less teacher-centered.

Effective teachers use a variety of teaching methods including, among others, lecturing, inquiry learning, case studies, journal keeping, and story telling. Constructivism is a popular teaching method in the new millennium. Constructivists believe that individuals must create their own understanding by tying new information to prior experiences. Constructivist teachers use such qualitative research methods as journal keeping, problem solving, story telling, and concept mapping to help students make these connections. This chapter encourages teachers to conduct simple action research studies that focus on teaching to enhance both their grant writing and the quality of their teaching.

Recap of Major Ideas

- Action research doesn't require the investigator to master any particular research designs, nor does it require any special statistical skills.
- All people are researchers in the sense that everyone conducts informal experiments daily.
- The questionnaire gives a very high rate of return for the investigator's time and energy.
- Extending questionnaires beyond one page significantly diminishes the return rates.
- By answering their own questionnaires, investigators can identify ambiguity in the questions.

References

Henson, K. T. (1996). "Teachers as researchers." Chapter 5 in J. Sikula, T. J. Buttery, and E. Guyton (Eds.). *Handbook of research on teacher education* (2nd ed.). Arlington, VA: Association of Teacher Educators.

Henson, K. T. (2001). *Curriculum planning: Integrating multiculturalism, constructivism, and education reform* (2nd ed.). New York: McGraw-Hill.

Jalongo, M. R., & Isenberg, J. P. (1995). *Teachers' stories*. San Francisco: Jossey-Bass.

5

Developing an Appropriate Writing Style

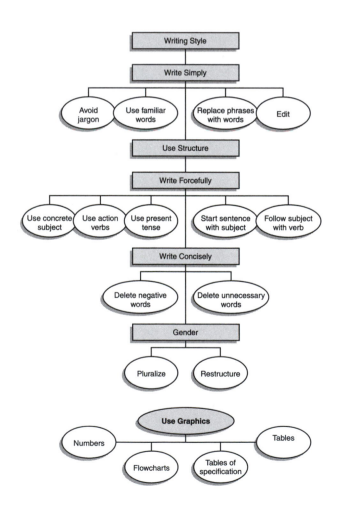

The Mystery of Writing

Most grant proposals are evaluated by a team of readers: men and women who have been assigned the task of spending hours, days, and often weeks reading and discussing dozens or even hundreds of proposals. The enormous number of proposals received for a single grant, coupled with the poor writing style employed by many of the writers, often renders the evaluation job almost impossible. You can use this knowledge to increase the likelihood that your proposal will be among those few that will be selected and approved for funding. Although you cannot change the number of proposals received, you can make your proposal stand out among its many competitors by developing an effective writing style.

A strange thing happens to people when they begin writing for any type of scholarly works, whether these are papers written in graduate classes, manuscripts to be submitted to editors for professional articles or books, or grant proposals intended to be funded. All of these writings have one thing in common; they will be evaluated. The authors' awareness of this forthcoming evaluation has mystical powers over their minds. *Mystical* may sound a little strange or far-fetched, but it is a carefully chosen and accurate word because just knowing that their work will be evaluated casts a spell over writers. They are unaware of the spell, but their behavior is dramatically affected. Unfortunately, the change in behavior is not for the better. On the contrary, it diminishes the quality of their work. For the few writers who are aware of this mysterious phenomenon, this is good news; they can use this knowledge to produce grade A papers, published books, and funded grants.

In the event that you are skeptical about mysticism and spells, consider the work of Muses. Many fiction writers say that the characters in their stories or plays sometimes come to life and take over the plot. At first, this sounds crazy, until you consider that once characters are fully developed, they must behave accordingly. But that is fiction writing, so now let's return to the business of grant writing. Knowing that the competition is keen and assuming that to make their proposals fundable, they must make them scholarly, grant writers often make their works unnecessarily complex. Several strategies are employed to achieve this goal—unusually long sentences and paragraphs, unfamiliar words, and sentence structures that leave the reader wondering whether the author meant this, or does the passage mean something else. Ironically, instead of impressing the evaluators and leaving them thinking that the author is a real scholar, the evaluators are at best disappointed and at worst put out because they cannot understand the proposal. When this happens, rejection is virtually guaranteed.

The good news is that an alert writer can reverse the results. All that is required to make your proposal more attractive than the competition is to unravel those strategies that made it obtuse, and use just the opposite approach. In other words, writers can make their proposals attractive by developing a simple, straightforward writing style. There is further good news; this is easy to do. The rest of this chapter is a simple recipe for developing a style that will get the attention and respect of your proposal evaluators.

Writing Simply

Have you ever noticed the change that comes over our vocabulary when we are introduced to strangers? The change also happens when we speak publicly. We are like medieval archers. In medieval times, archers were extremely valuable in wars. They served the same role that cannons served during the Civil War and heavy artillery played in later wars. Like today's jet bombers, the arrows and heavy artillery had the ability to reach out and strike over a distance. To appreciate the importance of these long-distance weapons, consider the alternative; without these long-distance warriors, all war becomes hand-to-hand combat and each soldier has to meet the opponent face-to-face.

The soldiers who used bows and arrows carried quivers over their backs, and each quiver contained a variety of arrows. Each type of arrow had a special purpose. We writers are like archers; we have quivers that we carefully load with words used to achieve specific purposes, and we use these words accordingly. Knowing that our proposals will be evaluated and assuming that the judges will be highly educated people, we choose words that we believe will make us sound highly educated. To impress, we use a lot of long words. These words don't have to have any special meaning; we use them because we believe that long words are evidence of scholarship. For example, when we are talking to a friend about the type of instrument we use to write grants, we might be embarrassed to say that we use a pencil or ballpoint pen and tablet. It sounds more impressive to say that we use our keyboard, computer, or laptop. If we want to further impress our audience, we can even crank it up a level and instead of saying that we *use* our computer to write, we might say that we *utilize* it. The word *utilize* has a scientific ring, implying a high level of precision. But, guess what? It doesn't have any meaning that the shorter, more familiar word *use* has. The only difference in these two words is that the one we choose when we write is about three times as long and has three times as many syllables. So, the next time you read a book on grant writing and you notice that the author advises you to choose words that grant writers use, take this advice with caution and skepticism. Your attempt to spice up your proposal by using language to impress the readers can easily backfire and have the opposite effect.

Through crisscrossing the country several times a year to give grant-writing workshops and writing-for-publication workshops, and watching the smiles on the faces of the participants, who incidentally are always keenly alert, I know that you, too, recognize that even the humblest of us are guilty of switching arrows. We can't resist the temptation to select a word, now and then, that we know some of our readers won't recognize, thinking that surely this will somehow leave the impression that we really know our stuff. Several years ago, I read the word *defenestration* and, since then I have been itching to use that word in an article or book. All of our teaching fields have highly specialized words that are necessary to make distinctions. But this word has nothing to do with my teaching fields and the only reason I want to use it is to let others know that I know a word that they probably don't know. When I think about this at all, I realize how juvenile and ridiculous this is, for all of my readers know words that I don't know. For those who might argue that on rare occasions we may need to select a word that is unfamiliar to some of our colleagues, my response is that these occasions should, indeed, be rare occasions because the behavior is totally necessary.

A good precaution against using unnecessary jargon is to imagine that you are meeting with one of the evaluators of your proposal. Pretend that you are sitting down in front of this person, just talking as you would talk to a colleague. Simply put the words in your proposal that you would use if you were having an informal chat, explaining the proposal to your colleague. This does not suggest that you should appear folksy, but rather that you should avoid using unfamiliar words.

In my writing-for-publication workshops, I caution writers against using two-dollar words when a twenty-five-cent word will suffice. Following is a list of unnecessarily long words along with a corresponding list of shorter words:

utilize	use
prioritize	rank
origination	origin
medication	medicine
established	set
administer	run
irregardless	regardless

Of course, the word *irregardless*, though common, isn't even a legitimate word, but that stops only a few writers.

Take a moment to examine your own tendency to use unnecessary, high-toned words. Make a list of two or three words that you frequently use, and for each word, list a shorter, more common word.

Using Simple Structure

Imagine an evaluator who is exhausted from hours of reading over dozens of grant proposals, and you will appreciate the need for making your proposal quick and easy to read. Replacing unnecessary jargon with everyday words is just one of several techniques you can use to write simply. You can also clarify your meaning by shortening your sentences and paragraphs. Strunk and White (1979, p. 23) said it clearly, "A sentence should contain no unnecessary words, a paragraph no unnecessary extra words for the same reason that a drawing should not have extra lines and a machine unnecessary parts." Imagine the damage that could be done to a drawing by adding an unnecessary line or the damage that would be done to a machine by adding just one extra part. One extra cog in your watch would render it comply dysfunctional. Just one unfamiliar word can draw the reader's attention away from the proposal. Consider the additional damage that could result from a few unnecessary paragraphs or pages. The same is true with a paragraph. Each paragraph should have only one idea. Any additional sentences should be deleted. If your paragraph runs for longer than a quarter of a page, it is probably too long and should be made into two paragraphs.

Having too many words often ruins sentences. Our language is filled with phrases that are unnecessary because they can be replaced with a single word. Consider the bulky and concise terms listed in Figure 5.1. Give yourself a test. Cover the column of words and see how many terms you can replace with fewer words.

This list includes just a few of the many expressions that make our writing awkward and murky. When you are drafting your proposal, don't worry about them. Yes, you read this sentence correctly. As a writer, your main goal is to get your ideas down on paper. Once the first draft is complete, you will have time to return and tighten your sentences. Look for adverbs. Adverbs slow down the reader. Use them sparingly or not at all. After your draft is complete, delete adverbs. Substitute long phrases with shorter ones or, when possible, with single words. Good writing is good self-editing. Is it work? Yes. Does it require self-discipline? Yes. Is it difficult? No.

> Using the list of bulky terms in Figure 5.1, identify some bulky terms that you frequently use. For each term, write down the word that can be substituted to replace the bulky term.

Writing Forcefully

Clarity is unarguably the most important quality in any serious, nonfiction writing, particularly in grant proposals, and as a grant writer, you must write clearly. But grant writers must go beyond this goal. Because grant writing is

Bulky Terms	Concise
until such time as	until
a high rate of speed	fast
on account of	because
in the event that	if
provides information	tells
in the majority of cases	usually
each and every one	all
has to do with	concerns
has the capability of	can
in spite of the fact that	although
cancel out	cancel
mandatory requirement	requirement
at that point in time	then
at this point in time	now
in attendance	there
improve the quality of	improve
a new innovation	an innovation
in short supply	scarce
in the final analysis	finally
in the foreseeable future	soon
she is a woman who	she
in view of the fact that	because
on a daily basis	daily
in a hasty manner	hastily
in close proximity	near
there is no doubt that	certainly
a large percentage of	most
once upon a time	once
during the past year	last year
can't help but think	think
almost everyone	most
need to be established	needed
filled to capacity	full
give consideration to	consider
rank order	rank
put in an appearance	attend
revert back to	revert to
with the exception of	except
have no other choice	must

FIGURE 5.1   Replacing Bulky Terms with Concise Terms

a buyer's market, meaning that the supply of proposals greatly exceeds the demand, and those who read and evaluate proposals are quickly lulled into a dull stupor, you must develop a style that reaches out and grabs the reader. One of the best examples of grabbing the readers is found in the opening lines of Charles Dickens's *A Tale of Two Cities*.

> *It was the best of times, it was the worst of times, it was the age of wisdom, it was the age of foolishness, it was the epoch of belief, it was the epoch of incredulity, it was the season of Light, it was the season of Darkness, it was the spring of hope, it was the winter of despair, we had everything before us, we had nothing before us, we were all going direct to Heaven, we were all going the other way.*

In these few short lines, Dickens grabs the reader's attention and, like an assailant with a firm grip on the neck, shakes the reader back and forth. Notice that each short phrase is a paradox. Dickens uses contrast to hold attention. Notice, too, the length of the phrases. Each phrase is short. Dickens is able to keep the readers totally involved and deliver tons of information without the use of complex paragraphs, unfamiliar words, or complicated sentences.

This is powerful and forceful writing. Because of the supply and demand mentioned earlier, grant writers must write powerfully and forcefully. Following is a clear formula for achieving this goal.

Begin by using a concrete noun for the subject of each sentence, and put this noun at the beginning of each sentence. This noun should be the focus of the sentence. For example, suppose you are writing a grant to improve traffic safety on snowy, icy highways. Instead of saying, "There are many times in January when the weather makes driving on the highways dangerous," just chop off the front of the sentence. Notice that this sentence begins with the word *there*. But *there* refers to location, and this sentence is not about location; it's about the effect that January weather has on driving. So, why not begin with the subject, *January weather?*

Next, follow the subject immediately with an action verb written in the present tense. So, now you have, "January weather makes driving dangerous." Does this sentence say the same thing that the longer sentence says? Yes. The big difference is that it uses fewer and more exact words. Precision and economy are essential to powerful writing. Notice, too, that the verb is written in the present tense. Past tense slows down the reader because it requires reading additional words.

Most people who have written dissertations or theses were taught to preface almost every meaningful statement with a conditioner, a qualifying statement intended to ensure that the writer and committee would not be sued for saying something that wasn't absolutely true. A similar practice, on a smaller scale, was found in high school where many of us were taught to avoid all-inclusive terms, such as *all* or *always*, and all-exclusive terms, such as *none* or *never*.

In summary, to be successful, you must keep the evaluators of your proposals interested, and you can do this by (1) using a concrete noun for the subject, (2) using an action verb, written in present tense, (3) putting the subject at the beginning of the sentence, (4) following the subject immediately with the verb, and (5) deleting all unnecessary words. The results will be short, crisp, clear, and powerful sentences.

Here is a final suggestion to help you write forcefully. Notice that this paragraph starts with the word *here,* and yet this sentence has nothing to do with location. Your author should use the advice given about starting each sentence with a concrete subject and other advice in this book as a good guideline, not as a strict recipe. For example, a final suggestion to help you write forcefully is to begin with a concrete subject. I had several reasons for beginning this sentence with the word *here.* To be honest, it was the first word that popped into my head, which exemplifies our need to always edit our own writing. Author and editor David Gilman said this about his own writing, "Often, I find myself saying, 'I didn't know I knew that.' " Editing and rewriting clarifies the product. More amazing, it clarifies our thinking. Occasionally breaking a few rules is all right and is actually recommended because it can keep your work from being stilted; yet, the closer you follow the guidelines, the more competitive your proposal will be.

Writing Concisely

I use the exercise shown in Figure 5.2 to give participants practice in editing to shorten their sentences.

> *Examine Figure 5.2 and, in the top box, delete as many words as you can from each sentence without changing the author's meaning. Sometimes this is difficult because you don't always know another author's intended meaning. Fortunately, this is not a problem when you are editing your own writing. Once you have finished editing the top box, check your revision against the second box. Perhaps you have gone further and tightened your statements even more. That's good. For example, the first sentence could read,* the company failed. *You may wish to continue tightening the rest of the sentences.*

The first sentence begins with, "The truth of the matter is." Because this is nonfiction writing, we can assume that it is true; therefore, this phrase can be eliminated. Next, notice the word "not." Negative words usually slow the reader, so "unsuccessful" is preferred over "not successful." The sentence can be further improved by simply saying, "The company failed." Notice that even when editing such a simple sentence, the process occurred in steps. Good editing seldom occurs in a single step. It is like shining a piece of furniture; each treatment makes a slight improvement and, if polished several times, the furniture will take on an entirely new glow. To illustrate that even the

Delete the unnecessary words.

1. The truth of the matter is that the company was not successful.
2. The judge, who was a distant cousin, set him free.
3. She is a woman who does not usually stumble forward without giving considerable thought to the possible consequences.
4. His cousin, who is somewhat older than he, himself is, will stand a good chance to inherit the entire estate.
5. The fact is, he's finished.
6. His job is a highly demanding one.
7. There is no doubt but that he responded in a highly hasty manner.
8. The reason why is that the Hawthorne control group was shocked out of its complacency by the supervisor's presence.
9. There is no doubt that the jury was right in finding him guilty.
10. Were you aware of the fact that excessive salt produces hypertension?

Note the effect of close editing.

1. The company was not successful.
2. The judge, a distant cousin, set him free.
3. She does not usually proceed without considering the consequences.
4. His older cousin will stand a good chance to inherit the entire estate.
5. He's finished.
6. His job is highly demanding.
7. There is no doubt that he responded hastily.
8. The reason is that the Hawthorne control group was shocked out of its complacency by the supervisor's presence.
9. No doubt the jury was right in finding him guilty.
10. Were you aware that excessive salt produces hypertension?

FIGURE 5.2   Writing Concisely

best writers must edit and rewrite their work again and again, consider this bit of data. Archives hold 119 copies of the final chapter of Ernest Hemingway's *A Fairwell to Arms*.

Writing concisely is not difficult, but it does take time. Noted writer Samuel Johnson once began a letter to a friend by apologizing for writing such a long letter, saying that he would have written a much shorter letter if he had had time. Clarity is achieved through editing, and it does take time. Figure 5.3 shows several sentences being rewritten to achieve clarity. You may wish to cover all columns except the left one and see how much you can improve each sentence.

Original Sentence	First Revision (to shorten)	Second Revision (to shorten more)	Third Revision (to make active)
It will help if teachers will identify routines that need to be established.	It will help if teachers will identify necessary routines.		Teachers should identify necessary routines.
Teacher preparation programs typically spend a great deal of time acquainting prospective teachers with how to teach information.	Teacher preparation programs typically spend considerable time acquainting prospective teachers with how to teach.	Teacher preparation programs typically spend considerable time on teaching about methodology.	Most teacher preparation programs emphasize methodology.
Such fear may well be a result of a lack of understanding of some ways of preventing problems and responding to them once they do occur.	Such fear may result from a lack of understanding of ways to prevent problems and respond to them.	Such fear may result from a lack of understanding of ways to prevent and respond to problems.	Not knowing how to prevent and respond to problems can frighten teachers.
However, repetition should not be overdone. If it is boredom can set in.	Repetition should not be overdone. If it is boredom can set in.	Excessive repetition can result in boredom.	Excessive repetition can cause boredom.
In general, people who are acknowledged to have a great deal of expertise in a given area exercise considerable influence over others.	In general, experts in a given area exercise considerable influence over others.	Experts in a given area exercise considerable influence over others.	Experts often influence their peers.
Efforts are being taken in nearly every industrialized nation to improve the quality of their schools.	Efforts are being made by most industrialized nations to improve their schools.		Most industrialized nations are working to improve their schools.

FIGURE 5.3 Good Editing Is a Step-by-Step Process

Writing Positively

Sometimes negative words have their purpose, but, like adverbs, they slow down the reader. Overuse them and you will sap your proposal of its energy, losing the evaluators' attention. Consider the following example:

"Grant writers do not often need to use more negative words." You can use several easy strategies to improve this sentence. Did you notice that it breaks several rules? The sentence begins with a noun, but this noun is not the focus of this sentence. The sentence begins by talking about grant writers, yet, the sentence is not so much about grant writers as it is about negative words and the effect they have on writing. Another warning to the experienced writer is that the sentence contains the negative word, "not." Sometimes using this word is appropriate, but when you see it in your writing, consider it a warning.

Try to rewrite the sentence so that the word is unnecessary. For example, you might change "do not often" to "seldom." "Grant writers seldom need . . ." But, remember that the subject belongs at the beginning of the sentence and "grant writers" is not the subject; this sentence is about the use of negative words. Take a breath, step back, and think. Why shouldn't grant writers use more negatives? Because negatives weaken the sentence. Why not say, "Too many negatives weaken a proposal" or "The overuse of negatives weakens the author's message"? Either of these rewrites is a major improvement.

Treating Genders Fairly

For centuries the English language practically ignored females, but this ended in the 1970s with the women's liberation movement. Authors wanted to be fair, but they didn't know how to achieve gender equity without constructing very awkward sentences. The results were sometimes highly entertaining: "He or she wants to develop an effective grant-writing style so that his or her proposals will be funded." A similar version of the same sentence often read like this: "He/she wants to develop an effective grant writing style so that his/her proposals will be funded." Speakers often embarrass themselves when their attempts to be equitable result in the combination, "he/she/it."

The easiest resolve is to pluralize, replacing "he/she" with "they" and "his/her" or "his or her" with "their." When pluralizing does not work, pause and rewrite the sentence. In the sentence "He/she wants to write excellent grants so that most of his/her grants will be funded," pluralizing will improve the sentence, but not enough. The subject of this sentence needs to be moved to the beginning of the sentence: "Excellence in grant writing enhances funding." Perhaps you can improve this sentence even more.

Do not be discouraged if you have to rewrite a sentence or paragraph several times to make it clear and powerful. All good writers know that the best writing usually takes the form of editing. Some of us have very weak backgrounds in grammar, but we have creative minds that are capable of good ideas. We should never let our writing limitations deter our desire to write grants. Appendix H is the *first draft* of a proposal for a small grant, showing the enormous amount of improvement made during the first edit. This grant reinforces the principle that the first business of a grant writer is to write grants; get your ideas on paper and later you can go back and edit. After several edits, this proposal was submitted and funded.

Using Graphics

Apart from the actual writing, another thing that affects the clarity of writing is organization or structure. You can strengthen the clarity of your grant proposal by using a combination of devises to organize the major concepts in the readers' minds. Among others, these include using numbers, tables, graphs, graphic organizers, flowcharts, and tables of specification. Following is a brief discussion on the use of each of these to enhance clarity.

Numbers.   Some grant writers are naturally quantitative; they think and express their ideas using numbers. Other grant writers are qualitative; they think in prose and explain their ideas using prose. All grant writers can benefit by using numbers. Numbers draw readers' attention. Numbers communicate expectations more accurately than verbal descriptions. Grant writers can use numbers to make commitments. This is important in garnering evaluators' support for the proposal. It is also valuable when the writer conducts a self-evaluation. For example, a grant proposal author who is asking for money to improve the dental health in a community assesses the existing condition before the improvement program begins. If that assessment is recorded in the number of cavities per one hundred patients, then after the treatment is given, a reassessment of the condition can be made accurately and easily. Put simply, grant evaluators like numbers because they communicate expectations clearly and because they make evaluation accurate and easy.

Tables.   Tables offer a way to view a wide range of data all at once, thus making comparisons easy. Tables should be used for this purpose, in lieu of pages and pages of words, which often bog down the reading of proposals.

Graphs.   Graphs are visual representations of variations. Perhaps the most familiar of all graphs is the bell curve, which shows the varied distribution of all sorts of things in nature. Some of the many things that are subject to this type of distribution are the weight and height of animals and plants, the margin of error of both humans and machines, and of course, the intelligence quotients of human beings. Of course, not all phenomena in the universe are distributed so evenly. For example, if high and low temperatures in a single year are plotted on a graph, or the highs and lows of the stock market, one would not expect to see the bell (or normal) curve.

Occasionally, I am surprised when my grant-writing workshop participants express concern that perhaps they should not use projections in their grant proposals. They worry that if their predictions fail to come true, then this could be interpreted as false representation on their part. This concern is absolutely unfounded. Graphs showing projected trends should be used because they can be a powerful communicator and a convincing tool. Like all visuals, graphs facilitate the mind's ability to grasp complex concepts that would be difficult to communicate in words only.

Abstract and Graphic Organizers. If a proposal is very long, a written abstract is often required to help the evaluators gain an overall mental grasp of the entire proposed project. Even if the RFP doesn't require an abstract, proposal writers always have the option to include one. The fact that many RFPs give a maximum word limit for abstracts testifies to their purpose, which is to facilitate quick and easy understanding of the proposal. Although, to some writers, the absolute word restriction may seem unnecessarily harsh, it should always be followed because some evaluators will refuse to read proposals that do not adhere to all of their guidelines.

Abstracts enable the reader to get a quick view of the overall project and its individual parts, acting as advance organizers. Graphic organizers are visuals designed to do the same. The main difference between the use of abstracts and graphic organizers is that the graphic organizer can be interpreted at a glance. For example, each chapter in this book is prefaced by a graphic organizer showing the relationships among its major parts.

Flowcharts. Flowcharts are graphics that are designed to show the sequence of events. Each flowchart has boxes or circles separated by arrows. Programmed instructional materials make extensive use of flowcharts, replacing the need for a teacher to be present to tell students what to do next. In Chapter Three, Figure 3.1 shows a sample flowchart.

Tables of Specification. A table of specifications is a particular type of chart, which is unique in that it uses labeled rows and columns. Tables of specification can be used by grant writers who want to make certain they are covering all elements they intended to cover. Failure to do this could be catastrophic. For example, a grant writer can lose credibility fast if an evaluator reads about part of the grant and learns that this part was overlooked in the table of contents, the body of the proposal, or the budget.

Each table of specifications uses a matrix with labeled columns and rows. For example, Table 5.1 was developed to be used in a city grant written to curb red light violations. A quick glance at this table of specifications shows, in a convincing fashion, the need for a solution to a rash of accidents resulting from red light violations in this particular town. Future grant writers could extend their investigations to test different devices to measure and compare their ability to deter red light violations.

TABLE 5.1   *Table of Specifications for Traffic Light Violations Grant*

Intersection	Frequency of Violations per Ten Minutes Time Interval																			
Washington and	1	2	3	4	5	6	7	8	9	10	11	12	13	14	15	16	17	18	19	20
1st	x																			
2nd		x																		
3rd		x																		
4th						x														
5th										x										
6th																				
7th	x																			
8th						x														
9th													x							
10th			x																	
Rose Avenue and	1	2	3	4	5	6	7	8	9	10	11	12	13	14	15	16	17	18	19	20
1st							x													
2nd																				
3rd													x							
4th	x																			
5th	x																			
6th								x												
7th																				x
8th																				
9th													x							
10th														x						

Summary

Successful grant writing demands a special writing style and that style can be developed by anyone. The major goal is clarity. The best approach to achieving clarity is to ignore style and grammar until the first draft is complete. Then go back and edit your draft copy several times, removing unnecessary paragraphs, sentences, and words.

Powerful and clear sentences can be written by placing a concrete subject at the beginning of the sentence and following it immediately with an action verb written in the present tense. Jargon and other unnecessary unfamiliar words should be eliminated or replaced with shorter, common words.

Such visuals as graphics, tables, graphic organizers, and tables of specifications can simplify and clarify your proposals. Do not be afraid to make projections part of your proposals.

Recap of Major Ideas

- Successful grant writing demands a special style, and that style can be developed by anyone.
- The most important feature of writing style is clarity. The proposal must be carefully crafted until its wording will be completely clear to the evaluators.
- Style should be of little or no concern until the writer completes the first draft.
- Self-editing and rewriting are essential steps in preparing all grants.
- Brevity facilitates clarity.
- Sentences should begin with concrete subjects and be followed quickly by action verbs written in the present tense to increase the power of writing.
- Whenever possible, past tense should be avoided because it slows down the reading.
- We tend to use fancy words when we write, and these words often confuse readers.
- In grant writing, the use of qualifiers should be limited because they rob each sentence of its power to communicate clearly.
- Unnecessary jargon confuses readers and, therefore, should be avoided.
- Many common phrases can be replaced with single words.
- Overuse of adverbs diminishes clarity.
- Negative words are a signal that a sentence may need to be rewritten and tightened up.
- Grants should represent the genders fairly. The easiest way to achieve gender equity is by pluralizing.

- Such visuals as graphs, tables, graphic organizers, and tables of specification should be considered because these can improve communications with evaluators.

References

Henson, Kenneth T. (1999). *Writing for professional publication: Keys to academic and business success*. Needham Heights, MA: Allyn & Bacon.

Strunk, W., Jr., & White, E. B. (1979). *The elements of style*. New York: Avon Books.

6

Keeping Your Grant

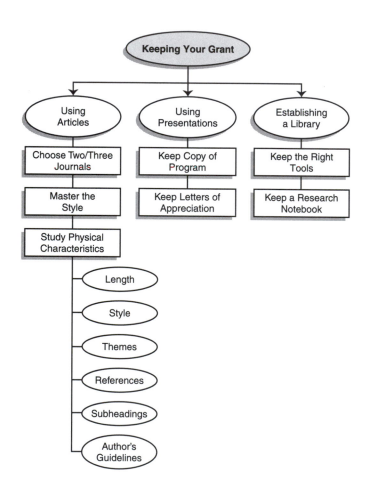

The first chapter in this book focuses on attitudes because our attitudes shape our behavior. So, as shown in Chapter One, several attitudes significantly impact our grant writing success—some positively, some negatively. Without doubt, the most important attitude a grant writer can have is one of self-confidence: "I can succeed at grant writing and, furthermore, I can succeed at the level I choose." Perhaps the second most important attitude of a grant writer is the perception that grant writing is not a one-shot, hit-or-miss activity, but rather an ongoing part of professional life. "I must establish my own grant-writing program and nurture it the same as professors or teachers must continuously nurture their teaching skills, or business owners must manage their businesses daily to earn a profit, or clergy or government workers must diligently watch their budgets to avoid overspending."

An axiom mentioned earlier is that each grant proposal is easier to write than the preceding grant proposal. This is true, but only if the grant writer stays focused and learns from each grant proposal. The teacher burnout grant discussed in Chapter Four netted its writers a total of just over one-third of a million dollars ($385,450). It also received a national award, proclaiming it the second best innovative program in the country for the year. Unfortunately, because this was the first grant ever written by this team, none of its members had the foresight to correctly document its existence, at least not in a way that could help its producers get future proposals funded. Once a grant proposal is funded, grant writers have several tools they can use to ensure that their grants are funded again and again. Perhaps the most powerful of these tools are articles published in magazines and journals.

Using Articles to Support Your Grants

Consider the advantage that would have resulted had the writers of this grant had the foresight to write an article about the program that this grant produced. Just a short piece in the local newspaper would have been useful to refer to when writing future grant proposals. Every state has newsletters, and an article in a professional statewide newsletter would have been even better. The very best way to have documented this program would have been to write an article for a professional journal. Each future grant proposal written by any of these authors could have had a copy of this article enclosed, or, if the lack of space prohibited this, could have, at least, cited the article. The article, or reference to the article, would attest to the investigators' grant-writing skills, including their human relations skills, management skills, and evaluation skills. A second article could have been written when the program received the distinguished national program award. This article would attest to the authors' credibility, as viewed by their professional peers.

Getting articles accepted in professional journals requires a special set of skills. Successful authors study the journals in their discipline and select two or three that make similar requirements of their authors. In retrospect, no authors are exempt from having some of their manuscripts rejected. By choosing similar journals, authors can immediately send each rejected manuscript to another journal. The goal is to become very familiar with these two or three journals. My biennial surveys sent to some fifty editors have consistently found that the number one reason manuscripts are rejected is the authors' failure to know the journals. Some of the comments of these editors include the following:

- "The authors do not understand the journal's purpose."
- "Read articles in the journal to which you are submitting."
- "Most mistakes . . . could be avoided if authors studied our journal . . . beforehand."
- "Authors need to read the editorial in the journal to which they plan to submit to find out what's appropriate."
- "Read a few copies."

Knowing a journal means many things, including knowing who reads the journal and the types of topics these readers consider important and knowing the services the journal provides. Is its main purpose to give the readers a review of articles? That's the purpose of *The Academy of Management Review*. Is the journal's purpose to help its readers draw relationships between the theory they read and practices in the real world? Such is the purpose of *Theory Into Practice*. The *Training and Development Journal* is aimed at providing its readers with the skills they need to enter and advance in their businesses. Or, perhaps the journal focuses primarily on policy, as does the *Phi Delta Kappan*. In a sense, each journal is specialized in that it has its own mission; knowing that mission is a requirement for attaining a high rate of success in being published in each journal.

Another part of knowing the journal is being aware of the types of topics the articles in this journal include. For example, the readers of the *Journal of Allied Health* have expectations different from those of the readers of the *Journal of Health Education*. Librarians read the *Journal of Education for Library and Information Science* for different content than that sought by the readers of *Library and Information Science Research*. The reason that knowing the purpose of the journal is so important is because without this knowledge, you cannot deliver substantive information that your audience expects and demands. Furthermore, many authors submit manuscripts that lack substance. Halpin and Halpin (1986, p. 24) reported that a "lack of contribution to the literature is one of the reasons research manuscripts are not accepted for publication." When I asked why so many of their manuscripts are rejected, some of the editors in my survey reported the following:

- "Old hat, old stuff"
- "Much ado about nothing"
- "No data base"
- "Not making a contribution"

A look at these responses reveals two things: Editors expect some data to be reported, however little, and they expect each article to advance their discipline. The rule is simple: If you are going to write, have something to say. Writers make two mistakes: Some ignore the advice and submit empty manuscripts, while others interpret this advice to mean that they must conduct major, comprehensive, empirical research studies so that they can have enough substance to justify writing an article. Do not be discouraged by the thought that each article should report some data. In fact, as stated in Chapter Five, a simple questionnaire can produce enough data for at least one or two good articles. Appendix I gives the preferences of journals in several disciplines.

Physical Characteristics of Journals

Another part of knowing the journals is knowing their physical characteristics. Journals and magazines are rigid, in the sense that they do not change dramatically from issue to issue. For example, their layouts are the same from one issue to another. If the readers of *Southern Living* want to read the section called "The Southern Journal," they know to turn to the very end of each issue because this section is never located in the front or the middle; it is always at the end.

A major physical characteristic of some journals is subheadings. The first manuscript I submitted to *USA Today* was returned with a letter saying that I had a great idea and had written it well except that it was too academic and lacked subheadings. When I followed the editor's advice, inserted a subheading every three pages and took out the jargon, it was immediately accepted. Fortunately, the manuscript had enough content that the editor considered important for the readers that he was willing to tell me of these shortcomings and give me an opportunity to correct them. Don't depend on such kindness; most rejections are accompanied by generic letters, each saying that the manuscript does not fit the current needs of the journal, which, incidentally, can mean anything from the literal message embedded in this puzzling phrase to the fact that your manuscript is poorly written. Poor writing style is among the top three reasons manuscripts are rejected. Because an entire chapter of this book (Chapter Five) was devoted to style, it will not be addressed again, but you should know that failure to follow proper style is consistently among the top five reasons that manuscripts sent to the journals in my surveys are rejected.

Another important physical characteristic of journals is their use of article references. Most magazines and some journals publish no references at all; some journals print a few references, and some journals print many references. Examine the journals to which you expect to target your manuscripts. If they include references, you should, too. How many should you include? I always try to include about as many as anyone else, because references give the work credibility.

Using Themes

Because this next suggestion is so important and because it can give you so much control over the success of your manuscripts, I want to use a little drama to introduce it. In my writing workshops, to ensure that my participants return to the workshops after lunch, I always end the morning session by promising to begin the afternoon session by showing them how they can increase the acceptance rate of their manuscripts by over 300 percent without their having to do any extra work. When the workshop resumes, usually with everyone present, I show the bar graph shown in Figure 6.1.

Examine the bar graph shown in Figure 6.1. This graph shows the number of manuscripts accepted for each of these issues. Notice the dramatic difference in the ratio of acceptance. Can you offer a hypothesis for the dramatic difference in acceptance rates for separate issues of the same journal? If you can discover this cause, you can eliminate over two-thirds of the competition for each of your

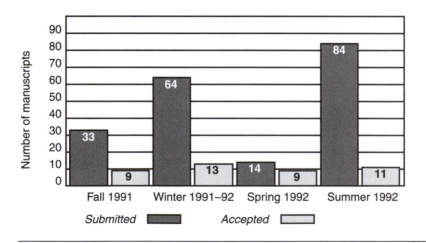

FIGURE 6.1 Percentage of Articles Accepted

manuscripts, thereby increasing the probability by over 300 percent that your manuscripts will be accepted.

The difference in the number of manuscripts submitted for these different issues of the same journal can be attributed to the fact that each year two of the four issues of the journal are generic issues and the other two issues are themed. Many authors avoid ever sending to themed issues; yet, the issues receiving the most manuscripts are the generic (nonthemed) issues. This means that by simply learning which issues of your journals are themed and then writing manuscripts that fit these themes, and by submitting your manuscripts before the respective deadlines set for these themed issues, you can effect a lot of control on the success rate of your manuscripts.

This is the point when you should ask, "How can I know the coming themes and the deadline for each theme?" This is easy. Annually, one or more issues of each journal contain an announcement of upcoming themes, along with the submission deadline for each. A word of caution is needed here, though; because most journals will not return to a theme for at least a year or two, if they return at all, you *must* make certain that you prepare your manuscript and submit it before the given deadline. Otherwise, your strategy will backfire, and you will ensure the rejection of your manuscript.

Perhaps the single most important part of any journal is a section of "Guidelines to Authors," included to help contributors prepare manuscripts for that particular journal. Like *Southern Living's* feature called "The Southern Journal," and like many journals' announcements of coming themes, guidelines to authors are usually found in the same part of the journal, issue after issue and year after year. Once you find this section, follow these guidelines as rigorously as you follow your RFPs.

Occasionally, journals will print a section titled "Call for Manuscripts." This is an extremely important tool. Generally, magazines and journals receive far more manuscripts than they have space to print, meaning that generally the acceptance rates are relatively low. When you see a "Call for Manuscripts," you know that this ratio has been reversed. For some reason, the editor needs more manuscripts. You should never ignore this opportunity. Remember to apply the grant-writing flexibility rule to writing. If you are working on a manuscript or you have a finished manuscript that has been rejected, you may be able to use your data, alter the thrust of the manuscript, and make it fit one of the journal's upcoming themes.

By now, I hope that you have begun to see that you have a lot more control over the fate of your manuscripts than you ever thought possible.

Select journals with the same referencing style (APA, Chicago, etc.) to avoid having to retype each article that gets rejected. Select journals with similar lengths. A journal with articles averaging 12 manuscript pages is almost sure to refuse manuscripts that run 30 pages long, and vice versa. Do not confuse manuscript lengths with journal article lengths. What you need to know is the lengths of manuscripts. (To convert journal article pages to manuscript pages, count the number of words in a journal article and divide by 250.)

Consider your professional goals and your personal goals; take time to select two or three journals.

Writing articles about your own grants is easy and quick. This is especially true of grants that produce programs. Just write a paragraph or two describing the needs and purposes of your grant. Then, step-by-step, describe the process used, and end by showing the readers exactly how they can develop similar grants and programs. Appendix J shows an example of such an article.

Articles written to share success stories of new programs, funded or not, are among the easiest types of articles to write. Notice that the article shown in Appendix J begins with a simple introduction of a problem. This first paragraph is actually a brief abstract of the program. It could be strengthened by citing some current references and by making a statement to help the readers generalize this program and see how it could work in their locale. For example, at the time this article was written, partnerships between universities and schools was a subject of much discussion in the professional literature. Suppose this paragraph said, "partnerships between universities and public schools are being encouraged throughout the country (Smith 2002; Jenkins 2003)." This sentence would accomplish some important goals. It would suggest that the program presented here could be used anywhere. Citing two recent sources of literature would give the article both some needed credibility and a sense of currency.

Now, skip to the last two paragraphs in this article. Notice that they are different from the preceding paragraphs in that they do not describe steps in the program. Instead, the next to the last paragraph explains how the program will be evaluated. This makes this a natural template for articles written about grants, because evaluation is an essential part of any grant. Of course, since grant evaluations are more detailed and explicit, you would want your evaluation paragraph for an article describing a funded grant to be more explicit and detailed. The final paragraph tells the advantages of this particular program. You could also add any insights you have gained through your work with this program.

Think about projects you have conducted or participated in, projects that you know could benefit others. These projects can be formal, funded projects or they can be informal, unfunded projects. They can be large or small. Each can be the subject of an article that you can use to support your future grant proposals. Now, using this article as a blueprint or template, write a short article to share a grant you have written or to share an unfunded program with which you have worked.

Using Presentations to Support Your Grants

As noted earlier, perhaps the best single source of documentation for grant writing is journal articles. Another excellent source is presentations and papers delivered at professional meetings. These, along with a page from the conference program, inform the potential funder that your work has been scrutinized and approved by your profession. If you receive positive reviews or letters complimenting your presentations or workshops, these, too, should be included as evidence of your credibility.

Using a Research Binder

Be proactive and do not wait, just hoping the media will pick up on your programs. Give awards to your participants and arrange for the media to be present during the award ceremonies. If you create partnership programs with others and if these affiliates compliment your programs, ask them if they would send you a brief letter or note typed on their letterhead stationary. Maintain a file of these letters in a ring binder in sheets that do not require holes to be punched in your records.

Invite your legislators and other key individuals, such as experts in your field, to give presentations or workshops. Keep copies of each program or workshop announcement. Invite media representatives and keep copies of their articles. Cite radio and television news coverage, listing the station or channel and the dates of the newscasts. Grant evaluators will be strongly influenced to select the proposals of those investigators they know they can trust to manage their resources responsibly and with the utmost care. These documents can give you indispensable credibility as a grant writer and can be included in the appendix of each of your future grant proposals.

In addition to maintaining a ring binder for publicity materials, each serious grant writer would do well to keep a second binder for research and articles on topics of ongoing interest. See Figure 6.2. Some writers prefer to photocopy articles for their files. A less expensive way to track the articles of special interest that appear in your own journals involves the use of small (2 inch) Post-It notes. Each time you receive a new issue of one of your journals, scan the contents section for articles on topics that you pursue. Each time you find an article, turn to the first page of that article and affix a Post-It note as a tab sticking out of the journal. On the exposed side of the tab, vertically write one word that identifies that topic. Continue this process throughout the issue.

When you have completed tabbing the entire issue, place the journal in your bookshelf, putting the spine first so that the name tabs will be showing. Always keep your journals ordered by month and year. The next time you begin writing a grant proposal, you can quickly glance at your bookcase and

(Middle School Methods Research)

Hannon, J. (2002). "No time for time out." Kappa Delta Pi Record 38. (3), 112-118.

behavior

"Many of the children benefit from well-timed and clear discussions or demonstrations concerning developmentally appropriate behavior. (p.114).

Hamm, M. and Adams, D. (2002). "Collaborative inquiry: Working toward shared goals." Kappa Delta Pi Record 38 (3), 115-118.

sense of community

"A common element in successful schools is a shared sense of community and a socially integrated sense of purpose." (p.116).

collaborative inquiry

"Implementing collaborative inquiry means defining students and teacher responsibilities. One of the first steps is instructing students in how to work together." (p.116).

group interdepenrce

"A key element in collaborative classrooms is group interdependence. The success of each individual depends on the success of each group member." (p.117).

problem solving

"Whatever the subject, it is more important to emphasize the reasoning involved in working on a problem than getting "the answer." (p.117).

FIGURE 6.2   Creating a Binder for Research

pull off the shelves only those few journals with tabs on the topic of your new grant project. Put only these tabbed issues on the table. This eliminates 90 to 95 percent of the information on your shelves and enables you to get to the heart of your project in record time.

Take a few moments to jot down some single words that symbolize the major concepts or theories that you enjoy learning about. Keep this list and use it to tab your articles each time you receive a new copy of one of your journals.

Now, referring to your chosen journals, make a profile of each, using all of the characteristics you have just read about. Starting with your next article, choose

*one of these journals and craft your article to make it fit the profile you have just
developed for this journal.*

Creating a Grant-Writing Library

A well-kept secret in grant writing is that successful grant writers develop
highly efficient behaviors, such as these, making each of their efforts produce
a high rate of results. A carefully developed grant-writing library is a good
example, and it does not require a lot of space or costs. The research binder
introduced earlier in this chapter is an excellent start. The professional journals to which you subscribe are also essential materials for your library. All
professionals have indispensable reference books, such as the accountant's
interest tables, the insurance representative's annuities tables, or the chemist's
table of elements. These important and useful documents should be kept in
your grant-writing office so they will be readily accessible.

Even though you may have learned to depend on your computer to
help you with your spelling and sentence structuring, a good dictionary is
essential. Robert Louis Stevenson said that the job of writers is to affect the
readers exactly as they choose to. A thesaurus can help you select the exact
word you need to affect your potential funders so that they will see the logic
in your proposal and so that they will also feel that you can be trusted to give
them exactly what they want to get for their money.

In addition to these professional tools, your grant-writing office should
have several common office supplies, such as a pencil sharpener, a holder for
a good supply of pencils, a tape dispenser, a hole punch (a small, hand-held
punch will suffice), scissors, and tabs such as Post-Its. Although these may
seem unimportant, their absence can send you running to another part of the
house looking for them, and this distracts your attention and wastes your
time. A list of these tools is shown in Figure 6.3.

Office furniture is equally important. While many items are optional,
for me, at least the following items are not. I require bookshelves to hold my
books and journals. I also need a simple table just large enough to stack a
few journals and to write on. Incidentally, I write everything in longhand
and then type it into my computer. For me, the keyboard has always been a
distracter. When I type, I unconsciously try to produce perfectly written and
perfectly punctuated sentences as I go. This means that I get distracted from
my major ideas; so, I never worry about spelling, punctuation, and syntax.
Possibly, you would find my office a bit austere. I want a straight-back chair,
not a recliner or an especially plush chair that might lull me to sleep. I certainly do not want a television, radio, crossword puzzles, leisure magazines,
newspapers, or anything else that might distract me from my work.

But, I also believe it is important to have a few elements in the office
that make you feel good. Perhaps an award-winning plaque or trophy, or

- Computer
- Dictionary (hard copy)
- Thesaurus
- Professional journals
- Professional books
- Yearbooks
- Style manual
- Research binder
- Grammar books
- Calculator
- Hole punch
- Tape and dispenser
- Scissors
- Pens
- Post-It tabs

FIGURE 6.3   Common Tools for Grant Writing

perhaps even a photo or picture or other items that make you feel good. A successful salesman friend shares his business office with several coworkers who hold degrees from Ivy League schools, made obvious by prominently displayed diplomas. My friend, who did not graduate from an Ivy League school, displays his beautifully framed GED diploma.

Take a moment to reflect on your own writing requirements, and make a list of those office items that you consider essential to your grant writing. Then add an item or two that really make you feel good.

Summary

Grant writers have at their disposal several tools they can use to encourage funders to fund their grants again and again. One of the most powerful of these tools is a collection of recent journal articles. Successful publishing, itself, requires a special set of skills. First, writers must know the journals to which they submit their articles, and this involves such things as knowing their audiences and what these readers want and demand from their journals. A good place to begin is by selecting two or three journals with similar audiences, purposes, writing style, and reference style.

A leading cause for rejection is failure to know the journal audience, the purpose of the journal, and the journal's physical characteristics. Get a recent copy of the chosen journal and check these properties; then design your articles accordingly. Authors can dramatically increase their chances of getting their manuscripts accepted by reading the guidelines to authors and following them precisely, and by selecting and writing to particular upcoming themes. A common major mistake of authors is failure to contribute significant content, which can be gathered with a short questionnaire. Grant writers can increase their levels of acceptance by making presentations at professional conferences and documenting each presentation.

Many serious grant writers develop their own grant-writing libraries or offices. Each library should contain those articles that are needed to craft competitive manuscripts, including the writers' journals with the topics they pursue carefully tabbed.

Recap of Major Ideas

- Grant writers can write articles and use them to build credibility for their grant-writing program.
- Successful writing for publication requires a special set of skills.
- Leading causes of manuscript rejection include failure to know the journal and failure to know the journal's audience.
- Writers can increase the acceptance level of their manuscripts by writing for themed issues.
- The target journal provides an excellent blueprint for designing articles.
- A special grant-writing library can reduce the time required to write publishable manuscripts.
- Grant writers can enhance their programs by keeping an ongoing notebook of research and articles in their areas of expertise.
- Each successful manuscript must make a contribution.
- Failure to make a contribution is the leading cause for rejection in research journals.
- Grant writers should follow their target journals' guidelines for authors with the same level of precision that they should follow RFPs.
- Calls for manuscripts announce special opportunities for publishing.

Reference

Halpin, G., & Halpin, G. (1986). "Guidelines for publication of research." *Thresholds in Education, 12*(4), 23–28.

7

Tapping Other Resources

All previous chapters in this book have one focus and one goal: to help you prepare grant proposals that have a high chance of being selected for funding. Grants are the most versatile method of getting money, but they are not the only source you can go to when you are seeking additional funds. This chapter is not intended to be used as a substitute or alternative to grant writing; rather its purpose is to provide sources to tap in addition to grants. As in the earlier chapters, the samples described in this chapter are actual approaches that have been tried and proved. You, too, can use these methods to find funds for new programs or funds for improving existing programs and practices.

The Teachers-in-Residence Program

The old adage that "need is the mother of invention" has some truth; when we feel a need for something we don't have, we are motivated to write grant proposals. Our need can be as varied as our imaginations allow.

I was serving as an area head at a major research-type university. An area head oversees and is responsible for the work of several departments. An area is a group of related departments and a head is like a chair, except with more authority. The area that I headed had several departments, so I had several department chairs reporting directly to me. These departments had ongoing programs throughout Central America.

Because I am a natural experimenter, I am always looking for better ways to meet my unit's goals; therefore, I encourage others to think "outside the box" and envision better ways of attaining our goals. I was sitting at my desk one day when one of our department chairs brought me a couple of problems along with an unusual proposal for resolving each.

"Our elementary education department is getting a lot of criticism. People are saying that our professors of courses on methodology have been away from schools so long that they are no longer able to identify with today's classrooms."

"Tom, you know that isn't true. All of our teachers are working in schools every week."

"I know, but that is the perception, and, right or wrong, it doesn't serve us well. We have another problem, too; our student teacher supervisors are telling me that the cooperating teachers are failing to live up to their responsibilities. We have a handbook that clearly explains the role of the students, the supervisors, and the cooperating teachers, and they simply have become relaxed and are no longer filling their responsibilities. So, I've been giving these concerns some thought and I believe I have good solution for each of them."

I listened as this department chair continued, "What if we could hire a couple of the best teachers in town and give them dual assignments? Each would teach methods courses and supervise student teachers. Nobody could accuse these teachers of not being in touch with today's schools because we would take them right out of their classrooms and put them in this assignment. And in contrast to our teachers, who find it difficult to tell teachers in the public schools that they are not doing their jobs, these teachers would not hesitate to tell their colleagues that they needed to perform their cooperating teacher responsibilities more carefully and completely."

I like ideas that are practical, and this proposal seemed very practical; it seemed like it would work. So I complimented my colleague on his good ideas and promised to follow through by inviting the superintendent of the local city schools and the superintendent of the local county schools to have lunch with both of us. I was careful to avoid telling them too much too fast, so all I said was that we had some ideas that we very much would like to share with them. I did say that we had some ideas that might be of mutual advantage to them (the public schools) and to us (the university).

I have always felt fortunate to live and work in college towns. College communities tend to be progressive, and the school principals and superintendents seem to be open to experimentation. Such was surely the case with these two superintendents; both were enthusiastic about the idea of experimenting.

The Role of Each Party

The four of us met for lunch at our university club, which was housed in a beautiful antebellum mansion. After making the introductions, we ordered our lunch and I explained the idea, saying that I wished to buy the contract of each superintendent's best teacher. I would pay these teachers' salaries for two years and would use them to teach methods courses and supervise student teachers. The superintendents would have three responsibilities: (1) they would ask their faculties to identify the three top teachers in the system and send me the vita of each of these teachers; (2) they would continue paying the fringe benefits for these teachers and make sure that the two years counted toward retirement; and (3) they would promise to hold each teacher's position so that these teachers could return to their own classrooms following their two years of absence.

During these two years, we would all remain flexible. At the end of the first year, if any party was uncomfortable, including the university, the schools, or the teachers, the teachers involved could return to their classrooms without any kinds of penalties. The program would be called the "Teachers-In-Residence Program."

Benefits to Each Party

Quickly, before the superintendents could decline, I explained the benefits of this arrangement to all participants, at least as I envisioned them. "The participating schools would receive a lot of positive publicity for having the best teacher in their respective districts. The participating teachers would receive expensive plaques, with their names recognizing each as a Teacher-of-the-Year. Each plaque would be awarded at a regular school board meeting, making sure that reporters from the local television stations and newspapers would be present. Once a teacher's two-year term was completed, both the university and the school districts would have the added benefit of having someone in the schools who understood the operations of the university. In the future, when either party needed the cooperation of the other, both would benefit from having a teacher who understood the operations of both the university and the public schools. These former teachers-in-residence could act as mediators and facilitators for future cooperative ventures."

My department chair and I were very pleased when both superintendents smiled and said that they would give this proposed program a try. Incidentally, this was a win-win program for all parties. The teachers were given professorial status and treated the same as the other professors. The only costs to the school districts were the fringe benefits. The program was free to the university; I simply took the next two vacancies in this department and assigned the positions to this program. When a teacher fulfilled the two-year term, another was put into the same slot. After more than a dozen years, the program continues to be a favorite. Furthermore, it has been emulated by other university/school partners in other cities. The year it was initiated, the program won the state award for being the most innovative program.

> *Albert Einstein said that the ability to identify problems was more important than the ability to solve problems. Now that you have read a story about a creative response to a couple of related problems, reflect on this story and see if you can identify the behaviors that led to solving the problems. First, you might begin by stating the problem as directly and succinctly as possible. Then list the behaviors that led to its solution.*

The Educational Leadership Institute

I had been working at a regional state university for only a few months when I learned that the widow of a former school superintendent who had been an alumnus of the university was planning to help the university at some time in the future, perhaps several to many years to come. The university's foundation officer told me that he would like me to meet this generous woman. When we met, I found her to be direct, no-nonsense, yet, charming and alert, with a good head for business. Fortunately, I arrived at the meeting prepared. She shared her intentions to help the university. I asked her if she had any interest in helping some now and shared my plan.

"I have heard that your husband was a progressive superintendent, and I think I have a plan that he might have liked. I hope you do, too. Because the state recently introduced a highly demanding education reform program, many school principals have chosen to take early retirement. Consequently, the state has a severe shortage of principals. Because of the new demands of the reform program, the schools need especially competent leaders. My idea is to establish a summer institute to prepare educational administrators. We would take a few of the brightest teachers who aspire to become administrators and pay their tuition and other expenses."

"How much would this program cost?"

"Each summer institute would need a cohort of ten participants. We could run each institute for ten thousand dollars."

"When could we begin?"

"If we initiated the planning and advertising now, we could offer our first institute this coming summer."

"I have just one request. I want each institute to have at least one woman participant."

"That should be no problem."

"Then, what are we waiting for? Let's do it."

So, we lost no time in seizing this opportunity. The first summer institute for educational leaders was held that summer, and it was a huge success. Our benefactress was pleased because over half of the participants were females.

Each participant in this institute learns how to use technology to plan and operate programs and to plan and track budgets. Participants also learn a lot about the qualities of those schools whose students score well on standardized tests. The real winners in this program are the tens and perhaps hundreds of thousands of elementary, middle, and secondary students who will benefit from having progressive, well-trained principals and superintendents running their schools.

Ten years have passed, and this program has supported some one hundred new, highly trained superintendents. Again, you can benefit by reflecting on this short story. What behaviors led to the funding of this institute?

This leadership institute leaves a few important messages. Many grant proposal writers equate grants with getting large sums of money, but there are other ways to get money such as through gifts from individuals. To get these gifts, the recipient must be creative, always on the lookout for ways to improve, always having an interesting idea in mind for making that improvement.

The institute experience suggests another salient truth about grants and gifts: Little gifts must never go unappreciated because, over time, they can amount to major sums of money.

Proposal Letters

Another popular, non–grant proposal approach to securing funds is simply writing a short letter. Some funders require such a letter as a precursor of a grant proposal; those investigators who submit the best letters are invited to follow their letters with a full-blown proposal. Other funders require letters in lieu of grant proposals.

Because letter proposals are much shorter (usually no longer than three or four pages, and often only one page long), many investigators do not give the attention that is required to produce a *successful* letter. Well-written and well-constructed letters often produce millions of dollars and, furthermore, establish relationships that enable the investigators to return again and again with successful letters for extensions to the original grant or for new grants.

Before you begin writing your letter, consider the mission and goals of the potential funder. Abraham Lincoln once said that in preparing for a court case, he usually spent about a third of his preparation time thinking about what he was going to say and the remaining two-thirds of his time thinking about what the opposing attorney was likely to say. This shift in perspective gives a competitive edge that works just as well in grant writing as in law. You can gather information by examining the RFP or by looking up the prospective funder in the Federal Register or in similar funding sources including the computer. By gathering and using information about the funding agency, you are able to understand how the funder thinks and feels, enabling you to craft a letter to garner the particular funder's support. Should your letter be rejected, it is imperative that you rewrite it to include the special goals and values of your next targeted potential funder.

Steps in Writing a Proposal Letter

When writing a proposal letter, include (1) a clear statement of the need or *problem,* (2) your proposed solution to the problem, (3) an explanation of why you are better prepared than others to solve this problem, (4) an invitation, including a statement about why you have chosen this particular funder, to help solve this problem, (5) the amount of support you are requesting, and (6) how you plan to measure the effectiveness of your treatment of the problem. A sample proposal letter is shown in Figure 7.1.

> *Examine the sample proposal letter in Figure 7.1. Look critically to see whether this letter meets the six criteria spelled out in this chapter section. If not, add any missing criteria. Can you think of any way(s) to alter this letter to make it more persuasive?*

Statement of Need or Problem. A needs statement should specifically describe an existing need. The need should always be realistic; that is, one that can possibly be resolved or improved. Ideally, it should be a need that relates to the mission or goals of the targeted funder. If you propose a multistep process or program to address this need, the needs statement should briefly discuss, or at least list, the steps. In this part of the proposal letter, the steps should be addressed in the order that they will be taken during implementation. Like all

[Use appropriate letterhead.]

Statement of purpose:	Provide an overview of the project including some general activities. (One brief paragraph)
Balance of letter:	*Situation and Problem.* (One paragraph)
	Capabilities. What your organization has done and its ability to carry out the project if support is received. (One paragraph)
	Program Methods and Operation. What you will do, how you will do it, who will be involved—community agencies, other organizations, donors? (Two paragraphs)
	Impact. How will youth, schools, or the community benefit? (One paragraph)
	Evaluation, Reporting, and Visibility. How will success be measured, how will the donor be informed, and what visibility will the donor receive? (One paragraph)
	Budget. The amount being requested. Include when you need the pledge, when you need the contribution, and your IRS number. (Short answer)
	Summary. A brief recap of the significance of this program for people, the community, and the donor. Add telephone number if not on the letterhead. (One paragraph)
Signatory:	Someone needing *no* introduction (e.g., president of organization).
Length:	Keep the entire letter to about two pages.
Best Use:	Companies, businesses, plants, foundations, local family charities, community trusts, individuals.

FIGURE 7.1   Sample Proposal Letter

other parts of the proposal letter, the needs statement should communicate well; this means that it should be kept short and clear. Figure 7.2 shows an instrument designed to be used to evaluate the needs statement.

> *When money is given through grants, it is given to fulfill a need or solve a problem. Use one or two sentences to describe a problem that you wish to solve or improve. Review the literature for data to support your claim.*

Below is a series of criteria to be used in judging the needs or problem statement. Evaluate each criterion by circling the number to the right of the statement.

4	Very apparent
3	Somewhat apparent
2	Not readily apparent
1	Missing
NA	Not Applicable

1. Appropriate introduction is provided.	4	3	2	1
2. Logical lead to problem or needs statement.	4	3	2	1
3. Problem or need is feasible to address.	4	3	2	1
4. Statistical data support statement.	4	3	2	1
5. If a training project, the "target" group has provided support to the need or problem.	4	3	2	1
6. Assumptions or hypotheses are clearly stated.	4	3	2	1
7. Need or problem appears to be credible.	4	3	2	1
8. Statement is clearly written.	4	3	2	1
9. The statement is presented in a logical order.	4	3	2	1

10. What is your overall impression of statement?

11. Strengths:

12. Comments for improvement:

FIGURE 7.2   Sample Evaluation of Problem or Needs Statement

Check the Physics Summer Institute Proposal shown in Appendix E. The first three paragraphs in this proposal identify the existing problem or need. Use the form shown in Figure 7.2 to evaluate this statement of needs. Is the statement specific enough? Could it have been made stronger by stating that over 85 percent of the nation's high school physics teachers are teaching out of their field? What adjustments would you make to strengthen the needs statement in Appendix E?

Your Proposed Solution.   Tell exactly how you plan to approach this problem. If your program involves a multistep approach, clearly distinguish among the steps, and keep these steps in the chronological sequence that you anticipate will occur.

Why Are You the Right Person or Team to Solve This Problem?   This is your opportunity to explain why you are the best choice to solve this problem. Most investigators make a mistake at this juncture and emphasize the degree of their own needs. But the funders are likely to be less interested in your needs and more interested in their own needs. Use this space to display your strengths. Tell the funder about your resources (both physical and human), and include some resources that you know will be unique to your proposal.

An Invitation.   Use a sentence or two to invite the funder to partner with you in solving this problem. If you are responding to an RFP, check it to see exactly what job this funder is wanting to get done. If you are not responding to an RFP, look the funder up on the Internet or in a grants book, such as the Federal Register, and consider using some of the language the funders have used to describe their agency or mission.

Support.   Check with the RFP or on the Internet to see the range of funds this donor gives for each project and, keeping within this range, state exactly how much money you need to solve this problem.

Evaluation.   Anyone who invests money is likely to be concerned with how successfully this money has been spent. Some funders require external evaluators because they believe they will be more objective than the investigator. Even if the funder makes no such limitations, consider hiring an outside evaluator; it lends credibility to your project. Explain how this money will be used.

All of these parts should be included in you letter; furthermore, your letter should be short and clear.

Summary

Writing grant proposals is a good way to provide support for creating new programs, solving problems, and addressing unmet needs. Yet, there are other ways to meet these needs. Getting funds requires the ability to see problems clearly. When viewed from several angles, unseen solutions often become visible.

The Teachers-in-Residence Program typifies the ability to solve some problems without seeking a grant. It also shows that sometimes, through cooperation and collaboration, individuals and groups can find joint solutions that benefit all parties, and sometimes, as in this program, solutions can be found without additional costs to anyone.

Many individuals consider grant writing synonymous with getting the money they need to solve problems. There's no doubt about it; having million dollar grants funded can open many doors and enable investigators to perform many services they otherwise could never afford. But investigators should not overlook the value of small grants and gifts. The administrators leadership institute exemplifies the long-term value that can result from a small beginning. Serious grant writers should remain alert to opportunities to get small funding as well as large grants. As in this example, these smaller funds may come more informally to those who remain alert to a variety of possibilities.

Some funders prefer receiving letters rather than full-blown grant proposals. To be successful, these letters must be crafted with equal or greater care than that which is required for large proposals. Some writers say that writing a good, short social letter is more difficult than writing a longer letter. Writing successful grant letters is a challenge because the letters must be kept short and must contain at least the following parts: (1) a clear statement of a problem, (2) a proposed solution to this problem, (3) an explanation of why you are the best person or group for doing this job (why you can do it better than others), (4) an invitation, explaining why you have chosen the particular funder, (5) a statement of the exact amount of support required to do this job, and (6) how you plan to measure your success. Each letter must be clear and brief.

Recap of Major Ideas

- Some funders prefer letters over full-blown proposals.
- Letters are often used to screen applications.
- Letters require the same careful crafting as proposals.
- Sometimes creative problem solving can replace the need for a grant.
- Problem-identification skills can be as important as problem-solving skills.
- Collaborative problem solving can produce advantages for all parties.
- Letters should be written with one eye on the funder's goals and the other on the investigator's special skills and resources.
- The ability to convince funders that you can do a good job is often a greater influence than an extensive discussion of your need.

8

Using Technology to Write Grants

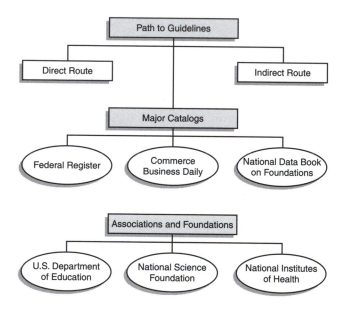

This chapter is about using technology to write grants. More specifically, it is about using the Internet. When computers first became accessible, courses were developed to teach students facts about the computer and to teach students how to write programs. Right away, students learned that using the computer was a very linear process. You either wrote your own program or you used an algorithm that someone else had written, following it step-by-step. But this chapter is not about program writing or algorithms. In fact, this chapter works with the Internet, and, of course, it works just opposite to program writing and algorithms. Instead of channeling their thoughts in one focused direction, use of the Web requires the user to think divergently; and instead of following the one-and-only path to the problem, the Web requires a lot of trial and error. This divergent nature of the Web makes it a perfect vehicle for grant writing because grant writing is not like an algorithm; there is no single correct method to follow. On the contrary, each grant writer, even the most experienced and most successful, has methodology that is somewhat unique. As explained in Chapter Two, effective grant writers develop generalizations that they use as guidelines, not hard and fast rules.

Surfing the Internet

Each grant project begins by conducting a search. One grant writer may begin by using terms that seem logical. But, quickly, the writers ask themselves, "What other terms should I use?" Experienced surfers know that the slightest alteration can produce major differences in the results. For example, an investigator might begin by calling forth a favorite search engine and entering the term *grant writing*. Another grant writer might begin by typing in the same words, but enclosing them in parentheses, and this writer would get a different set of information. Or the investigator could get an even different set of information by typing in *requests for proposals* or *"requests for proposals."*

Using the Internet to Validate

Once the investigator locates some guidelines, the next step is to decide what to do with them. When using the Web, a skeptical scientist's attitude is healthy. Instead of accepting the information as fact, it is far better to look up several guidelines and compare them. Chapter Two discussed guidelines for writing a grant proposal. The Web can be used to validate the essential parts of a proposal. For example, I wanted some assurance that the views I shared in Chapter Two about the parts of a proposal that I consider essential were shared by others who give advice on proposal writing. So, I typed in *grant proposal letters*. Then I scrolled until I found a heading that read *writing a grant proposal*. When I clicked on this option, I found an article by this same title written by Indiana Congressman Pete Visclosky, who explained that a proposal must be more than a report; it must be a convincing presentation.

I remembered reading on another website that grant writers must have passion. The congressman's article said that in addition to meeting all the requirements of the funding source, each proposal must have the following qualities:

- The proposal should have a clear and descriptive title.
- The proposal should be a cohesive whole, building logically with one section leading to another.
- Language should be clear and concise, devoid of jargon; explanations should be offered for acronyms and terms that may be unfamiliar to someone outside the field.
- Each part of the proposal should provide as brief a narrative as possible, with supporting data relegated to an appendix.

Reading this article made me feel confident because he was giving the same advice that I had given. The one additional piece of advice that he gave was to be cohesive and ensure that each part of your proposal flows logically to the next. Later, I added this tip to this book. So, the Web can be useful for discovering information to put into your grant proposals.

When using the Web, each source should be used to validate your previous understandings, and you should also look for additional information. Some surfers find this aspect of the Web irresistible; you never know what will be ahead.

I first used this article to validate my prior understandings. Incidentally, this article listed the components of a successful proposal. I felt somewhat reassured to see that the parts listed included the same parts that I had included when I wrote Chapter Two, namely, a cover letter, summary or abstract, introduction, problem statement or needs assessment, objectives, methods or procedures, evaluation, further funding (what happens to the project when the funding dries up?), budget, and appendix.

This article also gave the readers a hotline for the *Catalog of Federal Domestic Assistance*, which is *www.cfda.gov*. This site is composed of three sections: First-Time User's Guide, Browse the Catalog, and Find Assistance Programs. I was curious, so I checked out the First-Time User's Guide, and discovered a large database of federal programs for state and local governments. The site also had a list of answers to frequently asked questions. At this site, I also learned how to apply for money to start a business. Under the heading "Where can I find assistance to start a business," I hit the hotline *small business* and found forty-one programs, shown in Figure 8.1. You can download application forms for these programs by going to *www.adobie.com*. Finding that this website also had a section titled, Developing and Writing Grant Proposals, I took that path.

Home | FAQ | Privacy | About The CFDA Web Site

Programs For Functional Area Of Small Business

Your search returned 40 programs from the functional area of *Small Business*

CFDA #	Agency	Program Title
10.212	USDA	Small Business Innovation Research
10.406	FSA	Farm Operating Loans
10.767	RBS	Intermediary Relending Program
10.768	RBS	Business and Industry Loans
10.769	RBS	Rural Business Enterprise Grants
10.773	RBS	Rural Business Opportunity Grants
11.108	ITA	Commercial Service
11.110	ITA	Trade Development
11.150	BXA	Export Licensing Service and Information
11.313	EDA	Trade Adjustment Assistance
11.611	NIST	Manufacturing Extension Partnership
11.800	MBDA	Minority Business Development Centers
11.806	MBDA	Minority Business Opportunity Committee Development
14.412	FHEO	Employment Opportunities for Lower Income Persons and Businesses
15.124	BIA	Indian Loans_Economic Development
21.003	IRS	Taxpayer Service
36.001	FTC	Fair Competition Counseling and Investigation of Complaints
39.001	GSA	Business Services
44.001	NCUA	Credit Union Charter, Examination, Supervision, and Insurance
59.002	SBA	Economic Injury Disaster Loans
59.005	SBA	Business Development Assistance to Small Business
59.006	SBA	8(a) Business Development
59.007	SBA	Management and Technical Assistance
59.008	SBA	Physical Disaster Loans
59.009	SBA	Procurement Assistance to Small Businesses
59.011	SBA	Small Business Investment Companies
59.012	SBA	Small Business Loans
59.016	SBA	Bond Guarantees for Surety Companies
59.026	SBA	Service Corps of Retired Executives Association
59.037	SBA	Small Business Development Center
59.041	SBA	Certified Development Company Loans (504 Loans)
59.043	SBA	Women's Business Ownership Assistance
59.044	SBA	Veterans Entrepreneurial Training and Counseling
59.046	SBA	Microloan Demonstration Program
59.049	SBA	Office of Small Disadvantaged Business Certification and Eligibility
59.050	SBA	Microenterprise Development Grants
59.051	SBA	New Markets Venture Capital
81.082	DOE	Management and Technical Assistance for Minority Business Enterprises
81.105	DOE	National Industrial Competitiveness through Energy, Environment, and Economics

://www.cfda.gov/public/browse_sub.asp?subcode=BK&st=1   4/29/2002

FIGURE 8.1   Programs for Functional Area of Small Business

I continued to look for ideas that have not been addressed in this book, and I found a couple of excellent ones. To increase your organization's credibility, consider including the following:

- A brief biography of board members and key staff members
- The organization's goals, philosophy, track record with other grants, and any success stories
- Data that are relevant to the goals of the grantor and to the applicant's credibility

While Chapter Six suggests keeping a grant-writing binder, this source suggests, "Throughout the proposal writing stage, keep a notebook handy to write down ideas. Periodically, try to connect ideas by reviewing the notebook. Never throw away written ideas during the grant writing stage." I find this advice to be especially appropriate for when you are using the Web because once you leave a site, the chances of finding it again without a written reference are small.

Using the Yahoo search engine, I entered "grant writing" in quotes. Next, I went to EPA grant writing tutorial. Then, I saw EPA Purdue University. By choosing Mock Grant Writing Activity, I found the following table of contents:

- Proposed summary
- Introduction to the organization
- Problem statement (or needs assessment)
- Project objectives
- Project methods or design
- Project budget
- Appendix

The site for EPA Purdue University listed the following tips to enhance grant proposal writing:

- Read the request for proposal (RFP) carefully.
- Organize your proposal according to the RFP.
- Pay attention to the point allocation before you begin writing.
- Explain things—don't declare them.
- Don't make assumptions of your reviewers.
- Avoid jargon and ACRONYMS.
- Don't simply reiterate buzzwords.
- Be innovative—new audiences, new techniques, and so forth.
- Be passionate.
- Be realistic.
- Be specific. "I would like this much in order to do this."

- Show the funder the return on its investment.
- Check grammar, spelling, and typos.
- Ask someone else to review it.
- Solicit partners.
- If the funder says, "No," ask why.
- Volunteer to be an evaluator.

This program is user friendly—written to help novice grant writers. By clicking on any one of the parts listed in the table of contents, you can get SOURCES. All serious grant writers should be familiar with some publications that provide funding agency sources. The Web can help you become acquainted with these and many other sources.

Sources Available on the Internet

At a minimum, sources available on the Internet include (1) the *Federal Register*, (2) the *Catalog of Federal Domestic Assistance*, (3) the *Commerce Business Daily*, (4) the *National Data Book of Foundations*, (5) MedWeb, (6) GrantsNet, (7) the U.S. Department of Education, and (8) the National Science Foundation.

The Federal Register

The *Federal Register* is a daily government newspaper. As shown in Figure 8.2, this website includes information on applying for grants in each major U.S. government department.

The Catalog of Federal Domestic Assistance

The *Catalog of Federal Domestic Assistance* is a must for many serious grant writers. This document lists over 1,400 different programs, tells who can apply for each, and gives the rules and regulations for applying. An aspect that is especially helpful and should be noted for each source is the range of dollars each program funds along with the average amount of dollars given per program. Hard copies of this document sell for about $70 each and can be obtained by writing to the following:

> Superintendent of Documents
> U.S. Government Printing Office
> Washington, DC 20402

Ask for stock # 922-014-00000-1.

December 12, 2002 (Volume 67, Number 239)

Table of Contents

ADMINISTRATION FOR CHILDREN AND FAMILIES

Notices

BUREAU OF LAND MANAGEMENT

Notices

CENTERS FOR DISEASE CONTROL AND PREVENTION

Notices

DEPARTMENT OF AGRICULTURE

Notices

DEPARTMENT OF COMMERCE

Notices

FIGURE 8.2   Federal Register

The Commerce Business Daily

You may wish to check this document on the Web if your area is business rather than research. The U.S. government uses this publication to solicit bids from businesses.

National Data Book of Foundations

Because the federal government requires everyone who gives money to file an IRS form 990, you can look up any grant in the *National Data Book of Foundations* to learn what groups any party has funded and how much was awarded for each grant.

MedWeb

This public health website lists who is getting the grants in the field of health. You may wish to study the approaches of others who are writing successful proposals.

GrantsNet

This is the official website for the U.S. Department of Health and Human Services. This source lists many small and medium health grants.

U.S. Department of Education

This website gives information on funding opportunities and information on who is successful.

National Science Foundation

The National Science Foundation gives grants to support innovative programs in the sciences. The address is as follows:

> National Science Foundation
> 4201 Wilson Boulevard
> Arlington, VA 22230

Another source that might be helpful to students who read this book is the Pell Grants. Using Yahoo, you can type in "grants" and scroll to Federal Pell Grants. This source provides to undergraduates funds that do not have to be repaid. The maximum per year is about $3,000 per student. Of course, this varies each year depending on the appropriations.

While visiting Yahoo, you might also want to check out the National Institutes of Health (NIH) grants. Simply, do the following:

> Enter in quotes, "NIH Grants".
>
> Scroll to NIH Guide for Grants & Contracts.
>
> Click this header and get a list of comprehensive archives of published NIH guide articles, listed by year over the past eleven years.

Choose a year and a weekly list.

Choose a week and scroll to "Requests for Applications".

Summary

The Internet has unlimited potential for those grant writers who learn how to use it effectively. In contrast to the use of algorithms, which are commonly used to write computer programs and require convergent thinking, successful internet use requires the user to get out of the box and think divergently. As all surfers know, this is fun, but it has some limitations. Because much of the information on the Internet is not copyrighted, its quality is always suspect; therefore, the user must view it with suspicion, paying close attention to the sources. Secondly, as all internet surfers know, it is easy to waste a lot of time without making any progress, unless you identify some clear goals and keep them in focus. Two common uses that grant writers make of the Internet are (1) the gathering of information to expand their knowledge and (2) the gathering of information to verify or validate their understanding. The writing of this chapter was a good example of both of these uses.

This chapter provides examples of the diversity of paths an investigator can take when searching for topics and the totally different results that can occur from such minor changes as using or not using quotes, changing only one word, or changing search engines. The chapter also identifies major grant directories and grant sources, and provides directions and internet addresses for the same.

Recap of Major Ideas
- The Web has unlimited information, but some of it is inaccurate.
- Successful Internet use requires much trial-and-error exploring.
- The Internet can be used to verify or validate information.

Appendix A

Sample Proposal Rating Form
ECIA, Chapter 2
Mathematics and Science
Improvement Program

INSTRUCTION TO THE REVIEWER: Study entire proposal before beginning the rating process because information relevant to a single rating criterion may be found in several sections of the proposal. Respond to each item on the rating form by (1) commenting on the strengths or weaknesses of the proposed project and (2) indicating the earned point-value on the scale, 0 through 5. The highest composite scores will identify the meritorious proposals. It may be helpful to note in your comments where in the proposal you found the significant data.

Indicate the total number of points awarded to the proposal at the bottom of page 3. On page 4 suggest any revisions that would better meet the overall objective of improving statewide teacher qualification in mathematics, chemistry, and physics.

Complete the reviewer identification section below. Send two copies of each review, one signed and one unsigned, to _____

Reviewer Name: _____

Address: _____

Office   Home
Telephone: _____   Hours: _____   Telephone: _____

Reviewer Signature: _____

Date Signed: _____

A. Are the objectives to be achieved in the institute precisely stated and reasonable?

Comment(s): _____

Points earned: ____   ____   ____   ____   ____   ____
                 (0)   (1)   (2)   (3)   (4)   (5)

B. Are the recruiting and selection procedures appropriate?

Comment(s): _____

Points earned: ____   ____   ____   ____   ____   ____
                 (0)   (1)   (2)   (3)   (4)   (5)

C. Do the proposed courses give reasonable assurance of achieving the objectives of the institute?

Comment(s): _____

Points earned: ____   ____   ____   ____   ____   ____
                 (0)   (1)   (2)   (3)   (4)   (5)

D. Is the instructional staff appropriate to the successful implementation of the institute?

Comment(s): _____

Points earned: ____   ____   ____   ____   ____   ____
                 (0)   (1)   (2)   (3)   (4)   (5)

E. Have adequate provisions been made for management and support personnel?

Comment(s): _____

Points earned: ____   ____   ____   ____   ____   ____
                 (0)   (1)   (2)   (3)   (4)   (5)

F. Are sound evaluation procedures included that will assure obtaining usable information about the degree of attainment of project objectives?

Comment(s): _____

Points earned: ____   ____   ____   ____   ____   ____
                 (0)   (1)   (2)   (3)   (4)   (5)

G. Has the sponsoring institution committed the necessary facilities, including instructional equipment, to the institute?
Comment(s): _____

_____

Points earned: ____   ____   ____   ____   ____   ____
                   (0)   (1)   (2)   (3)   (4)   (5)

H. Does the proposal indicate an adequate level of fiscal and in-kind support from the sponsoring institution?
Comment(s): _____

_____

Points earned: ____   ____   ____   ____   ____   ____
                   (0)   (1)   (2)   (3)   (4)   (5)

I. Is the proposed budget consistent with the size and scope of the proposed institute?
Comment(s): _____

_____

Points earned: ____   ____   ____   ____   ____   ____
                   (0)   (1)   (2)   (3)   (4)   (5)

TOTAL POINTS AWARDED _____

Appendix B

ESCAPE Modules

I. Organizing and Teaching Subject Matter

  A. Planning

    101. **Curriculum**—fitting the curriculum of a subject or grade level into the total academic program

    102. **Planning and Teaching a Unit**—developing, executing, and evaluating plans with a central theme

    103. **A Daily Lesson Plan**—developing, executing, and evaluating a daily lesson plan

    104. **Conference Planning**—familiarizing the student (teacher) with procedures and organization of conference planning for an entire class

  B. Techniques for Teaching Subject Matter

    111. **Principles of Reinforcement**—identifying and applying various reinforcement methods in the classroom

    112. **Asking Questions**—asking higher order questions

    113. **A Module on Modules**—identifying parts of a module

II. Human Dynamics of Teaching

  A. Teacher-Pupil Interaction

    201. **Motivation**—using Maslow's Hierarchy of Human Basic Needs to assist motivational learning activities

    202. **Consistency**—demonstrating using consistency with pupils in and out of the classroom

    203. **Classroom Management**—demonstrating skills and techniques utilizing the democratic process in the classroom

    204. **Reinforcement Techniques in Written Work**—using written reinforcement techniques on written work

205. **Handling Discipline Problems Objectively**—recognizing and handling discipline problems
206. **Humor in Education**—demonstrating a sense of humor in the classroom

B. Diagnosing Classroom Climate

211. **The Sociogram: Social Isolates**—using the sociogram to identify social isolates and prescribing a suitable remedy
212. **Learning Difficulties**—diagnosing learning difficulties and prescribing appropriate teaching-learning strategies
213. **Children's Misbehavior Goals**—identifying and dealing with children's misbehavior goals as described by Adler

C. Teacher-Pupil Relationships

221. **Empathetic Responses**—aiding and developing empathetic responses
222. **Group Structure and Dynamics**—reviewing group processes and their effects on dynamics and task achievement
223. **Attitude Feedback**—measuring and finding a means to a positive attitude
224. **Value Clarification**—defining values and related behavioral problems
225. **Recognizing Enthusiasm**—identifying verbal and nonverbal behaviors that demonstrate enthusiastic teaching and assessing the consequences of those behaviors

III. Developing Teaching Skills

A. Technical Skills of Teaching

301. **Handwriting**—demonstrating the ability to form letters according to the curriculum guide of the student's (teacher's) school
302. **Use of Instructional Media**—developing and executing an instructional presentation demonstrating the proper operational techniques of audio-visual media
303. **Plan Book/Grade Book: Development and Utilization**—developing and using a plan book and a grade book to meet the needs of a student's (teacher's) teaching situation
304. **Utilizing and Supplementing Cumulative Records**—familiarizing the student (teacher) with ten pupils through cumulative records, observations, and interviews
305. **Parent Conferences**—conducting a parent-teacher conference
306. **Field Trips**—planning or executing a field trip

B. Varied Approaches to Teaching

311. **Individualizing Instruction**—demonstrating techniques of individualizing instruction
312. **Guided Discovery**—using the guided discovery technique
313. **Problem Solving**—using the problem-solving technique
314. **Performance-Based Education in the Classroom**—preparing and implementing a performance-based lesson plan identifying specified skills or competencies
315. **Creativity**—describing and demonstrating the humanistic teaching technique of creativity
316. **Individual Needs**—using activities for meeting individual performance levels

C. Verbal Communication in Teaching

321. **Enunciation**—Focusing attention on and corrective measures for commonly mispronounced words
322. **Communicating on the Pupil's Level**—restating a school directive at the pupil's level of understanding
323. **Voice Simulation**—using voice simulations in story telling, story reading, and role playing
324. **Listening Skills**—using listening variables and reacting to pupil comments to facilitate better pupil understanding
325. **Lecture and Demonstration**—describing and practicing lecture and demonstration techniques

IV. Professional Responsibilities

A. Policies and Regulations for the Classroom

401. **Rules and Regulations**—familiarizing the student (teacher) with state and local regulations, requirements, and curriculum policies
402. **Emergency Preparedness**—demonstrating knowledge of and developing a plan for federal, state, and local Emergency Preparedness Plans
403. **School Policy**—demonstrating knowledge of local policies and procedures as presented in policy handbooks
404. **Good Health**—demonstrating the importance of a working knowledge of health factors in education

B. Professional Contributions of the Classroom Teacher

411. **Professional Organizations**—learning about professional educational organizations
412. **Code of Ethics**—demonstrating a knowledge of ethical behavior

413. **Legal Responsibility of the Teacher**—demonstrating legal responsibility
414. **School Communication and the Community**—demonstrating the ability to communicate with the community through various media
415. **Co-Curricular Activities**—identifying common problems of and participating in activities that are not part of the regular academic program
416. **Professional Growth**—demonstrating a knowledge of professionalism, an awareness of impedances to it, opportunities and resources for growth, and professional responsibilities

Appendix C

A Module on Modules

Objective(s)

The purpose of this module is to enable the student (teacher) to write and understand the component parts of a module by being able to do the following:

1. Write one or more behavioral objectives on a topic of the student's choice.
2. Write a rationale that supports the objectives.
3. Write a module guide that provides a step-by-step procedure for working through the modules.
4. Identify any pre-assessment measures that will allow the pupil to test out of the module.
5. Design appropriate instructional activities that will enable the pupil to realize the objectives.
6. Write the evaluation procedures in objective terms.
7. Provide for any necessary remediation.

Evaluation of the prepared module will be based on the assessment of the module resources person(s) using the evaluation checklist on page 129.

The prepared learning package may be used in the classroom, but such activity is not required for this module.

Rationale

Modules can be defined as a type of teacher-learning packet that includes the following:

1. A list of competencies that a student (teacher) is expected to have at the end of a unit

2. An explanation of any teacher/learning activities that are designed to help the individual to achieve what is expected of him
3. Statements of how each student's performance and progress is to be evaluated
4. Standards each student must meet in order to complete or master those things expected of him

The nature of teaching is determined by what the pupil to be taught needs to learn and how he or she best may learn it. The nature of the acquisition process by which teaching competency is acquired is determined by what the teacher is to learn and how he or she may best learn it. The rationale for competency-based teacher education pertains to the latter. The former determines its content.

The rationale for competency-based programs derives from concepts about the nature of what is to be learned (in this case, teaching competency) and from a model of the system most likely to enhance this acquisition.

Learning modules are becoming popular educational tools in schools today. This module designed to help a student (teacher) learn about modules by going through a self-instructional module on the concept of modules.

Module Guide

See Figure C.1 for a flowchart of how to proceed through the module.

Pre-Assessment

None

Instructional Activities

The following activities are optional but are designed to help the student (teacher) complete the module satisfactorily.

1. Read *Preparing Behavioral Objectives* by Robert Mager.
2. Study other modules in Project ESCAPE to learn types of content—the component parts.
3. Study the categories on the post-assessment checklist.
4. Read *Measuring Instructional Intent* by Robert Mager.

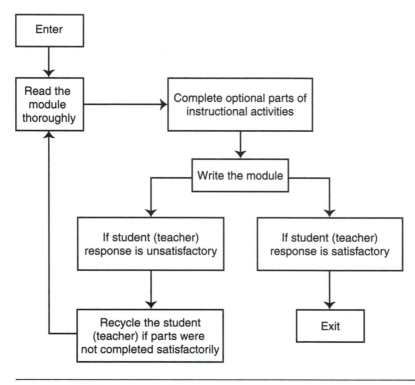

FIGURE C.1   How to Proceed through the Module

Post-Assessment

The student's (teacher's) prepared module should be evaluated by the module resource person(s) using the following checklist.

Evaluative Checklist for Learning Modules

Name of Evaluator _____

	Yes	Not Sure	No	If Not Sure or No, Please Comment
I. Objective(s)				
1. Specifies what is to be done	____	____	____	_____
2. Identifies condition	____	____	____	_____
3. States how it is to be done	____	____	____	_____
4. Provides criteria for completion	____	____	____	_____
II. Rationale				
1. Identifies relevant research	____	____	____	_____
2. Shows relationship to topic	____	____	____	_____
3. Is consistent with objective(s)	____	____	____	_____
4. Shows importance of objective(s)	____	____	____	_____
III. Module Guide				
1. Identifies prerequisites	____	____	____	_____
2. Identifies procedures for completing module	____	____	____	_____
IV. Pre-Assessment				
1. Is consistent with objective(s)	____	____	____	_____
2. Allows student to test out of module	____	____	____	_____
V. Instructional Activities				
1. Is consistent with stated objective(s)	____	____	____	_____
2. Reasonable amount of time required	____	____	____	_____
VI. Remediation				
1. Procedure to be followed in event of unsatisfactory progress	____	____	____	_____

Suggestions for improvements (additional prerequisites, instructional activities, etc.)

_____

_____

_____

_____

_____

Reference

Mager, R. F. (1984). *Preparing instructional objectives.* 2nd ed. Belmont, CA: Pitman Management and Training.

Appendix D

Teachers as Researchers

Definitions

The term *teacher as researcher* is polymorphous; it continuously changes and it stimulates about as many concepts as the number of individuals who consider it. Any attempt to study the subject requires attention to its many definitions.

The number of ways the term *teacher as researcher* has been defined is matched by the diversity among the definitions; some of the definitions are all encompassing, some are narrow and specific, and most are somewhere between these ranges (Bracey, 1991). The definition used at any particular time may be determined by the context in which the term is found (McKernan, 1988).

The differences among the definitions of *research* are more than accidental and can be of significant consequence because they reflect different sets of values and assumptions (Shannon, 1990). An examination of these differences can lead to a better understanding of the individual terms and of how they are interrelated.

Vockell (1983) used a general definition of *research* that can lead to a broad definition of *teacher as researcher*. According to Vockell, research has three levels: (1) descriptions of processes (what actually happens); (2) descriptions of relationships (what is associated with what); and (3) research supporting a causative relationship, even without relationship to an overall theory.

Those who define *research* so generally will probably agree with Shalaway (1990) who said that "(for many teachers) research is more a verb than a noun" (p. 34). Shalaway pointed out that the work of researchers is similar, regardless of whether teachers work alone or collaborate with a research team: "no matter where they work, teacher researchers all engage in the same basic

This appendix appeared as Chapter Four of *Handbook of Research on Teacher Education*, 2nd ed., a project of the Association of Teacher Education, John Sikula, Senior Editor. New York: Macmillan, 1996. Reprinted with permission.

process—systematic inquiry" (p. 34). Although Shalaway's definition is general, it does specify "systematic" behavior.

Classroom/Action Teacher Research

The Reading/Language in Secondary Schools Subcommittee of the International Reading Association's (IRA) (1989) perception of the term is reflected in the following passages:

> Any time you try an experiment with one group in the classroom and set up another group as a control for comparison, you have the foundation for research. When you decide a method worked or didn't work as judged from the results, you have done some classroom research.
>
> Classroom action research may be as formal or informal as the teacher chooses. It may be done alone in the privacy of the classroom or teachers may prefer to collaborate with a university educator or other members of their faculty or district staff. (p. 216)

Lytle and Cochran-Smith (1990) defined *teacher research* as "systematic, intentional inquiry by teachers" (p. 83). They say that this definition is consistent with the idea that to learn deliberately is research, with the notion that every lesson should be an inquiry for the teacher (see Goswami & Stillman, 1987, p. 15). Steinhouse (see McKernan, 1988) defined *research* as systematic, self-critical inquiry made public. McKernan (1988) said that this definition of *teacher research* is useful because "it suggests rigorous examination of one's own practice as a basis for professional development; the idea is that each school, and indeed each classroom, is a laboratory in which the curriculum and problems experienced as problems by teachers (not outside researchers) are subjected to empirical examination by practitioners" (p. 154). McCutcheon and Jung (1990) defined *action research* as "inquiry teachers undertake to understand and improve their own practice" (p. 144). Oberg and McCutcheon (1987) said that action research is "any systematic inquiry, large or small, conducted by professionals and focusing on some aspect of their practice in order to find out more about it, and eventually to act in ways they see as better or more effective" (p. 117). McKernan (1988) listed four self-recommending features of action research over fundamental or traditionally defined research:

1. It assists participants in gaining and *increasing their own understanding* of personally experienced educational or curriculum problems.
2. Action research as opposed to fundamental research focuses on problems of *immediate concern.*
3. Research is geared toward practical short-term solutions—thus, it is a form of *operational* or *applied* research.
4. Action research often encourages (though it does not have to be collaborative) *collaboration* of a number of participants on an equal footing. It is for equality

of partnership, not simply in engaging of participants in a cooperative research enterprise. (p. 155)

Carr and Kemmis (1986) defined *action research* as a form of self-reflective inquiry undertaken by participants in social situations in order to improve the rationality and justice of their own practices, their understanding of these practices, and the situations in which the practices are carried out (p. 162).

These definitions (Carr & Kemmis, 1986; McCutcheon & Jung, 1990; McKernan, 1988; Oberg & McCutcheon, 1987) create an image of action researchers as teachers who each day pursue relevant topics to improve their teaching.

History

Teacher Involvement with Research

The concept of classroom teachers as researchers is not new. As early as 1908 concerted efforts were being made to involve classroom teachers in research (Lowery, 1908). Two years later the topic appeared in a professional journal (Bagley, Bell, Seashore, & Whipple, 1910). As Olson (1990) said, "it is interesting to note that early in the twentieth century teachers were recognized as persons to identify educational problems pertinent to teaching. Furthermore, teachers were charged with investigating solutions to those problems, although the practice was never called research" (p. 3). Even with encouragement to become involved with research, the type and level of involvement was limited throughout the first half of the twentieth century. Initially teachers were not conductors of research, nor were they full investigative partners; rather they remained primarily recipients of research (Peik, 1938).

Teacher-conducted research in the United States accelerated in the 1920s (Olson, 1990) as a consequence of encouragement from several sources (Buckingham, 1926; Cushman & Fox, 1938; Dewey, 1929; Good, Barr, & Scates, 1936; Peik, 1938; Waples & Tyler, 1930). Initially teachers were encouraged to conduct action research as a means of curriculum development (McKernan, 1988). In the 1950s, Corey (1953) and Shumsky (1958) urged teachers to become researchers in their own classrooms. Stevens, Slanton, and Bunny (1992) cited several studies that have described classroom teachers performing the role of researchers (Allen, Combs, Hendricks, Nash, & Wilson, 1988; Busching & Rowls, 1987; Copenhaver, Byrd, McIntyre, & Norris, 1982; Fischer, 1988–1989; McDaniel, 1988–1989; Reading/Language in Secondary Schools Subcommittee of IRA, 1989).

Teacher Attitudes

Some clear differences exist in the way teachers and university researchers view research. This disparity frequently serves as a major barrier to effective collaboration. J. Myron Atkin (1989) addressed the problem.

> Teachers are at best peripheral to the conduct of educational research. They are often studied, but they are seldom encouraged to undertake systematic studies of educational problems. As a result, serious gaps exist in our understanding of schools, and a great many teachers and administrators believe—and say, with conviction—that educational research is irrelevant, wrong-headed, or both. (p. 200)

Hastie (1992) reported that university researchers are concerned that "teachers do not attempt to attain up-to-date information about research, while teachers suggest that the information provided by researchers does not transfer well to the teaching context" (p. 371). Teachers also often perceive researchers' topics as too theoretical or, conversely, too superficial (Chattin-McNichols & Loeffler, 1989). Cuban (1992) said that the teacher's usual world is characterized by action, concrete knowledge, and the ability to work in actual settings. Cuban attributed this difference in perceptions among teachers and researchers to the different cultures in their daily lives; a teacher's world is more concrete. For example, researchers are comfortable in exploring possibilities such as possible products to come from collaboration, whereas teachers ask questions to remove the uncertainty, such as "What should the products look like?" "What does the collaboration want?" or "When?"

The literature is replete with expressions of concern over the bases for teacher decisions. For example, Egbert (1984) said, "Teachers ignore research and overestimate the value of personal experience" (p. 14). Garrison (1988) noted, "If they could, many if not most teachers would ignore research on teaching entirely . . ." (p. 489). Brown (1990) said that teachers usually do not base their planning on the factors that affect achievement. When Marshall (1991) asked teachers why they teach as they do, they reported:

> It's the way I was taught.
> It's the way I learned.
> It's the easiest way to cover the material. (p. 227)

Bellon, Bellon, and Blank (1992) attributed teachers' failure to develop effective teaching strategies to the absence of opportunities to develop an adequate research knowledge base. These authors reported:

> We have found that the most able teachers do not want simple prescriptions that are intended to help them be more effective. They know teaching

is a complex process that is individual and highly contextual. . . . Successful teachers want to have a broad knowledge base that will help them make the most appropriate instructional decisions. (p. 3)

Historically, the level of teacher involvement in research has been low (Olson, 1990). This low involvement is attributable, at least in part, to the failure of preservice programs to prepare and require students to conduct research. Another contributor is poor communications between teacher and researcher (Bain & Gooseclose, 1979; Odell, 1976; Rainey, 1972; Travers, 1976). Even when teachers were involved, they usually had little or no voice in the desired outcome (Atkin, 1989; Fenstermacher, 1987). Often research involved teachers who were reluctant subjects of studies (Glatthorn, 1993). Tyack (1990) pointed out that most of the important changes that have occurred in the schools since the 1960s have resulted from federal laws. Yet, many educators (Haberman, 1992; Kirk, 1988; Kowalski & Reitzug, 1993; Ravitch, 1992) agree that if the conceived changes are to be effectively implemented, teachers must be involved in their planning. Intrinsic motivators (e.g., involvement with the results of an innovation) are exceedingly more powerful motivators than are extrinsic motivators (Herzberg, Mausner, & Snyderman, 1959; Wright, 1985; Young, 1985).

A major barrier to teacher involvement is teachers' schedules. Put simply, today's teachers have so many responsibilities that they have little or no time left in their schedules for doing research. Through the years, noneducators have viewed teaching as an act that requires little planning. Darling-Hammond (1993) concluded that American teachers are denied time to plan because they are stereotyped as being relatively unimportant; however, teachers' behaviors significantly affect the quality and amount of learning that occurs in their classrooms (Bellon, Bellon, & Blank, 1992; Chimes & Schmidt, 1990; Good & Brophy, 1987).

Given the important influence that teachers have on student learning, teachers need to keep up with the latest developments in their fields, and they need to develop the deepest possible level of understanding of the important concepts in their content specialties (Doyle, 1990). This can be done effectively through involving teachers in action research. The expansion of research on teaching in recent years has made research consumerism more important for teachers. Bellon, Bellon, and Blank (1992) explained: "now there is so much current research available that we have to carefully select findings that are consistent across studies and which are based on sound research techniques" (p. 7). Many resources are available to those who wish to know more about the relationships between teaching and research. These include commercially published books (Bissex & Bullock, 1987; Schon, 1987), books published by professional associations (Curtis, 1932; Elliott, 1980; Monroe, 1938; Olson, 1990), theme issues of journals (Oberg & McCutcheon, 1987), university projects (Oja & Pine, 1983), clearinghouse publications (Myers, 1985), research and development center publications (Houston, 1979; Huling & Griffin, 1983; Tikunoff, Ward, & Griffin, 1979), and federal publications (U.S. Department of Education, 1987). Resources also are available on the case study method (Bissex & Bullock, 1987; Kowalski, Henson, & Weaver, 1994).

Involvement in conducting research provides teachers a means of reaching goals. After monitoring and evaluating the behavior of teachers who were involved in conducting research, Bennett (1993) reported:

> Teacher-researchers viewed themselves as being . . . better informed than they had been when they began their research. They now saw themselves as experts in their field who were better problem solvers and more effective teachers with fresher attitudes toward education. (p. 69)

Involvement in research can improve teachers' understanding of why they behave as they do. Oberg (1990) reported that those teachers who are aware of the reasons underlying their behavior can make better choices of behavior.

Levels of Involvement

Although teachers have been slow to get involved with research, they have been involved at three levels. The levels reflect the teacher's degree of decision-making power throughout the research process and particularly with the identification of the problem, design of the study, and use of the data. As shown in Table D.1, at level 1 the teacher's behavior can be described as that of helper. For example, at this level the teacher's main role is to provide a classroom and students to be studied by an outside researcher. Also at this level the teacher may gather data to give to a university researcher.

At level 2 the teacher is a junior research partner who has little or no involvement in decisions that guide the research process. At level 3 the teacher is either a full research partner (collaborator) who participates equally in the decision-making process or a lone researcher who makes all of the decisions.

Three areas of decision making are especially important to teachers who work with research: (1) identifying the problem (Tripp, 1990), (2) designing the study, and (3) using the data (see Table D.2). At level 1, the teacher

TABLE D.1   *Levels of Teacher Involvement*

Level 3	Teacher as researcher
	Lone researcher or collaborator (equal partner)
Level 2	Teacher as junior partner
Level 1	Teacher as a helper

TABLE D.2   *Levels of Teacher Involvement: A Comprehensive View*

	Identifying the Problem	Conducting the Research	Use of Results
Level 3	The teacher, either alone or in cooperation with equal partners, identifies a current classroom problem.	Either alone or in cooperation with equal partners, the teacher chooses to design and conduct the study or to let a partner who has more expertise in research design the study.	Either alone or with equal partners, the teacher uses the results to improve teaching.
Level 2	The teacher provides minimal input into identifying the problem to be studied.	The teacher may make suggestions about the design of the study, but the ultimate decision is made by the senior partner.	At this level the teacher seldom sees the results.
Level 1	The teacher is excluded from the process used to identify the problem to be investigated.	The teacher offers a classroom and students to be studied. The teacher may or may not assist with the collection of data. The data are turned over to the "real" researcher.	At this level the teacher typically does not ever see the results.

has no input into the selection of the problem to be investigated; rather, an outside researcher, traditionally a university professor, selects the problem, sometimes using as the major criterion the type of problem that can help lead to tenure, promotion, or merit pay. At this level the teacher facilitates by providing the necessary subjects for the study (e.g., classroom, students). These arrangements do not require the teacher's input into the design of the study. At this level the teacher collects the data and turns them over to the researcher. The teacher may or may not see the results.

At level 2 the teacher's level of input into the selection of the problem is minimal and the senior researcher has the final word. The teacher may make suggestions about the design of the study, but the final decisions will be made by the senior partner. The level 2 teacher seldom has access to the results once the data are turned over to the research partner.

At level 3 the teacher has equal or total choice of the problem, choosing a problem that can help improve one of his or her classes. The teacher may design the study or may choose to rely on a research partner who has more expertise. The results are returned to the teacher who uses them to improve the class. When partners are used, often they are university personnel, faculty, and doctoral students who may wish to use those same data to produce an article for publication. Usually the article is mutually written and becomes the joint property of all research team members.

In this chapter the terms *collaborator* and *collaboration* refer to the teacher as an equal partner in research. Throughout the remainder of this chapter, the term *teacher as researcher* refers to both the teacher as an equal partner in research and to the teacher as a lone researcher, but not to the teacher as assistant or junior partner.

Effects of Teacher Involvement with Research

Effects on Teachers

A review of the literature shows that concern over the removal of most teachers from research has been growing during the past decade. Atkin (1989) gave several reasons why teachers should be more highly involved with research.

> Research is needed for educational improvement to occur, of course. Teachers need new knowledge to cope with the complex issues they face, and they are continually seeking information. For example, they want to know how they can use their instructional time most effectively, how students can learn more, how children can teach other children, and how students' educational progress can best be evaluated.
>
> They also want a deeper understanding of how the various subjects taught in school relate to one another and to the lives of young people, of what subject matter is most worth teaching and when and how students might best be engaged in activities with long-term educational payoffs, of what classroom implications stem from the rapidly changing characteristics of the student body, of how schools themselves might change to take advantage of growing community interest in the purposes and effectiveness of public education, and of how to capitalize on local (and often unanticipated) events that have potential for enriching life in classrooms. (pp. 200–201)

The Reading/Learning in Secondary Schools Subcommittee of the IRA (1989) identified the following benefits of action research:

Helps solve classroom problems
Encourages effective change
Revitalizes teachers

Empowers teachers to make decisions in their classrooms
Identifies effective teaching and learning methods
Promotes reflective teaching
Promotes ownership of effective practices
Verifies what methods work
Widens the range of teachers' professional skills
Provides a connection between instructional methods and results
Helps teachers apply research findings to their own classrooms
Enables teachers to become change agents (p. 217)

During the 1980s, the expression "teacher as researcher" commanded a strong emphasis in the literature (Chall, 1986; Hanna, 1986; Santa, Isaacson, & Manning, 1987; Stansell & Patterson, 1988). The literature consistently reports that those teachers who participate in research bring from the experience a variety of positive changes in themselves (Boyer, 1990; Carr & Kemmis, 1986; Carson, 1990; Chattin-McNichols & Loeffler, 1989; Goswami & Stillman, 1987; Kirk, 1988; Lieberman, 1986a; Lytle & Cochran-Smith, 1990; Nixon, 1981; Rogers, Noblit, & Ferrell, 1990; Sardo-Brown, 1992; Shalaway, 1990; Stevens, Slanton, & Bunny, 1992). As previously mentioned, when teachers initially became involved in research, the typical teacher's role was to offer their classes to the study. Yet, teachers have moved from this passive role to become equal partners in research and, indeed, in many instances to identify the problems to be studied and either conduct or co-conduct the studies. This shift in the role that teachers play in research has greatly increased the positive changes that teachers experience from being involved with research.

Effect on Teachers' Ability to Teach (Instructional Empowerment)

Does involvement in research really help teachers to improve their teaching? To find the answer to this question, Stevens, Slanton, and Bunny (1992) administered a questionnaire to a group of teachers who had been participating in a research project for 1 year. These researchers reported that "When asked to complete a brief questionnaire about their first year with the research group, each classroom teacher stated that the membership in the group helped him/her do a better job" (p. 8). These researchers further concluded that this improved teaching resulted in part from an "increased awareness of effective instructional practice" (p. 8).

There is evidence that involvement in research expands teachers' commitment to developing a variety of teaching methods and to keeping abreast of new information. Dicker (1990), Fullan (1982), Santa (1990), and Santa, Isaacson, & Manning (1987) reported that involvement with research expanded the teachers' possible approaches. Sardo-Brown (1992) reported that involvement in research gave teachers a renewed desire to stay current.

Teacher burnout takes a major toll on teachers in every school. Involvement in action research offers teachers a rich source of vitality (Sucher, 1990). One teacher who became involved in a research project had the following to say about burnout and the effect of involvement in research on teacher burnout:

> Teacher burnout is really feeling that you have stopped growing as a person in the classroom. Learning how to do research in my own classroom has started me growing again. (Chattin-McNichols & Loeffler, 1989, p. 25)

Another major change that involvement in research fosters is an openness toward learning more about everything in general and about teaching in particular. By conducting research, teachers become ongoing learners (Boyer, 1990; Brownlie, 1990). As Boyer (1990) explained, "As teachers become researchers they become learners" (p. 57).

Neilsen (1990) identified several changes that occur when teachers become more open and when they commit their energy to learning about teaching by becoming involved in research.

> As an observer, guide, and sometimes confidante, I have seen teachers grow in wisdom and confidence, learn to be eloquent speakers and group leaders, become assertive and knowledgeable advocates for change, forge new and affirming relationships, create support groups, and produce magnificent pieces of writing. (p. 249)

Marriott (1990) reported on his personal growth experience, which involved opening up and taking on new challenges.

> The drudgery of complacency has been replaced with a sense of mission. I have experienced more professional growth than at any other period in my career. (p. 2)

Rogers, Noblit, and Ferrell (1990), however, warned that this growth may not always be in directions that teachers prefer. The goal should be to prepare teachers to change their classrooms as they would like to have them. Consider, too, that while successful action researchers can decide to make the changes they perceive necessary, they also have the ability to hold those practices that they perceive important. Nixon (1981) said that "Action research serves primarily to sharpen perceptions, stimulate discussion and energize questioning" (p. 9).

A professor who required graduate education students to complete an action research project (Bennett, 1993) reported a positive change in the students' attitudes toward themselves and toward research.

> I noted that teachers went into the research component of the program feeling anxious, and hostile, but emerged feeling positive about the

experiences and their newly formed identities as teacher-researchers . . . as teachers gained experience and success with research, their attitude toward research greatly improved . . . teacher-researchers viewed themselves as being more open to change, more reflective, and better informed than they had been when they began their research. (p. 69)

Obviously, action research affects different teachers in different ways. Furthermore, different people seek different benefits from action research. Rogers, Noblit, and Ferrell (1990) did not see this as a problem.

Action research is a vehicle to put teachers in charge of their craft and its improvement. Yet there is considerable variation in what people see action research accomplishing for teachers. These variations range from mundane technical improvement in classrooms to transforming a teacher's identity. (p. 179)

Involvement with research makes teachers more critical (in an analytical sense), causing them to question their own beliefs and the assertions of others (Goswami & Stillman, 1987; Neilsen, 1990). Neilsen (1990) said, "As teachers substantiate what they know through research, they typically develop keen observational powers and a critical sensibility and are less likely to accept, without question" (p. 249). In their book, *Reclaiming the Classroom: Teacher Research as an Agency for Change,* Goswami and Stillman (1987) described the effects of research on teachers who do research.

They collaborate with their students to answer questions important to both, driving on resources in new and unexpected ways.

Their teaching is transformed in important ways: They become theorists, articulating their intentions, testing their assumptions, and finding connections with practice.

Their perceptions of themselves as writers and teachers are transformed.

They step up their use of resources; they form networks; and they become more active professionally.

They become rich resources who can provide the profession with information it simply doesn't have . . . teachers know their classroom and students in ways that outsiders can't.

They become critical, responsive readers and users of current research, less apt to accept uncritically others' assertions, less vulnerable to fads, and more authoritative in their assessment of curricula, methods, and materials.

Lytle and Cochran-Smith (1990) said,

As teachers begin to participate in the generation of knowledge about teaching, learning, and schooling, they become more critical of both university-based research and standard school practices. They challenge taken-for-granted assumptions about theory and practice. (p. 101)

Shalaway (1990) summed up the attitudinal change that involvement in research has on teachers by saying,

> That's a typical pattern of teacher researchers. Above all, they illustrate the fact that good teachers never stop learning to teach—and research provides the means to do so. (p. 36)

Allan and Miller (1990) and Bennett (1993) reported positive changes in teachers' problem-solving skills (after having been involved in an action research project). "They (the teachers) now saw themselves as experts in their field who were better problem solvers . . ." (p. 69).

Effects on Students

Reed, Mergendoller, and Horan (1992) suggested broadening the membership of action research teams. Involvement in action research increases all parties' awareness of student needs (Kirk, 1988; SooHoo, 1993). Haberman (1992) reported that teachers who are directly involved in curriculum development tend to shift their style from prescriptive to more interactive, enabling the teacher to increase the interaction with students and to more effectively evaluate student needs.

> As teachers feel more involved in the development of curriculum, it is clear that their personal commitment will be a primary factor in motivating the student to be more interested in the material being presented. Further, improvements in teacher-student relationships will not only enhance teaching, but will be evidenced in student achievement as well. Thus, curriculum development becomes curriculum renewal as the chain of communication from student to teacher to curriculum committee becomes a continuous cycle of analysis and problem solving. (p. 15)

Prerequisites for Successful Teacher Research

A prerequisite for teachers' research success is the opportunity to reflect on the consequences of findings. Clandinin (1992) said that teachers' stories are a powerful means of helping teachers reflect on their teaching practices. Collaboration in reflection offers additional advantages. Reporting on a study at the Professional Development Center in Palo Alto, California, a participant said, "Teachers in our study were encouraged to interact with other teachers . . . as they documented and reflected on their practice" (Shalaway, 1990, p. 38). The teachers reported that this interaction provided a wonderful growth opportunity. This participant concluded that "Perhaps one of the best ways for a teacher to grow is to get together with colleagues to talk about teaching" (p. 38). Neufeld (1990) referred to such growth as "an increased sense of professionalism" (p. 345). A Canadian teacher-researcher said, "The opportunity to contribute to educational research allows the teacher to become more confident and to grow in a very personal way toward a deeper understanding of what is meant by the act of teaching" (McConaghy, 1987, p. 631). Although collaboration itself does not constitute conducting action research, it enriches the benefits of action research.

Reporting on an action research project involving middle and secondary teachers conducted at Friends University in Wichita, Kansas, Schumm (1993) identified as a primary concern "the need for a support group to help sustain and guide the process" (p. 449).

The Reading/Language in Secondary Schools Subcommittee of the IRA (1989) listed the following steps, which it says are necessary for classroom action research:

1. Identify the problem, the experimental and control groups, and the change or strategy to try.
2. Establish a baseline by testing data, checklists, observations, behaviors.
3. Implement the change or strategy.
4. Analyze results and other influences that affect the outcome.
5. Share results with students, teachers, administrators, and others. (p. 217)

Models

Classroom-Based Model

Some teachers initiate their own research in the perimeter of their classrooms (Marks, 1989; Reading/Language in Secondary Schools Subcommittee of the IRA, 1989; Shalaway, 1990). This type of action research gives almost immediate feedback on questions that teachers have about their instructional and management practices. The intent is not to get published in a professional journal, but to see if the altering of practices can improve classroom performance or behavior. This context-based, classroom-based model is needed to improve teacher education (Cardelle-Elawar, 1993; Cross, 1990; Cunningham & Shillington, 1990).

Having access to knowledge that otherwise would not be available seems justification enough for classroom research, but as McKernan (1988) pointed out, "It is not enough that classrooms be researched, they need to be researched by teachers" (p. 154).

Traditional Collaboration Model

Although not all teacher involvement with research involves collaboration with universities or other agencies, most of this research is through cooperative efforts. Such collaborations usually involve universities. Most collaborative studies are initiated by university researchers (Van Manen, 1990). Definite problems (see Bracey, 1991) and benefits result when teachers and professors collaborate. A lack of agreement on the roles of teachers and ownership of the results is common. According to Porter (1990), "The research base relative to collaborative efforts is relatively non-existent" (p. 78). Porter says that this conclusion is supported by Fox and Faver (1984), Hord (1986), and Houston (1979); however, as mentioned earlier in this chapter, teacher involvement with research can be traced back to the early 1900s. At the beginning of teacher research, teachers linked with others (usually university faculty members or personnel in federal, state, or local school departments or districts). Since its beginning, teacher research has focused on a broad topic that was generated externally and that often had little apparent significance to the local teacher or classroom (Atkin, 1989; Fenstermacher, 1987; Houser, 1990). In fact, teachers often perceive the topics as either too theoretical or too superficial or both (Chattin-McNichols & Loeffler, 1989).

In recent years this model has come under much criticism. Critics (Chattin-McNichols & Loeffler, 1989; Neilsen, 1990) say the harshest of these criticisms is that a research problem is seldom perceived by teachers as significant. Houser (1990) said that teachers were minimally informed about the research project.

Although this model has existed since the 1930s, its limitations have grown as teacher empowerment has expanded. In addition to having an outside agency identify the problems to be studied without teacher input into the selection, the agencies have used teachers to gather data without knowing how these data were being used. Atkin (1989) addressed this problem.

> In turn, investigators in the research community watch teachers and listen to them—but only when the teachers are doing things that the researchers consider important or interesting. This condition dominates mainstream educational research. . . . The resulting loss is profound, both in our understanding of educational events and in the disheartening message sent to teachers that their role in educational change is simply discovering the site-level consequences of somebody else's ideas or implementing the classroom techniques that other people have devised. (p. 201)

The collaboration research model offers several advantages that come from the associations that teachers have with others outside their own classrooms. The degree to which these advantages will be realized (and therefore the level of effectiveness of each collaborative research program) is contingent on each teacher, researcher, school district, parent, and other outside agency correctly performing its role.

Collaboration forces teachers to expose their teaching practices to others (McElroy, 1990; Santa, 1990). A willingness to share their practices, classroom, and students is a prerequisite for success. Therefore, one of the first steps in the teacher's role in collaboration is to develop a willingness to share and a willingness to experiment at the cost of failing and having others become aware of these failures.

Collaboration also requires the ability to critically self-analyze, with the willingness to change when a change is warranted. This self-analytic evaluation process can take the form of keeping a portfolio or keeping a journal. Recording experiences in a journal helps teachers reflect on both their thoughts and their actions (Shalaway, 1990).

Student-Centered Problem-Solving Model

As early as the seventeenth century, John Locke (see Gay, 1964) developed the concept "tabula rasa," which proclaimed that the mind at birth is a blank slate that can be filled only through experiences. By the late nineteenth century, Europeans realized the motivational and retention benefits of active student involvement in lessons. Froebel, Herbart, Pestalozzi, and Montesorri (see Ikenberry, 1974) were quick to design curricula around planned student experiences. By the beginning of the twentieth century, Colonel Francis Parker (see Campbell, 1967) had brought the concept of learner-centered education to America and implemented it in the Quincy, Massachusetts, schools. By the early 1920s with the help of Colonel Parker, John Dewey had introduced a revolution in American schools called *progressive education.* This student-centered system dominated American education for more than two decades. The effectiveness of student-centered education was carefully measured in a famous Eight-Year Study (Henson, 1994). The results were that when compared to traditional teacher-dominated teaching, learner-centered teaching was far more effective in cognitive gains and in a host of other areas. Students in learner-centered classes were more creative, exhibited superior leadership skills, displayed more intellectual curiosity, and were more highly motivated.

Student involvement is just one example of the many principles of learning that guide teacher behavior. An awareness of these principles alone is inadequate; students and teachers need to be involved in discovering knowledge. Teachers also need to possess the skills required to measure the effectiveness of those principles when they are applied in the classroom (Marks, 1989).

Case Studies

One major benefit of teacher research is the knowledge that it generates (Houser, 1990; Learning from Children, 1988); case study development can contribute greatly. Shulman (1990) believes that a major goal of future education is to develop a collection of case studies.

Teachers need opportunities to learn to become independent thinkers (Cardelle-Elawar, 1993; Cross, 1990, Floden & Klinzing, 1990; Sagor, 1991). The case study method can provide opportunities for teachers to make judicious decisions, a skill that cannot be developed by traditional teaching methods (Kowalski, Henson, & Weaver, 1994). Cases developed by teachers can even become springboards for further teacher-conducted research (Atkin, 1989).

Barriers

Successful collaboration among teachers and researchers requires certain conditions (Gies, 1984; Hastie, 1992; Sanger, 1990). Reporting on a joint conference involving the Association International des Écoles Superieures d'Éducation Physique (AIESEP) and the National Association for Physical Education in Higher Education (NAPEHE), Hastie (1992) said that successful collaboration requires a reward system to encourage and reward success; yet, Gies (1984) warned teachers to first consider the significance the problem(s) under investigation has for them because no reward system is likely to be adequate to satisfy teachers who are not committed to the study. Other researchers and teachers have stressed the need for teachers to be involved in deciding the problems to be studied (Applebee, 1987; Kearney & Tashlik, 1985; Lieberman, 1986b; McKernan, 1988). Gill (1993) listed the following conditions as prerequisites to successful collaboration:

> Adeguate professional development, including a sufficient knowledge base and enough time
>
> Support from the union
>
> A credible leadership team
>
> Support from the school administration—philosophically and materially
>
> Continuing support by those who understand the new practice(s)
>
> Regular opportunities for reflection and problem solving
>
> Relief from the constraints of traditional evaluation and testing while new ways are learned
>
> Hope that structural changes teachers begin to find necessary to sustain their efforts can indeed happen (p. 41)

A major barrier for most teachers who wish to participate in collaborative projects is the time required of teachers (Gajewski, 1986; Houser, 1990; Schumm, 1993). The problem is exacerbated by schools' inflexible schedules (Arndt, 1984). Often teacher-researchers trade half of their teaching time for researching time. The responsibilities of both jobs can grow until the teacher has two full-time jobs (Porter, 1990). Projects should be designed so that they do not make extra demands on teachers' time (Hastie, 1992). The problem can be further ameliorated by making sure that all participants are organized and by clarifying the role of each participant (Stevens, Slanton, & Bunny, 1992).

Another barrier to teachers conducting research is lack of confidence. Many teachers believe that they do not possess the research and statistical skills needed to perform research. Some educators believe that this is more a perceived weakness than a true weakness (Winter, 1982; Woods, 1986). In reality, action research may involve the use of sophisticated research knowledge and skills, but teachers who lack such sophistication can design and conduct simpler studies.

Some teachers work in environments where research is not appreciated (McDaniel, 1988–1989). This introduces another barrier that seems to develop automatically—a status hierarchy that separates teachers and professors. In some collaborations, university partners are ranked above teachers (Gies, 1984). Where this hierarchy exists, teachers are relegated to the status of a second-class partner in the research process. This can lead to inferior expectations for teachers and even to inferior self-expectations. Ironically, the same teachers who suffer a loss of self-esteem can also suffer a deterioration in relationships among fellow teachers (Porter, 1990).

Sometimes the idea of the teacher as an inferior professional incapable of conducting research is just that—an idea in the minds of teachers (Avery, 1990). Participation in research can dispel this common misconception.

Contributions to Education Reform

Needed Support

Effective schools have principals who are effective instructional leaders (Beck, 1990); yet teachers do not perceive their principals as instructional leaders (Hall, 1986).

Recent education reform practices are holding schools (teachers and administrators, and in some states, parents) accountable for preparing students to apply learned knowledge. To assure that this goal is being reached, "performance evaluation" of student work has become common in states where education reform is extensive. Self-evaluation through portfolios has been introduced to help students learn how to record data and to measure progress. These practices reflect a broadening concept of evaluation. This change has been paralleled by a broadening concept of research strategies appropriate for education. Gitlin (1990) addressed this expansion by quoting Gage:

> Over the last two decades, dramatic shifts have occurred in the research methods that can be legitimately employed in the field of education.

Ethnography, once the primary method of anthropologists, for example, is now widely used and valued by the educational research community. And, more recently, it has been noted that "nothing about objective quantitative research preclude(s) the description and analysis of classroom practices with interpretive-qualitative methods." (p. 443)

As the century and millennium approach their ends, Americans are excited about their schools on a new level. The current wave of school reform was simmering at the turn of the 1980s when the National Commission on Excellence in Education's report, *A Nation At Risk* (1983), shifted the reform activities from low to high gear.

An analysis of school events since the 1960s shows that curricula have been implemented that give teachers a secondary role (Darling-Hammond, 1993). This trend was made obvious at the beginning of the 1960s when local curricula were being replaced by preconstructed curricula that put the student in the center of instruction, excluding the teacher. Programs developed at research and development centers, such as programmed instruction, were being sent to the schools along with paraphernalia to be used by students to solve problems. These programs were designed to be teacher-proof. Yet, teaching is a highly complex, demanding, and difficult activity (Cornett, 1990; Samuels & Jones, 1990), and major school reform success relies on teachers (Consortium on Chicago School Research, 1993; Cuban, 1993).

One way to promote reform is by involving teachers in research (Allan & Miller, 1990; Casanova 1989; Hovda & Kyle, 1984; McCutcheon, 1987; Sardo-Brown, 1992; Shalaway, 1990). By conducting research, teachers increase their self-efficacy regarding their ability to make a difference (Cardelle-Elawar, 1993; Sardo-Brown, 1992). This increased self-confidence is not empty emotions but results from increased ability to make important differences in the levels of learning occurring in their classrooms and in the school at large. Teachers who are involved with research become more reflective, critical, and analytical of their own teaching (Cardelle-Elawar, 1993; Carr & Kemmis, 1986). The process teachers use to develop theories from their classroom experiences and then to modify those theories through further experiences is called praxis. As Houser (1990) expressed, "If the ultimate goal of research and curriculum development is improved learning, then praxis, in the form of teacher-research, makes perfect sense" (p. 58).

This view of the praxis process is oversimplified. Although learning from research may occur in a simple, linear process, it is more likely to occur following questioning, pondering, and discussing the results (Kearney & Tashlik, 1985). This view of teacher research reflects Bertrand Russell's (1958) conception of "scientific temper" versus "scientific technique." Scientific temper recognizes that the investigator's work is never complete and the conclusions are never absolutely certain. Whereas some may question the application of this incomplete and uncertain investigative process to explore teaching, in fact, these apparent weaknesses of the scientific method are just the opposite, they are important strengths. Garrison (1988) explained,

> Of all the instruments of inquiry thus far fashioned there can be no doubt that the scientific method imparts the greatest power for solving our practical problems and achieving our daily purposes. The scientific method of inquiry is, in our time at least, the supreme knowledge gathering tool and the supreme form taken by knowledge. Let me hasten to add that for a philosophical pragmatist such as Dewey, science is supreme not because it yields necessarily "truth" but rather, as Russell indicates, it is systematically correctable and improvable. (p. 491)

Intensifying the need for teacher involvement in research, many of the reform reports either ignore or understate the importance of pedagogy, espousing the belief that teacher education programs should require fewer methods courses and more courses in the content areas. Cuban (1993) explained,

> Worse still, curriculum reformers ignore the power of pedagogy. They believe that content is more important than teaching. They are wrong. At the heart of schooling is the personal relationship between teacher and students that develops over matters of content. (p. 184)

Through conducting research, teachers develop a deeper and clearer understanding about their content areas and about how they are learned.

Restructuring

Throughout the 1980s and continuing into the 1990s, many education reform programs have stressed the need to restructure schools. Indeed, *restructuring* has been associated so loosely with *reform* that the two terms are often used interchangeably (Boe & Boruch, 1992). An integral part of the restructuring movement is accountability; schools (meaning administrators and teachers) and parents are being held accountable for student success (National Center for Education Statistics, 1993). Site-based decision-making councils have been the vehicle through which administrators, teachers, and parents are being held accountable.

Effective participation on site-based decision-making councils requires expertise of all members (Fullan & Stiegelbauer, 1990). Participation in research is a direct route to increased expertise (Atkin, 1989; Bennett, 1993; Kirk, 1988) and is a way for teachers to improve their self-confidence as professionals (Bennett, 1993; Neilsen, 1990; Sardo-Brown, 1992).

Constructivism

Increased student learning (the ultimate goal of education reform) depends on increased teacher expertise (Consortium on Chicago School Research, 1993). In fact, a purpose of all education is to enable people to think and to perform more effectively. Education is about learning how to deal with uncertainty and ambiguity (Eisner, 1992). "Its goal is for people to become more skilled, more dynamic, more vital" (Ayers, 1992, p. 260).

This skill enhancement requires developing new insights and learning new knowledge. The development of new insights and knowledge requires relating newly discovered knowledge to previous understandings. King and Rosenshine (1993) explained, "According to constructivist views, when presented with new information individuals use their existing knowledge and prior knowledge to help make sense of the new material" (p. 127). Constructivists describe learning in terms of building connections between prior knowledge and new ideas and claim that effective teaching helps students construct an organized set of concepts that relates old and new ideas (Markle, Johnston, Geer, & Meichtry, 1990).

Teachers who engage in research studies of their own instructional practices position themselves in permanent confrontation with new knowledge. Through praxis, teachers are provided with continuous opportunities to add clarity to their never complete or perfect understanding, thereby serving education reform by improving their own understanding of the education process.

Conclusion

The term *teacher as researcher* has many definitions and may vary as the teachers vary and as the context changes (McKernan, 1988). Many who have attempted to define it have agreed that it involves the teacher purposefully engaged in inquiry. *Action research* is a term used to refer to a teacher being engaged in inquiry for the purpose of understanding and improving his or her own practice (McCutcheon & Jung, 1990; Shalaway, 1990). The inquiry is into problems of immediate concern (McKernan, 1988).

As early as 1908, efforts have been made to involve teachers in research (Lowery, 1908). The types and level of teacher involvement with research have been limited (Peik, 1938). In essence, when teachers have been involved they have helped collect data, often without the benefit of even seeing the results of the study.

Teachers often perceive researchers' topics as too theoretical (Chattin-McNichols & Loeffler, 1989), saying that the results do not transfer well to the teaching context (Hastie, 1992), but today teachers are under fire for failure to use research (Hastie, 1992). Staying alert to and using research are necessary for teachers to stay current and to develop the important concepts in their fields (Doyle, 1990).

When teachers do become involved with research, several benefits accrue—they remain better informed in their fields (Bennett, 1993) and they gain a better understanding of why they behave as they do (Oberg, 1990), which prepares them to make better choices of behavior (Oberg, 1990). Furthermore, involvement with research revitalizes teachers (Reading/Learning in Secondary Schools Subcommittee of the IRA, 1989) and promotes continuous learning (Boyer, 1990, Shalaway, 1990) and self-confidence (Neilsen, 1990), leaving them feeling more positive toward themselves and toward research (Bennett, 1993).

Many of these benefits are contingent on a high level of involvement with research, a level where teachers either conduct the research independently or where teachers are equal partners in collaborative studies.

Teacher research responds positively to the current reform pleas for teachers to expand their professional roles beyond their immediate classroom walls. Involvement with research increases teachers' self-efficacy (Cardelle-Elawar, 1993; Sardo-Brown, 1992) and causes teachers to become more reflective, analytical, and critical of their own teaching (Cardelle-Elawar, 1993; Carr & Kemmis, 1986). Involvement with research sharpens teachers' problem-solving skills.

Educational reform efforts are expanding teachers' roles. For example, site-based decision-making committees place teachers in problem-solving roles. New assessment practices demand high levels of self-confidence from teachers. Many school districts are now requiring teachers to choose and use those practices that are research proven. Teachers must be able to use the current knowledge base to justify the methods or strategies they use in the classroom.

Future teachers will be expected to be problem solvers and more; they must be proactive problem solvers. They must use their problem-solving skills to predict and to plan to avoid future problems. Direct involvement in research is excellent preparation for becoming a proactive problem solver.

References

Allan, K. K., & Miller, M. S. (1990). Teacher-researcher collaborative: Cooperative professional development. *Theory into Practice, 29*(3), 196–202.

Allen, J., Combs, J., Hendricks, M., Nash, P., & Wilson, S. (1988). Studying change: Teachers who become researchers. *Language Arts, 65*(4), 379–387.

Applebee, A. M. C. (1987). Musings . . . teachers and the process of research. *Language Arts* 64(7), 714–716.

Arndt, R. (1984). Adjusting to contrasting tempos. *IRT Communication Quarterly, 7*(1), 2.

Atkin, J. M. (1989). Can educational research keep pace with education reform? *Phi Delta Kappan, 71*(3), 200–205.

Avery, C. S. (1990). Learning to research: Researching to learn. In M. W. Olson (Ed.), *Opening the door to educational research* (pp. 32–44). Newark, DE: International Reading Association.

Ayers, W. A. (1992). The shifting ground of curriculum thought and everyday practice. *Theory into Practice, 31*(3), 259–263.

Bagley, W. C., Bell, J. C., Seashore, C. E., & Whipple, G. M. (1910). Editorial. *Journal of Psychology, 1*(1), 1–3.

Bain, H. P., & Gooseclose, J. R. (1979). The dissemination dilemma and a plan for uniting disseminators and practitioners. *Phi Delta Kappan, 61*(2), 101–103.

Beck, J. J. (1990). Preparing principals for an educational research agenda in the schools. In M. W. Olson (Ed.), *Opening the door to classroom research* (pp. 97–111). Newark, DE: International Reading Association.

Bellon, J. J., Bellon, E. C., & Blank, M. A. (1992). *Teaching from a research knowledge base.* New York: Merrill.

Bennett, C. K. (1993). Teacher-researchers: All dressed up and no place to go. *Educational Leadership, 51*(2), 69–70.

Bissex, G. L., &: Bullock, R. H. (Eds.). (1987). *Seeing for ourselves: Case study research by teachers of writing.* Portsmouth, NH: Heinemann.

Boe, E. E., & Boruch, R. F. (1992, December). *Unpacking the concept of educational restructuring with a focus on the entrepreneurial approach.* Research report No. 1992-ERI, Center of Research and Evaluation in Social Policy.

Boyer, E. (1990). *Scholarship reconsidered: Priorities of the professoriate.* Princeton, NJ: Carnegie Foundation for the Advancement of Teaching.

Bracey, G. W. (1991). Teachers as researchers. *Phi Delta Kappan, 72*(5), 404–405

Brown, D. S. (1990). Middle level teachers' perceptions of action research. *Middle School Journal, 22*(1), 30–32.

Brownlie, F. (1990). The door is open. Won't you come in? In M. W. Olson (Ed.), *Opening the door to educational research* (pp. 21–31). Newark, DE: International Reading Association.

Buckingham, B. R. (1926). *Research for teachers.* New York: Silver, Burdett.

Busching, B., & Rowls, M. (1987). Teachers: Professional partners in school reform. *Action in Teacher Education, 9*(3), 13–23

Campbell, J. K. (1967). *Colonel Francis W. Parker: The children's crusader.* New York: Teachers College Press.

Cardelle-Elawar, M. (1993). The teacher as researcher in the classroom. *Action in Teacher Education, 15*(1), 49–57.

Carr, W., & Kemmis, S. (1986). *Becoming critical: Education, knowledge, and action research.* London: Falmer.

Carson, T. (1990). What kind of knowing is critical to action research? *Theory into Practice, 29*(3), 167–173.

Casanova, V. (1989). Research and practice: We can integrate them. *NEA Today, 7*(6), 44–49.

Chall, J. S. (1986). The teacher as scholar. *Reading Teacher, 39*(8), 792–797.

Chattin-McNichols, J., & Loeffler, M. H. (1989). Teachers as researchers: The first cycle of the teachers' research network. *Young Children, 44*(5), 20–27.

Chimes, M., & Schmidt, P. (1990). What I read over my summer vacation: Readings on cultural diversity. *The Clearing House, 64*(1), 44–46.

Clandinin, D. J. (1992). Creating spaces for teachers' voices. *Journal of Educational Thought, 26*(6), 59–71.

Consortium on Chicago School Research. (1993). Chicago elementary school reform: A midterm exam. *The Education Digest, 59*(3), 4–8.

Copenhaver, R. W., Byrd, D. M., McIntyre, D. J., & Norris, W. R. (1982). Synergistic public school and university research. *Action in Teacher Education, 4*(1), 41–44.

Corey, S. M. (1953). *Action research to improve school practices.* New York: Teachers College Bureau of Publications, Columbia University.

Cornett, J. W. (1990). Utilizing action research in graduate curriculum courses. *Theory into Practice, 29*(3), 185–195.

Cross, P. (1990). Making teaching more effective. *Journal of Freshman Year Experience, 2*(2), 59–74.

Cuban, L. (1992). Managing dilemmas while building professional communities. *Educational Researcher, 21*(1), 4–11.

Cuban, L. (1993). The lure of curricular reform and its pitiful history. *Phi Delta Kappan, 75*(2), 182–185.

Cunningham, R. C., & Shillington, N. M. (1990). Mentoring preservice teachers through interdisciplinary teams: A school-university partnership. *Action in Teacher Education, 11*(4), 6–12.

Curtis, F. D. (1932). Some contributions of educational research to the solution of teaching science. In *Thirty-first yearbook of the National Society for the Study of Education, Part 1* (pp. 77–90). Bloomington, IL: Public School Publishing.

Cushman, C. L., & Fox, G. (1938). Research and the public school curriculum. In G. M. Whipple (Ed.), *The scientific movement in education. Thirty-seventh yearbook of the National Society for the Study Education, Part 2* (pp. 67–68). Bloomington, IL: Public School Publishing.

Darling-Hammond, L. (1993). Reframing the school reform agenda: Developing capacity for school transformation. *Phi Delta Kappan, 74*(10), 752–761.

Dewey, J. (1929). *The sources of a science of education.* New York: Liverright.

Dicker, Mary (1990). Using action research to navigate an unfamiliar teaching assignment. *Theory into Practice, 29*(3), 203–208.

Doyle, W. (1990). Themes in teacher education research. In W. R. Houston (Ed.), *Handbook of research on teacher education* (pp. 3–24). New York: Macmillan.

Egbert, R. L. (1984). The role of research in teacher education. In R. L. Egbert & M. M. Kluender (Eds.), *Using research to improve teacher education: The Nebraska consortium* (pp. 9–21). Lincoln, NE: American Association of Colleges for Teacher Education.

Eisner, E. (1992). *The educational imagination: On the design and evaluation of school programs* (2nd ed.). New York: Macmillan.

Elliott, J. (1980). Implications of classroom research for professional development. In E. Hoyle & J. Megarry (Eds.), *World yearbook education: 1980. Professional development of teachers* (pp. 308–324). London: Nichols.

Fenstermacher, G. D. (1987). On understanding the connections between classroom research and teacher change. *Theory into Practice, 26*(1), 3–7.

Fischer, R. L. (1988–1989). When schools and colleges work together. *Action in Teacher Education, 10*(4), 63–66.

Floden, R. E., & Klinzing, H. G. (1990). What can research on teacher thinking contribute to teacher preparation? A second opinion. *Educational Researcher, 19*(5), 15–20.

Fox, M. F., & Faver, C. A. (1984). Independence and cooperation in research: The motivations and costs of collaboration. *Journal of Higher Education, 55*(3), 347–359.

Fullan, M. G. (1982). *The meaning of educational change.* New York: Teachers College.

Fullan, M. G., & Stiegelbauer, S. (1990). *The new meaning of educational change* (2nd ed.). Toronto: Ontario Institute for Studies in Education.

Gajewski, J. (1986). Teachers as full partners in research. *IRT Communication Quarterly, 1*(4), 2.

Garrison, J. W. (1988). Democracy, scientific knowledge, and teacher empowerment. *Teachers College Record, 89*(4), 487–504.

Gay, P. (Ed.). (1964). *John Locke on education.* New York: Teachers College Bureau of Publications.

Gies, F. (1984). The efficacy of educational research. *American Education 20*(6), 15–16.

Gill, A. J. (1993). Thinking mathematics. *Educational Leadership, 50*(6), 40–41.

Gitlin, A. D. (1990). Educative research, voice, and school change. *Harvard Educational Review, 60*(4), 443–466.

Glatthorn, A. A. (1993). *Learning twice: An introduction to the methods of teaching.* New York: HarperCollins.

Good, C. V., Barr, A. S., & Scates, D. E. (1936). *The methodology of educational research*. New York: Appleton-Century.

Good, T. L., & Brophy, J. E. (1987). *Looking in classrooms* (4th ed.). New York: Harper & Row.

Goswami, D., & Stillman, P. (1987). *Reclaiming the classroom: Teacher research as an agency for change*. Portsmouth, NH: Boynton Cook.

Haberman, M. (1992). The role of the classroom teacher as a curriculum leader. *NASSP Bulletin, 76*(547), 11–19.

Hall, G. (Ed.). (1986). *Beyond the looking glass: Recommendations and critical warnings for teacher education practitioners, policy makers, and research*. Austin: Research and Development Center for Teacher Education, University of Texas.

Hanna, B. (1986). Improving student-teaching effectiveness through action research projects. *Action in Teacher Education, 8*(3), 51–56.

Hastie, P. A. (1992). Prospects for collaboration between teachers and researchers. *Clearing House, 65*(6), 371–372.

Hattrup, U., & Bickel, W. E. (1993). Teacher-researcher collaborations: Resolving the tensions. *Educational Leadership, 50*(6), 38–40.

Henson, K. T. (1994). *Curriculum development for education reform*. New York: Harper-Collins.

Herzberg, F., Mausner, B., & Snyderman, B. (1959). *The motivation to work*. New York: Wiley.

Hord, S. M. (1986). A synthesis of research on organizational collaboration. *Educational Leadership, 43*(5), 22–26.

Houser, N. O. (1990). Teacher-researcher: The synthesis of roles for teacher empowerment. *Action in Teacher Education, 12*(2), 55–60.

Houston, W. R. (1979). Collaboration—See "treason." In G. E. Hall, S. M. Hord, & E. Brown (Eds.), *Exploring issues in teacher education: Questions for future research* (pp. 331–348). Austin: University of Texas, Research and Development Center for Teacher Education.

Hovda, R. A., & Kyle, D. W. (1984). Action research: A professional development responsibility. *Middle School Journal, 15*(3), 21–23.

Huling, L. L., & Griffin, G. A. (1983). Educators work together with interactive research and development (collaboration is not a four-letter word). *Research and Development Center for Teacher Education Review, 1*(3), 1–2.

Ikenberry O. S. (1974). *American educational foundations: An introduction*. Columbus, OH: Charles E. Merrill.

Kearney, L., & Tashlik, P. (1985). Collaboration and conflict: Teachers and researchers learning. *Language Arts, 62*(7), 765–769.

King, A., & Rosenshine, B. (1993). Effects of guided cooperative questioning on children's knowledge construction. *The Journal of Experimental Education, 61*(2), 127–148.

Kirk, D. (1988). Ideology and school-centered innovation: A case study and a critique. *Journal of Curriculum Studies, 20*(5), 449–464.

Kowalski, T. J., Henson, K. T., & Weaver, R. A. (1994). *Case studies on beginning teachers*. New York: Longman.

Kowalski, T. J., & Reitzug, V. C. (1993). *Contemporary school administration*. New York: Longman.

Learning from children: Teachers do research (1988). *The Harvard Education Letter, 4*(4), 1–5.

Lieberman, A. (1986a). Collaborative research: Working with, not working on . . . *Educational Leadership, 43*(5), 28–32.

Lieberman, A. (1986b). Collaborative work. *Educational Leadership, 43*(5), 4–8.

Lowery, C. D. (1908). The relation of superintendents and principals to the training and professional improvement of their teachers. *Seventh yearbook of the National Society for the Study of Education, Part 1*. Chicago: The University of Chicago Press.

Lytle, S. L., & Cochran-Smith, M. (1990). Learning from teacher research: A working typology. *Teachers College Record, 92*(1), 83–103.

Markle, G., Johnston, J. H., Geer, C., & Meichtry, Y. (1990). Teaching for understanding. *Middle School Journal, 22*(2), 53–57.

Marks, M. B. (1989). Practice into theory: The teacher authenticates research findings. *Educational Research Quarterly, 13*(3), 17–25.

Marriott, V. (1990). *Transition*. Unpublished paper, Mount Saint Vincent University, Nova Scotia, Canada.

Marshall, C. (1991). Teachers' learning styles: How they affect student learning. *The Clearing House, 64*(4), 27–36.

McConaghy, T. (1987). Teachers as researchers: Learning through teaching. *Phi Delta Kappan, 68*(8), 630–631.

McCutcheon, G. (1987). Teachers' experience doing action research. *Peabody Journal of Education, 64*(2), 116–127.

McCutcheon, G., & Jung, B. (1990). Alternative perspectives on action research. *Theory into Practice, 29*(3), 144–151.

McDaniel, E. (1988–1989). Collaboration for what? Sharpening the focus. *Action in Teacher Education, 10*(4), 1–8.

McElroy, L. (1990). Becoming real: An ethic at the heart of action research. *Theory into Practice, 29*(3), 209–218.

McKernan, J. (1988). Teacher as researcher: Paradigm and praxis. *Contemporary Education, 59*(3), 154–158.

Monroe, W. W. (1938). General methods: Classroom experimentation. In G. M. Whipple (Ed.), *The scientific movement in education. Thirty-seventh yearbook of the National Society for the Study of Education, Part 2* (pp. 319–328). Bloomington, IL: Public School Publishing.

Myers, M. (1985). *The teacher-researcher: How to study writing in the classroom*. Urbana, IL: ERIC Clearinghouse on Reading and Communications Skills and the National Council of Teachers of English.

National Center for Education Statistics. (1993). *America's teachers: Profile of a profession*. Washington, DC: U.S. Department of Education, Office of Educational Research and Improvement.

National Commission on Excellence in Education. (1983). A nation at risk: The imperatives for educational reform. Washington, DC: U.S. Government Printing Office.

Neilsen, L. (1990). Research comes home. *The Reading Teacher, 44*(3), 248–250.

Neufeld, K. (1990). Preparing future teachers as researchers. *Education, 110*(3), 345–351.

Nixon, J. (1981). *A teacher's guide to action research*. London: Grant McIntyre.

Oberg, A. (1990). Methods and meanings in action research: The action research journal. *Theory into Practice, 29*(3), 214–221.

Oberg, A., & McCutcheon, G. (1987). Teachers' experience doing action research. *Peabody Journal of Education, 64*(2), 116–127.

Odell, L. (1976). The classroom teacher as researcher. *English Journal, 65*(1), 106–111.

Oja, S. N., & Pine, G. (1983). *A two-year study of teacher stage of development in relation to collaborative action research in schools*. Durham: University of New Hampshire Collaborative Action Research Project Office.

Olson, M. W. (1990). The teacher as researcher: A historical perspective. In M. W. Olson (Ed.), *Opening the door to classroom research*. Newark, DE: International Reading Association.

Peik, W. E. (1938). A generation of research on the curriculum. In G. M. Whipple (Ed.), *The scientific movement in education. Thirty-seventh yearbook of the National Society for the Study of Education, Part 2* (pp. 53–66). Bloomington, IL: Public School Publishing.

Porter, A. C. (1990). Collaborating with teachers on research. In M. W. Olson (Ed.), *Opening the door to classroom research* (pp. 77–96). Newark, DE: International Reading Association.

Rainey, B. G. (1972). Whatever happened to action research? *The Balance Sheet, 53*(7), 292–295.

Ravitch, D. (1992). National standards and curriculum reform: A view from the Department of Education. *NASSP Bulletin, 76*(548), 24–29.

Reading/Language in Secondary Schools Subcommittee of the International Reading Association (IRA). (1989). Classroom action research: The teacher as researcher. *Journal of Reading, 33*(3), 216–218.

Reed, C., Mergendoller, J., & Horan, C. (1992). Collaborative research: A strategy for school improvement. *Crossroads: The California Journal of Middle Grades Research, 2*(1), 5–12.

Rogers, D. L., Noblit, G. W., & Ferrell, P. (1990). Action research as an agent for developing teachers' communicative competence. *Theory into Practice, 29*(3), 179–184.

Russell, B. (1958). *Religion and science.* Oxford: Oxford University Press.

Sagor, R. (1991). What Project LEARN reveals about collaborative action research. *Educational Leadership, 48*(6), 6–7, 9–10.

Samuels, S. J., & Jones, H. L. (1990). A model of teaching and instructional improvement. In M. W. Olson (Ed.), *Opening the door to classroom research* (pp. 126–140). Newark, DE: International Reading Association.

Sanger, J. (1990). Awakening a scream of consciousness: The critical group in action research. *Theory into Practice, 29*(3), 174–178.

Santa, C. M. (1990). Teaching as research. In M. W. Olson (Ed.), *Opening the door to classroom research* (pp. 64–76). Newark, DE: International Reading Association.

Santa, C. M., Isaacson, L., & Manning, G. (1987). Changing content instruction through action research. *The Reading Teacher, 40*(4), 434–438.

Sardo-Brown, D. (1992). Elementary teachers' perceptions of action research. *Action in Teacher Education, 14*(2), 55–59.

Schon, D. (1987). *Educating the reflective practitioner: Toward a new design for teaching and learning in the professions.* San Francisco, CA: Jossey-Bass.

Schumm, J. S. (1993). Action research: What do secondary teachers think? (Summary of research by D. S. Brown). *Journal of Reading, 36*(6), 449.

Shalaway, L. (1990). Tap into teacher research. *Instructor, 100*(1), 34–38.

Shannon, P. (1990). Commentary: Teachers as researchers. In M. W. Olson (Ed.), *Opening the door to classroom research* (pp. 141–154). Newark, DE: International Reading Association.

Shulman, J. H. (1990). Now you see them, now you don't: Anonymity versus visibility in case studies of teachers. *Educational Researcher, 19*(6), 11–15.

Shumsky, A. (1958). *The action research way of learning.* New York: Teachers College Press.

SooHoo, S. (1993). Students as partners in research and restructuring schools. *The Educational Forum, 57*(3), 386–393.

Stansell, J., & Patterson, L. (1988). Teacher researchers find the answers in their classrooms. *Texas Reading Report, 10*(6), 2–4.

Stevens, K. B., Slanton, D. B., & Bunny, S. (1992). A collaborative research effort between public school and university faculty members. *Teacher Education and Special Education, 15*(1), 1–8.

Sucher, F. (1990). Involving school administrators in classroom research. In M. W. Olson (Ed.), *Opening the door to classroom research* (pp. 112–125). Newark, DE: International Reading Association.

Tikunoff, W., Ward, B., & Griffin, G. (1979). *Interactive research and development on teaching: Final report.* San Francisco, CA: Far West Laboratory for Educational Research and Development.

Travers, R. M. W. (1976). Impact of research on teaching. *Education Digest, 42*(4), 6–8.

Tripp, D. H. (1990). Socially critical action research. *Theory into Practice, 29*(3), 158–166.

Tyack, D. (1990). Restructuring in historical perspective: Tinkerking toward utopia. *Teachers College Record, 92*(2), 170–191.

U.S. Department of Education. (1987). *Teachers as researchers program.* Washington, DC: U.S. Department of Education, Office of Educational Research and Improvement.

Van Manen, M. (1990). Beyond assumptions: Shifting the limits of action research. *Theory into Practice, 29*(3), 152–157.

Vockell, E. (1983). *Educational research.* New York: Macmillan.

Waples, D., & Tyler, R. W. (1930). *Research methods and teachers' problems.* New York: Macmillan.

Winter, R. (1982). Dilemma analysis: A contribution to methodology for action research. *Cambridge Journal of Education, 12*(6), 161–174.

Woods, P. (1986). *Inside schools: Ethnography in educational research.* London: Routledge and Kegan Paul.

Wright, R. (1985). Motivating teacher involvement in professional growth activities. *The Canadian Administrator, 24*(5), 1–6.

Young, J. H. (1985). Participation in curriculum development: An inquiry into the responses of teachers. *Curriculum Inquiry, 15*(4), 387–414.

Appendix E

Sample Proposal for Funding

Proposal to the State Department of Education
ECIA, Chapter 2

Mathematics and Science Improvement Program
Closing Date: **February 15**

NAME OF APPLICANT INSTITUTION The University of		
NAME AND ADDRESS OF OPERATING UNIT		
TITLE OF PROPOSED PROJECT Summer Institute for Precollege Teachers of Physics	SUBJECT AREA Physics	
BUDGET TOTAL $30,245.00	DESIRED STARTING DATE June 10	DURATION 10 weeks

Certification and assurances:

The applicant institution has a State-approved teacher education program in the subject area of the proposed project. The person whose signature appears as project director is authorized by the applicant institution to make this proposal. If funded, the institute will be implemented as approved. The applicant institution will accept responsibility for complying with all applicable State and federal requirements including the resolution of any audit exceptions.

Endorsements for the applicant institution:

Signature _____

Name and Title _____

SECOND SIGNATURE, IF APPLICABLE:

Signature _____

Name and Title _____

Physics Teachers Summer Institute Proposal
Table of Contents

Proposal for Summer Institute
for Precollege Teachers of Physics

II. PROJECT DESCRIPTION

A. Objectives

Physics is the study of the laws of nature at the most fundamental level. As a result, all of modern science and technology derives much of its success from physics. It is because of scientific discoveries and applications that we live in such a technologically advanced world. For decades the United States has been the world leader in science and technology, and as a result, it is the most economically and militarily powerful nation on earth. These past developments are strongly tied to the successful education of our citizenry, and education will continue to be the key in the development of our nation.

Education in the sciences and mathematics is not only important in terms of training future scientists, engineers, and technicians, it is equally important for those who opt for other careers. We live in a highly complex country in which the results of science and technology affect us on a daily basis. We benefit from advances in communications, entertainment, and medicine, and at the same time, we must content with unwanted results such as pollution and the danger of nuclear annihilation. As consumers and as voting citizens, both scientists and nonscientists must be prepared to make intelligent decisions regarding science and technology.

Recent studies, such as *A Nation at Risk* by the National Commission on Excellence in Education, have shown that the United States has fallen behind many other industrialized countries in educating its citizens. In addressing the reasons for this decline, the Commission has pointed out a severe shortage of qualified science and mathematics teachers almost everywhere in the country. A recent survey of all the school superintendents in this state has documented the shortage of qualified physics teachers. While his study clearly identified secondary schools where inadequately prepared teachers are teaching physics, it did not include the many small, rural secondary schools throughout the state that do not offer physics at all because of the lack of a properly trained teacher. Both of these situations are of major concern.

Of the many alternatives that could prove to be effective solutions to this dilemma, the most immediate would seem to be to retrain secondary teachers who are already certified in other fields. It is for this reason that the university enthusiastically accepts the state department of education's call for proposals for summer physics institutes. The university proposes an institute that is planned to meet the following objectives. The program will provide 15 teachers from throughout the state opportunities to do the following:

1. Develop the knowledge and understanding that is expected in basic university physics courses.
2. Develop the understandings and skills needed to effectively teach the most commonly used physics textbook in this state's schools at this time. An experienced secondary school physics teacher will provide specific training to help participants use this text in the classroom and in the laboratory.
3. Develop laboratory skills associated with basic physics courses, including the use of computers in the laboratory. Emphasis will be placed on designing low-cost experiments that can be used in all secondary schools, including those with the least facilities, equipment, and supplies.

4. Enable each participant to earn 12 semester hours of credit toward Class B certification in physics. It will be communicated, however, in the announcement of this program, that this benefit to the participants is secondary in significance, that the actual number of hours it will reduce certification attainment will vary among the participants, and that neither the university nor the state department of education will be obligated to provide further grants to those students to help them complete their certification requirements. Indeed, the participants, themselves, will be encouraged to assume this responsibility.

The program will provide for follow-up reinforcement and evaluation during the coming school year.

B. Participant Selection

1. Number of participants

Fifteen participants will be provided total support. Up to three additional certified secondary teachers who wish to gain certification in the area of physics will be allowed to participate in the program without support. The university will provide tuition grants for these teachers.

2. Policy for admission

Of particular concern is that some teachers are now teaching physics in the state's secondary schools without having been certified. Hence, the selection of participants for this institute will give first priority to noncertified teachers who are already teaching physics in our secondary schools.

Other secondary teachers who teach courses in other fields have been offered opportunities to teach physics as replacements for retiring teachers and noncertified teachers. These teachers who also have positions awaiting them next fall will receive secondary priority in the screening of applicants for this institute.

If there are other teachers who hold secondary teaching certificates who wish to achieve certification in the area of physics, they will receive the next priority in the selection process.

Candidates within each of these groups will be rated on the basis of letters from their employers, previous scholarships as evidenced by their academic records, and their personal commitment to teaching physics as expressed in a letter which they will be required to write. An attempt will be made to select applicants from small rural high schools over a broad geographic area.

3. Selection procedure

a. All teachers holding temporary certification in physics will be identified through state department of education records. Each will receive a notice of this institute. All superintendents and curriculum supervisors will also receive a copy of the announcement. An announcement will also be sent to the state department of education with a request for inclusion in the state newsletter.

b. To be considered for this institute, applications must include a participant information form, a letter(s) of testimony from an appropriate school administrator(s) which specifies the candidate's expected teaching assignment, an academic transcript, and, when available, test scores. Applications must be received by April 30, 1985.

c. The selection will be completed and notification will be sent by May 10. Participants will be asked to respond by May 22.

C. Program Content

The institute will begin on June 10, and run continuously until August 17. The three courses, tutorials, and seminars will require a total of 266 contact hours. The courses involved are as follows:

Course	Title	Credit (semester hours)	Contact Hours
PHYSICS 110	Secondary Physics for Teachers[b]	4	60
PHYSICS[b]	Physics Electives[b]	8	88
PHYSICS[a]	Integrated Physics Lab[a]	0	78
PHYSICS[a]	Seminar for Teachers[a]	0	10
PHYSICS	Tutorial[a]	0	30

[a]New courses may be added specifically for summer institute.
[b]Participants may elect from the following:

PH 101–102 General Physics	4 semester hours
PH 105–106 General Physics with Calculus	4 semester hours
PH 253 Modern Physics	3 semester hours

The major components of this program are as follows:

1. Physics 110—Secondary School Physics for Teachers

The most immediate impact the proposed program can have on the teaching of high school physics is to improve the effectiveness and confidence of the participating teachers in the use of a text and related materials in their classrooms in the coming year. The most widely used of the state approved textbooks is *Modern Physics* (Holt, Rinehart and Winston, 1976). This text will be the focus of a four-credit-hour course meeting throughout the ten weeks of the institute (60 total contact hours). This course will concentrate mostly on the content of the text; laboratory work will be covered in a separate phase of the institute. Although all the institute staff will participate in this course in appropriate ways, the lead instructor will be an experienced high school teacher. The survey of the text will be intensive and detailed. The rationale for the course is that the most important prerequisite for effective use of the text is a teacher has a thorough competence in all the subject matter of the text and confidence in his/her ability to explain that subject material to students. Each concept in the text will be examined and developed to whatever depth is necessary in order to achieve that competence on the part of all participants.

This course will also cover methods for supplementing the high school physics text. Demonstrations will be used as an aid in teaching the textbook material, with an emphasis on the use of low-cost demonstrations for high school courses. Computer-aided instruction will also be covered. Many high schools are acquiring microcomputers which can be used as a tool to help teach physics, if adequate software is available. A part of the course will emphasize selecting and using software for computer-aided physics instruction.

2. Physics Electives

Each participant will select on appropriate undergraduate physics course during each session of the summer term. The courses that will be available are PH 101–102, General Physics; PH 105–106, General Physics with Calculus; and PH 253, Modern Physics. The course selected by the participant will depend upon his/her prior experience. Participants who have not taken a physics course in recent years will be open only to the institute participants. Participants with a sufficiently strong background may choose instead to take PH 105 or PH 253, which are offered as regular classes during the summer session at the university. In addition to regular classes attendance (44 contact hours), each participant will be scheduled for three hours per week (30 total hours) of tutorial meetings with the class instructor. The purpose of the tutorial meetings is to provide the extra in-depth explanations of course material that may be useful to participants who have been away from undergraduate study in the sciences for an extended period. Participants will be evaluated on their work in regular classroom activities as well as tutorial sessions.

3. Integrated Laboratory for Physics Elective and for Physics 110

Laboratory experiences are important both for the physics elective and the survey of a secondary school physics text. In the proposed program, these laboratory experiences will be integrated into a single laboratory organized for the institute participants. The laboratory will meet for thirteen three-hour sessions each term (78 total contact hours). Experiments will be selected from the regular lab of the physics elective and, wherever possible, will be conducted in parallel with similar experiments scaled for use in a high school laboratory. The purpose of this approach is to give participants two types of experiences. First, they need knowledge of the type of experiments currently conducted in undergraduate college level courses. More importantly, however, they need practical experience in setting up laboratory experiments appropriate for the high school physics laboratory (high school laboratories are more limited in time schedule and frequently in available equipment than college laboratories). The content of the integrated lab will be planned on an individual basis by the instructor of the physics elective and the consulting high school teacher. A graduate student will assist in the laboratory.

Some of the laboratory meetings will also be devoted to using microcomputers in the physics laboratory. Some experiments will be performed in which the computer is used to assist with taking and analyzing data.

4. Seminar for Teachers

In order that the separate components of the program may be brought together to form a more unified experience, a weekly seminar for participants in the institute will be held. The content of the seminar will, in part, be developed based on the perceived needs of participants. In part, however, the seminar will be directed toward supplemental material, such as articles from *Physics Today, Scientific American, Science Education, The Physics Teacher,* and other sources of information on topics of current interest, puzzles, and games that stimulate interest in physics.

D. Additional Components

1. Follow-up Activities

During the second half of the fall semester the co-directors will make an on-site visit to each participant's school. This follow-up visit will serve two purposes: (1) it will provide an opportunity to assess the value of the institute and (2) it will provide each participant opportunities to clarify any misunderstandings and to fill in any knowledge gaps about the content or skills set forth in the objectives of this institute.

2. Evaluation

The proposed program will be subjected to two types of evaluation.

(a) *Evaluation by participants.* Participants will be asked to evaluate the program at two stages. The initial evaluation will be made by a questionnaire administered near the end of the summer session. The effectiveness of each component of the institute will be evaluated. A second evaluation will be conducted near the end of the school year after participants have had classroom experience in using skills developed in the institute.

(b) *Evaluation by an outside observer.* At an appropriate point in the institute an evaluation will be sought from one or more outside observers. For this evaluation an effort will be made to obtain the services of an individual with supervisory experience and special knowledge in secondary level science education, in a state school system, the state department of education, and/or another institution of higher education in the state.

III. STAFF

Professional staff for the proposed institute will be composed of one coordinator, two assistant coordinators, a consulting high school teacher, the instructors of the physics electives, and the lab instructor. Résumés of principal participating staff are included as an appendix.

A. The coordinator of the program will be Kenneth Henson, Head, Area of Curriculum Instruction, College of Education. Phillip Coulter, Chairperson and Professor, Department of Physics and Astronomy, and J. W. Harrell, Associate Professor of Physics, will serve as assistant coordinators. Dr. Henson's responsibilities will include attaining publicity for the program, evaluation the program, and preparing an institute report. He will further provide assistance in announcing the program, selecting the participants, conducting the follow-up component, an participating in the weekly seminars. Dr. Harrell's responsibilities will include arranging the weekly seminars, correspondence related to selection and notification of participants, and paperwork associated with participant support. Dr. Coulter will coordinate the responsibilities of Physics faculty in the program, assist with the weekly seminars, and help with the paperwork associated with participant support.

B. Dr. Peggy Coulter, teacher of mathematics and physics at Central High School and Adjunct Associate Professor of Education, College of Education, is being asked to serve as lead instructor for PH 110 and as consultant for the integrated laboratory and the tutorial session for the physics electives. Dr. Harrell will assist in the instruction for PH 110 in the areas of computer-aided instruction and low-cost lecture demonstrations.

C. The instructors for the physics electives are as follows: PH 101—Professor J. W. Harrell; PH 105—Professor Chester Alexander; PH 102—Professor Richard Tipping; PH 253 and PH 106—Professor William Walker. These individuals will participate as tutorial leaders for participants who are enrolled in their classes. They will also serve as consultants for PH 110, the integrated laboratory, and the seminar for teachers.

D. A physics graduate student with experience in physics laboratories will supervise the integrated laboratory. The content of the laboratory will be a joint responsibility of the consulting high school physics teacher and the instructors for the physics electives.

IV. FACILITIES

A. Instructional Facilities

Participants in the program will make use of facilities of the Physics Building of the university for work associated with the physics elective course, PH 110, the integrated laboratory, and tutorials. The computer laboratory in the College of Education will be available for use by the participants at specified times. This computer lab serves as the statewide depository for hardware and software. Participants will have the opportunity to duplicate any of the available programs that are in the public domain. The Seminar for Teachers will be scheduled at a lunch period and will make use of a private dining area in the Continuing Education Center.

B. Housing Facilities

Residential participants will be house in _____
Hall, the Continuing Education Center of the university. Housing is available at the rate of $50 per week. Meal service is provided in the same building at the cost of $12.50 per day. Meal service is also available to commuting participants at the Continuing Education Center.

V. INSTITUTIONAL SUPPORT AND MANAGEMENT

The university is able to commit support to the proposed program in the following ways:

Released time for co-coordinators and secretarial staff (estimated in-kind contributions)

K. Henson	25% for 12 weeks	$2,861.54
P. Coulter	15% for 12 weeks	1,759.50
Secretary	10% for 14 weeks	276.00

Supplies for curriculum development projects,
correspondence, etc. (estimated cash contribution)   200.00
Travel for follow-up activities (estimated cash contribution)
Per-diem for six days @ $40/day   240.00
Tuition grants will be provided by the university
for up to three additional unsupported participants
3 participants @ $731.50   2,194.50
TOTAL IN-KIND CONTRIBUTION $7,531.54

VI. BUDGET

TUITION AND FEES:

Tuition	@	$552.00
University Fees	@	104.50
Lab Fees 3 @ 25.00		75.00
		731.50 × 15 = $10,972.50

FIRST-TIME APPLICANTS: 6 @   15.00   = $120.00

PARTICIPANT SUPPORT:

Commuters (4)

Mileage (3000 @ .22)	$660.00
Meals (50 @ $4.25)	212.50
Lab kits/materials	40.00
Textbooks	25.00
	937.50
	× 4 = $3,750.00

Residents (11)

Room (10 weeks @ $50)	$500.00
Mileage	60.00
Meals	577.50
Lab kids/materials	40.00
Textbooks	25.00
	1,202.50
	× 11 = $13,227.50

TOTAL PARTICIPANT SUPPORT	$16,977.50
TRAVEL FOR FOLLOW-UP ACTIVITIES	400.00
INDIRECT COST REIMBURSEMENT (16% of $11,072.50)	1,775.00
PROJECT BUDGET TOTAL for 15	$30,245.00

Appendix F

Student Satisfaction with Constructivism

Abstract

Education reform in the 1990s called for hands-on activities in elementary and secondary schools. The early 2000s saw education reform moving to higher education institutions, bringing the expectation of hands-on activities to college campuses. Although hands-on activities are welcomed by teachers and students, unless these activities are supported by a strong, theoretical, pedagogical framework, they will not bring forth sustained academic improvement. The constructivist methodology introduced over a half-century ago by Russian sociologist Lev Vygotsky and American psychologist John Dewey, and reinforced by today's teachers of the year were tested to see how well they are received today by prospective teachers. The conclusion was that constructivist strategies are a viable option to teachers who want to use proven learning methods to motivate and educate their students.

Attitudes of Teacher Education Students toward Selected Constructivist Practices

Throughout the 1990s education reform programs nationwide were calling for more *hands-on* learning in elementary and secondary schools. Since the beginning of the new millennium, these demands have reached higher education institutions, with the same expectations now being held of all university professors who teach future teachers. But, by themselves, hands-on activities are shallow and offer little promise for increased learning. Hope for continuous academic growth will require a clear grasp of a sound theoretical base to guide the application of hands-on activities.

Although a method that will succeed with all students under all conditions has yet to be discovered (Stedman, 2000), research on teaching effectiveness has shown that teachers whose students consistently reach high academic and social success levels tend to follow general patterns of instruction (Good & Brophy, 2000; Teddlie & Reynolds, 2000). An analysis of advice given to beginning teachers by fifteen teachers found recurring use of several constructive practices (Henson & Eller, 1999).

In the spring of 2000, an experiment was designed to measure the teacher education student satisfaction level toward several selected constructivist practices found in the advice given by teachers who received the Teacher of the Year award for their respective states. The subjects in this study were two sections of a junior-level human growth and learning courses: n=22 and n=24, respectively. Two instruments were used to collect data and measure student satisfaction levels: The IDEA student course evaluation form and a self-made student evaluation form. Following is a description of the approach used and the resulting evaluations.

Role of Experience in Learning

Constructivism has its early roots in the works of seventeenth-century English philosopher John Locke and his experimental theory, *tabula rasa*, the idea that at birth the minds of all individuals are like blank tablets, and the only way to fill them is through hands-on experience. Locke was not a teacher and, therefore, his ideas remained passive for the next hundred years until eighteenth-century Swiss/French philosopher Jean Jacques Rousseau put them into practice. Though also not a classroom teacher, Rousseau was tutor to two children who were brother and sister, Emile and Sophie. In this book *Emile*, he proposed a naturalistic, experience-based teaching method. Two and a half centuries later, the perceived importance of the role of experience in learning has not diminished, at least not as perceived by former Alabama teacher of the year Susan Lloyd (1999, p. 255) who advised future teachers to, "Go out there and experience life, have an adventure, and then translate that into your teaching." Experience tends to personalize information. Former Utah teacher of the year Marilyn Grondel (1999, p. 216), said, "To be meaningful, students need to see how the curriculum fits in with their everyday experiences and interests."

Story Telling and Confluency

Two sections of the course EPY 319: Human Development and Learning were used to test the effectiveness of selected constructivist practices when used to prepare teachers. Story telling was one of the more effective teaching methods used in these classes. Story telling, like writing, can help teachers organize their thinking about teaching. Jalongo and Isenberg (1995, p. xvii) said, "It is primarily through story, one student at a time, that teachers organize their thinking and tap into the collective, accumulated wisdom of their profession." Story telling also develops *confluency*, connecting the mind and the emotions. A major advantage of story telling is its ability to motivate students and open up a path for dialog.

Former Pennsylvania teacher of the year Howard Selekman (1999) uses journal writing with his students daily to enable them to make personal connections with their subjects. He said, "My best teaching occurs when students are writing daily and I am writing with them" (p. 59). Selekman encourages his students to write about topics that they know about and also about topics on which they know very little. The purpose is to achieve confluency; that is, to engage the students' minds and emotions. Abraham Maslow (1973, p. 159) gave a powerful testimony to confluent teaching when he said,

> As I go back in my own life, I find my greatest education experiences, the ones I value most in retrospect, were highly personal, highly subjective, very poignant combinations of the emotional and the cognitive. Some insight was accompanied by all sorts of autonomic nervous system fireworks that felt very good at the time and which left as a residue the insight that has remained with me forever.

Like most story tellers who have worked to improve their story telling, I find that the more stories I tell, the more students look forward to them, and I find myself getting just as caught up in my stories as my students do and laughing with my students about the stories and often about myself. Virginia teacher Mary Bicouvaris (1999, p. 124) testified to the appeal of story telling, saying, "The smartest students love story telling, the weakest students worship it."

Successful confluent teaching requires a particular attitude, one of enjoyment. Former Nevada teacher of the year John Snyder (1999, p. 476) said, "If you love what you are doing, the students can tell." The most common adjectives these teachers of the year used to describe their classes were *joy* and *fun*. My self-made course evaluation instrument included the statement, "The professor enjoys teaching." This item was rated "strong" by 100 percent of the respondents. Making stories fun requires the same joyous or fun-filled attitude. Former Utah teacher of the year Marilyn Grondel (1999, p. 316) referred to this attitude when she said, "I believe that wonder and joy are always in the attic of one's mind." I am being honest when I tell my students as I often do that even if I were independently wealthy, I would still want to teach; for doing what you enjoy doing most is truly being fortunate.

Concept Mapping and Connections

A review of the advice given by the fifteen teachers of the year analyzed in this study found that in addition to *joy* and *fun,* a word they repeatedly used to explain their success was *connections.* Former Pennsylvania teacher of the year Howard Selekman (1999, p. 59) said that his best teaching occurs when students are attempting to discover connections among the disciplines they are studying. John Dewey (1938) said that he believed that the failure to make connections with the world outside of school and with the students' lives might be the biggest failure of teachers: "Perhaps the greatest of all pedagogical fallacies is the notion that a person learns only the particular thing he is studying at the time" (p. 49). In the truest constuctivist vein, Dewey stressed the significant responsibilities of teachers to help all students connect material being studied to earlier experiences: "It is also essential that new objects and events be related intellectually to those of earlier experiences" (p. 90).

I use a type of concept mapping to help my students make connections among the concepts we are studying. For example, if they were asked to read this article, I might say, "At this point, we are going to stop and make some connections. If each of you will begin by writing the word *constructivism* in an oval ring drawn in the center of a blank sheet of paper, I will concurrently draw and write the same on the blackboard. Now, without your neighbors' help, during the next 5 minutes, recall any other ideas we have read and/or discussed so far that relate to constructivism." Timing them carefully, I then ask them to share their words with their group members. Then I ask them to compile all their individual drawings into one major group drawing and to draw lines to connect all the words, explaining the need for each line. In the constructivist spirit, I insist that every member must contribute something, if only a word or a connecting line, the member with the fewest entries on his or her paper going first.

Next, I ask for the student with the most complete map to draw that map on the board. The entire class assists by ensuring that all concepts and lines from each group are included. This gives students opportunities to rehearse the major concepts, and it lets everyone teach. My best teaching occurs when my students are teaching me. At this point in the lesson, the map would begin looking something like that shown by the continuous circles in Figure F.1. The dotted circles would be added later in the hour, after these topics had been introduced.

Negotiating Meaning

Next, using the map in Figure F.1 as a guide, I continue my story, introducing John Dewey and his well-known expression, "Learning by doing." I also introduce Lev Vygotsky and tell an interesting but sad story about his personal life

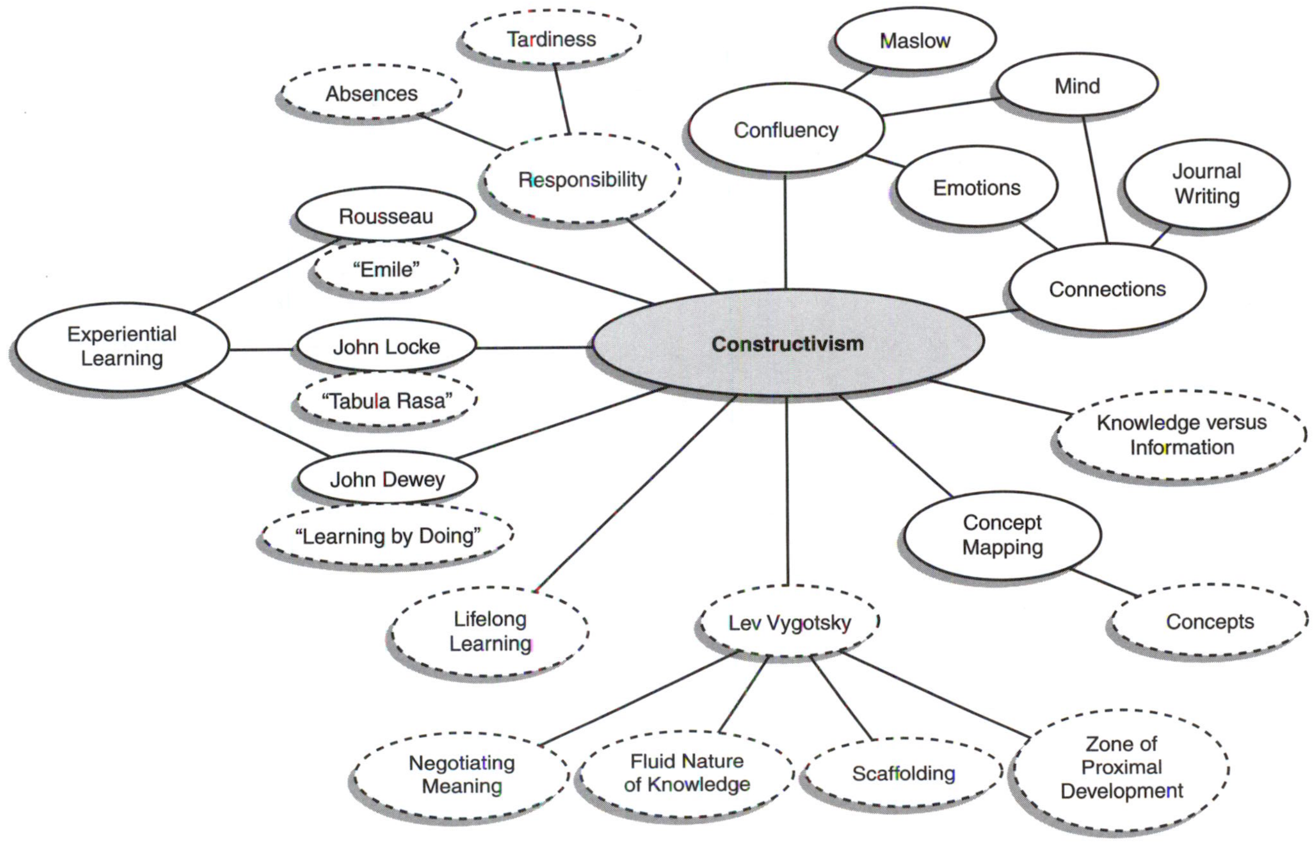

FIGURE F.1 Concept Map

and death. I tell about his noticing that as his students talked to each other, they led each other to understand the lesson, a process he labeled *negotiating meaning*. I point to literature that supports the current belief of educators that the same process works with adults, that dialoguing with colleagues can produce collective meaning (Garmston & Wellman, 1998, p. 30). I ask students to discuss what they think Vygotsky could have meant by the term *negotiating meaning*. As I wander throughout the room asking the students what they are doing, purposefully using a slightly accusing tone, they tend to get confused and a little defensive. Soon, someone will ask me if I didn't tell them to discuss the lesson. And I ask what they think Vygotsky would say they were doing. At this moment, they discover that they have been negotiating meaning.

Two major purposes of school are to enhance learning and social development (Dewey, 1938; Henson & Eller, 1999). The use of small-group discussions also helps meet the second major goal, social development. This is of special concern because many programs designed to meet individuals' academic needs actually deprive them of meeting their social needs. Kohl (see Scherer, 1998) investigated a large number of schools that use individualized learning programs and reported that, ironically, many of these schools have a dehumanizing effect, depriving students of the opportunity to develop socially. The same weakness had been noted of home schooling (Williams et al., 1999).

I ask how many students have traveled out West and whether they have ever seen an oil refinery. I remind them how unrefined oil smells, and we talk about why we remember bad odors so well, leading to a review or rehearsal of the concept *confluent learning*. This is a convenient opportunity to revisit this concept; so I ask if anyone can identify the raw product that we smell at a refinery. The odor comes from crude oil, which, in its crude or natural state has no value. I compare the crude oil to *information,* which, by itself, is the relatively worthless raw product in the learning process. When refined, however, the results are highly valued *concepts,* which are analogous to expensive oil, gasoline, and dozens of other valuable products. We then search for a finished product in the classroom. Someone says that its learning, but someone else says no, that it's *knowledge* because learning is the refining process. I draw a distinction between the terms *information* and *knowledge*. *Information* is material that remains crude and useless unless it is refined and turned into *knowledge* by connecting it to prior experiences and knowledge. This concept is at the heart of constructivism, which holds that all learning requires the learner to invent his or her own understanding by trying new information to prior knowledge and experiences.

The Temporary and Fluid Nature of Knowledge

I then ask if students know what I mean if I say that the rancher or farmer feeds his cattle fodder. Most of my students grew up in rural areas, and many on farms, but they don't know the term *fodder*. I tell them not to be ashamed, that none of us knows everything and even when we do know something, that knowledge that we think we know so well can change. This introduces the *temporary* and *fluid* nature of knowledge. We pick these words up casually as we return to the story of the fodder. I tell the students that fodder is dried plants, such as corn leaves and even corn stalks, which serve as cattle feed when better cattle food is unavailable. During our discussion, we decide that fodder is similar to what some refer to as *silage*, but that instead of being ground up and stored in a silo, fodder may or may not be ground and is usually stored in a barn loft. I tell them about a Mississippi superintendent who, when preparing to interview a teacher candidate, was told that the candidate was very bright and extremely knowledgeable in his field. "But," asked the superintendent, "can he put the fodder down to a level where the cattle can reach it?" Together, we analyze and interpret this statement.

Before leaving the idea that knowledge is fluid, I give a couple of examples from history when the whole world held erroneous ideas ranging from believing that the world was flat to using leeches to bleed away illness. Then I invite students to give other major misconceptions.

Scaffolding

So we talk about how useless the fodder is to cattle when it is up in the barn loft, unless we know a way to get it down to the cattle. Indeed, the barn loft could be full of fodder and the cattle would starve if nobody knew how to get it down to where the cattle could reach it. I ask the students to turn to their groups and make some sense from this fodder story as it relates to what happens in the classroom. When the connection is made, we compare the students to cattle (which a few students always find humorous) and the fodder to information, we talk about how the farmer or rancher has either a mechanical left or a built-in ladder used to bring the fodder down step-by-step until the cattle can reach it. This introduces Vygotsky's concept of *scaffolding*. From here we go to the *zone of proximal development* and so forth. We collectively decide where on our maps to put these terms, drawing lines that represent our individual and group thinking.

Responsibility and Respect

In addition to having a joyous attitude, these teachers-of-the-year award recipients repeatedly spoke of respect. Marilyn Grondel (1999, p. 316), former Utah teacher of the year, reminded us of the importance of respect in the classroom and the teacher's responsibility to promote respect:

> I've come to the frightening conclusion that I am the decisive element in the classroom. It's my personal approach that creates the climate. It's my

daily mood that makes the weather. As a teacher, I possess a tremendous power to make a child's life miserable or joyous. I can be a tool, a torture instrument, or an instrument of inspiration. I can humiliate or humor, hurt or heal . . . I love and respect each child. Each child that spends time in my classroom is a gift to me from his parents. It is my responsibility to cherish that gift, to dream for that child, to lift him to new heights, to help him be the best he can be.

Former Nebraska teacher of the year Duane Obermeier (1999, p. 12) fully agreed and explained the connection between respect and responsibility:

I firmly believe in treating students like fellow human beings who have feelings just like I do. They don't appreciate being embarrassed or humiliated or confronted with problems in front of their peers. But they do respond to kindness, encouragement, a friendly tease, and smile. I try to teach manners in my classroom by being mannerly to my students; but I am not one of those wishy-washy let-each-student-do-his-own-thing, we'll-all-get-along types. Seldom is progress made by protecting students from the consequences of their behavior. If you skip class you get detention. If you don't do your work you get a failing grade.

Notice that along with respect, Mr. Obermeier added *responsibility*. In my classes, I discovered that assessment can be designed and used successfully to teach both respect and responsibility.

Using Assessment to Develop Respect and Responsibility

On the first day of class, I put forth rules of the class very firmly:

Speak loudly and clearly, making eye contact with your intended audience, which means no eating or chewing gum while speaking and no baseball caps or other head gear in class that might threaten to obstruct vision. If you use poor grammar in this class, I will never correct you to embarrass you, but I will never ignore your errors to protect you. Likewise, if I make a grammatical error, it is more than your right to call my attention to it; it is your responsibility as a class member. You will never hear intended sarcasm or other forms of rudeness from me, and I expect you to reciprocate toward me and other class members.

Then, to assure students that I already respect them, I share a humorous story that is very complimentary to the citizens of this state.

Yes, like Mr. Obermeier, I work to show *respect* for my students, and I also share Mr. Obermeier's belief that good teachers hold students accountable and responsible for their actions. I work to shift *responsibility* from myself to them. For example, I refuse to play warden or truant officer. I don't call the role. I never worry about tardiness. I don't have to; my classes have the highest attendance and punctuality record in the college. But, as you would guess, students insist on bringing doctors' excuses to me. I tell them to keep them, for while I am sorry to learn that they were ill, I haven't anything to do with the absences or tardiness. I haven't missed anything, and I surely am not upset at them for missing; so why should their absences concern me? Of course, I do care very deeply about attendance and punctuality, and to an outsider, I might appear unsympathetic, but I refuse to let my desire to show compassion cripple my students by excusing undesirable behaviors such as absenteeism and tardiness. Haberman (1999, p. 73) warned that in our efforts to be compassionate, we often lead students to conclude that it is acceptable to be absent or tardy if you have a good excuse. He pointed out that later, when our students exhibit the same behavior on the job, they receive pink slips. I try desperately to avoid contributing to this self-destructive cycle.

My university has a policy that says that students must be given opportunity to make up work for "excused" absences. It also has a policy that says that missing over 15 percent of classes automatically results in failure. I devised an assessment that I believe complies with both of these policies and, yet, puts responsibility for attendance and promptness on the students. This is how my system works. We cover material in one lesson and have a quiz covering that material in the next lesson at the very beginning of the period. I read the questions orally and never revisit a question. So, if a student arrives when we are taking question nine, that student can respond only to the last three questions. Each quiz has 10 points on yesterday's material plus two bonus points. If students are absent because of illness, I still don't give make-up quizzes. The two bonus points take care of occasional absences; a student can miss a few classes and still *possibly* make 100 percent on the grading scale, although nobody ever does. If I have serious students who have missed a class or two because of circumstances, such as having to stay home with a sick child or taking advantage of an unusual educational opportunity elsewhere, I always have the option of dropping the lowest quiz score for the entire class.

The two bonus questions are taken from the items missed most frequently on previous tests and from information in the text that was not discussed in class. This practice reinforces the idea that teachers must train themselves and their students to be lifelong learners—just because we have moved on to another chapter, this does not mean we cannot and indeed should not return to material learned earlier and be held accountable for it again and again.

How about those written assignments? Suppose a student brings a medical excuse and asks to turn in an assignment after the deadline for that assignment has passed. I accept this, but only if this is a *required* assignment.

I give another major written assignment that is optional. Because this assignment is not required and is offered as an opportunity to earn extra credit, I do not accept optional papers that miss the deadline. To those who would say that this is harsh and lacking of compassion, I remind them, as I remind my students on the first day of class, that the teaching profession is very unforgiving on the issues of absences and tardiness; every time a teacher is tardy or absent, a principal and an entire school board are put in legal jeopardy. In educational psychology, we learn that the best predictor of future behavior is past behavior. If, indeed, we issue permissions or excuses for tardiness and absences, we contribute to the forming of these negative behaviors, and we have no basis for believing that our graduates will magically reverse this behavior just because they receive their diplomas.

Using the Text

Each chapter of our adopted textbook has six major pedagogical components: *Todd Williams* (a case study of a first-year teacher), *In the Classroom* (comments from a teacher of the year), *A View from the Field* (an educational psychologist's advice to future teachers), *Technology in the Classroom, Surfing the Web, Recap of Major Ideas,* and *Key Terms.* The Todd Williams component is a one- to two-page, silk-screened scenario about a first-year teacher. We first meet Todd in Chapter One and accompany him to school on his first day of teaching. The principal, Ms. Wikersham, escorts Todd to other teachers' classrooms, introducing him to teachers who have different philosophies and who use different practices. There, we get an inside glimpse of distinctly different classrooms. Todd revisits each chapter and holds informal discussions with a couple of his fellow first-year teachers. The case study of Todd is a way of showing the theory in the chapter in practice, as Todd and his friends confront the issues of the chapter. In the final chapter, we visit Todd on the last school day of the year and hear him say farewell to his first students, giving a moving speech delivered by Nelson Mandella and telling his students how proud he is that he chose teaching for his lifelong profession.

Because my best teaching occurs when my students are teaching, every day I arrange for all of my students to teach. The class is divided into six groups. Using the grid shown in Figure F.2, the groups locate the part of the chapter they are charged with teaching to the rest of the class. As I move throughout the class, monitoring the discussions, I make certain that each group covers the two or three concepts that I believe are most important, letting them choose the rest. Each week the group rotates, each teaching a different part of the chapter. The groups have exactly ten minutes to review their assignments and prepare their presentations. Each group prepares a concept map to accompany their presentation.

Chapter Part

W = Todd Williams
C = A Teacher's Class
V = A View from the Field
T = Technology in the classroom & Surfing the web
R = Recap of major ideas
K = Key terms

Group Assignments

Group	I	II	III	IV	V	VI
1	W	C	V	T	R	K
2	C	V	T	R	K	W
3	V	T	R	K	W	C
4	T	R	K	W	C	V
5	R	K	W	C	V	T
6	K	W	C	V	T	R
7	W	C	V	T	R	K
8	C	V	T	R	K	W
9	V	T	R	K	W	C
10	T	R	K	W	C	V
11	R	K	W	C	V	T
12	K	W	C	V	T	R

FIGURE F.2   Grid Used to Make Daily Group Work Assignments

Empowering Students through Problem Solving in a Risk-Free Climate

Like my attendance and tardiness practices, using the format described requires a willingness to empower students and to have enough confidence in their abilities to let them make up their own problems and find the solutions. Former North Carolina teacher of the year Renee Coward (1999, p. 174) said, "I can, however, empower my students and help them determine their own questions; and I can help guide them in gaining the skills needed to solve their questions. This requires a tremendous leap of faith on the teacher's part because it involves giving up a position of ultimate authority and assuming the position of facilitator of learning." This format also requires me to set a climate that allows students to make mistakes and feel good about them, knowing that it is through our mistakes that we learn best how to learn. An item on my self-made, student evaluation instrument asks for evidence that I am a lifelong learner. One student responded, "He learns from his mistakes," and another replied, "He learns from his students." The first response is a nice compliment, but I really like the second one because it elevates and empowers my students.

Martinez (1998, p. 609) explained the importance of climate during problem solving, "Errors are a part of the process of problem solving, which implies that both teachers and learners need to be more tolerant of them. If no mistakes are made, then almost certainly no problem solving is taking place. Unfortunately, one tradition of schooling is that perfect performance is often exalted as an ideal. Errors are seen as failures, as signs that the highest marks are not quite merited."

Evaluation

Because, when used by itself, no single measurement is sufficient for measuring student perceptions, I chose to use both the IDEA student evaluation form and my own self-made student questionnaire. Following is a brief discussion of the results from using each of these instruments.

IDEA Results

A sample IDEA summary statement for one of these classes is shown in Figure F.3. Students in this class identified twenty teaching strategies that they thought should *not* be relinquished under any circumstances (strength column) and zero strategies that they thought I should consider eliminating (weakness column).

Self-Made Questionnaire

Obviously, I was pleased with the IDEA results, but I also wanted feedback on some questions lurking in my own mind about some formal and informal constructivist practices reported by the teachers of the year that are not measured on the IDEA form; therefore, I constructed and administered my own questionnaire. I asked questions about promptness. Did the class usually start and end on time? If I insist on holding students accountable for this behavior, then I must hold myself accountable for modeling the same behavior. Were the written assignments and tests returned promptly? All students (100 percent) said the class usually started on time, and three-fourths said that it always ended on time. (Incidentally, according to our large wall clock, these classes always started and ended exactly on time.) All students (100 percent) said their assignments and tests were returned promptly (all were returned at the following class meeting).

Student-Centered Teaching Strategies

I asked whether students thought that the class had engaged them (a) less than other classes, (b) somewhat more than other classes, or (c) a lot more than

| Teaching Methods and Styles | Average Rating | Comparison with Classes of Similar Size and Level of Student Motivations |

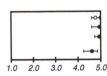

A. Student-Faculty Contact (Average of 1, 2, 20)
  *1. Displayed a personal interest in students and their learning
  2. Found ways to help students answer their own questions
  *20. Encouraged student-faculty interaction outside of class (office visits, phone calls, e-mail, etc.)

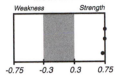

B. Involving Students (Average of 5, 9, 14, 16, 18)
  *5. Formed "teams" or "discussion groups" to facilitate learning
  *9. Encouraged students to use multiple resources (e.g., data banks, library holdings, outside experts) to improve understanding
  *14. Involved students in "hands on" projects such as research, case studies, or "real life" activities
  *16. Asked students to share ideas and experiences with others whose backgrounds and viewpoints differ from their own
  *18. Asked students to help each other understand ideas or concepts

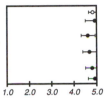
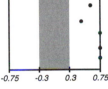

C. Establishing Expectations (Average of 3, 4, 8, 13, 15)
  *3. Scheduled course work (class activities, tests, projects) in ways which encourage students to stay up to date in their work
  4. Demonstrated the importance and significance of the subject matter
  8. Stimulated students to intellectual effort beyond that required by most courses
  13. Introduced stimulating ideas about the subject
  *15. Inspired students to set and achieve goals which really challenged them

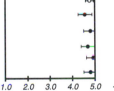
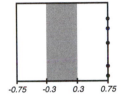

D. Clarity of Communication (Average of 6, 10, 11)
  6. Made it clear how each topic fit into the course
  10. Explained course material clearly and concisely
  11. Related course material to real life situations

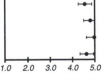
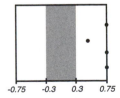

E. Assessment/Feedback (Average of 7, 12, 17, 19)
  7. Explained the reasons for criticism of students' academic performance
  12. Gave tests, projects, etc. that covered the most important points of the course
  *17. Provided timely and frequent feedback on tests, reports, projects, etc. to help students improve
  19. Gave projects, tests, or assignments that required original or creative thinking

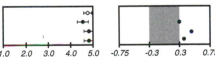

* New Item

⊢○⊣ *Average Category rating ± one standard error of measurement*
⊢●⊣ *Average item rating ± one standard error of measurement*

FIGURE F.3 Sample IDEA Student Evaluation

other classes. No students marked "less than," 75 percent marked "somewhat more than in their other classes," and the rest marked "a lot more than their other classes." I asked them to list the teaching strategies they could remember. Their responses included constructivism, cooperative learning, proximity control, overlapping, direct instruction, guided discovery, group work, hands-on activities, inquiry learning, lecture, rehearsal, and review. Surprisingly, and frankly somewhat disappointing, some of the most frequently used strategies were not mentioned at all. These included advance organizers, concept mapping, formative evaluation, and the most widely used teaching strategy, story telling. I have concluded that while modeling is essential, by itself, it is inadequate. The teacher must articulate the fact that a desired teaching behavior is being used; so, throughout the term, each time I used proximity control or overlapping, I called attention to these skills by asking students to name the skill I was using. It is no coincidence that they remembered to list these skills.

The Professor's Attitude

I asked questions to gather student perceptions of the professor's attitudes and behavior. All students (100 percent) said that the professor enjoys teaching and all (100 percent) said that he *reinvented* the course daily until it worked for them. All (100 percent) found the professor accessible. All students (100 percent) said that the professor understood their needs and was flexible. They expressed appreciation for my making rare exceptions for deserving students, and, without being asked by the other students, automatically extending this exception to the rest of the class. All students (100 percent) said that the professor is a *lifelong learner*, giving such evidence as "He relates news events to us," "He is always relating books and articles to us," "He learns from experience," and "He learns from his students."

Conclusions

An important result from this study was the reminder that all course evaluations are imperfect, substantiating the premise that multiple measuring instruments are essential, even when just measuring student attitudes. Even more so, we know that student opinions, alone, are inadequate for assessing teaching performance. Yet, both instruments used in this study clearly showed that teacher education students perceived all of the constructivist methods used in this study as being effective, and all students embraced these methods. To derive further benefits from this study, the results of the students' evaluations of the course, the course syllabus, the textbook, sample tests, sample assignments, student work, sample graphic organizers, transparencies, concept maps, and a Power Point presentation for each chapter of the text subsequently have been submitted to solicit feedback from others who teach this course.

Was I happy with the results of these evaluations? Yes. I am also happy to report that since receiving these data, a new semester has begun and the new students seem even more excited over the course; however, I have already changed the course in several ways. Each class is different and has to be dealt with slightly different—differently from other classes and differently today from yesterday (Armstrong et al., 2001). Jean Piaget (1973) provided a poignant definition of constructivism when he titled one of his books, *To Understand Is to Invent*. The fluid nature of teaching is a quality of life itself. The poet Antonio Machado addressed the fluid nature of life when he wrote, "Life is a path you beat while you walk it." I believe that teaching is the same; to understand it and make it work, each teacher has to keep analyzing, reinventing, and beating out a new path each term and each day.

References

Armstrong, D. G., Henson, K. T., & Savage, T. V. (2001). *Teaching today* (6th ed.) New York: Prentice-Hall.

Bicouvaris, M. (1999). A teacher's class. In K. T. Henson & B. F. Eller (Eds.), *Educational psychology for effective teaching*. Belmont, CA: Wadsworth, 124.

Coward, R. (1999). A teacher's class. In K. T. Henson & B. F. Eller (Eds.), *Educational psychology for effective teaching*. Belmont, CA: Wadsworth, 174.

Dewey, J. (1938). *Experience and education*. Reprinted in 1998. Indianapolis: Kappa Delta Pi.

Garmston, R., & Wellman, B. (1998). Teacher talk that makes a difference. *Phi Delta Kappan, 55*(7), 30–34.

Good, T., & Brophy, J. (2000). *Looking in classrooms* (8th ed.) New York: Harper-Row.

Grondel, M. (1999). A teacher's class. In K. T. Henson & B. F. Eller (Eds.), *Educational psychology for effective teaching*. Belmont, CA: Wadsworth, 316.

Haberman, M. (1999). The anti-learning curriculum. Part 2: The solution. *Kappan Delta Pi Record, 35*(2), 71–74.

Henson, K. T., & Eller, B. F. (1999). *Educational psychology for effective teaching*. Belmont, CA: Wadsworth.

Jalongo, M. R., & Isenberg, J. P. (1995). *Teachers' stories*. San Francisco: Jossey-Bass.

Lloyd, S. (1999). A teacher's class. In K. T. Henson & B. F. Eller (Eds.), *Educational psychology for effective teaching*. Belmont, CA: Wadsworth, 225.

Martinez, M. E. (1998). What is problem solving? *Phi Delta Kappan, 79*(8), 605–609.

Maslow, A. (1973). What is a Taoistic teacher? In L. J. Rubin (Ed.), *Facts and feelings in the classroom*. New York: Walker.

Obermeier, D. (1999). A teacher's class. In K. T. Henson & B. F. Eller (Eds.), *Educational psychology for effective teaching*. Belmont, CA: Wadsworth, 12.

Piaget, J. (1973). *To understand is to invent*. New York: Grossman.

Scherer, M. (1998). The discipline of hope: An interview with Herbert Kohl. *Educational Leadership, 56*(1), 8–13.

Selekman, H. (1999). A teacher's class. In K. T. Henson & B. F. Eller (Eds.), *Educational psychology for effective teaching*. Belmont, CA: Wadsworth, 59.

Snyder, J. (1999). A teacher's class. In . T. Henson & B. F. Eller (Eds.), *Educational psychology for effective teaching*. Belmont, CA: Wadsworth, 476.

Stedman, C. (2000). *Identifying good teaching: What research tells us.* Indianapolis: Kappa Delta Pi.

Teddlie, C., & Reynolds, D. (2000). *The instructional handbook of school effectiveness research.* New York: Falmer Press.

Williams, P. A., Alley, R., & Henson, K. T. (1999). *Managing secondary classrooms.* Boston: Allyn & Bacon.

Appendix G

Sample Survey Questionnaire

The Status of the American Middle School Teacher

A. Your Professional Preparation

1. What is the *highest college degree* you hold? Do not report honorary degrees. Check ONE.
   [ ] Two-year college diploma, degree, or certificate
   [ ] Bachelor's degree
   [ ] Master's degree
   [ ] Professional diploma based on six years of college study (Specialist Degree)
   _____ Major field bachelor's degree
   _____ Major field master's degree
   _____ Major field specialist's degree
   _____ Major field doctor's degree

2. In what *year* did you receive your highest college degree?
   _____ year

3. In what *type of institution* did you take the largest part of four years of college education? For each degree held, write in the number corresponding to the type of institution in which you took the largest part of your work. (Please answer in terms of the type of institution it was when you were graduated.)
   1 Public (tax-supported university or land-grant college)
   2 Public teachers college
   3 Other public college
   4 Nonpublic (privately supported) university
   5 Nonpublic teachers college
   6 Other nonpublic college
   _____ Bachelor's degree
   _____ Master's degree

_____ Professional diploma based on six years of college
_____ Doctor's degree

4. In terms of actual contribution to your success in teaching, how would you evaluate the amount and quality of your *undergraduate teacher preparation* program in the following areas? Check ONE space for EACH area.

PART I:

	Amount of preparation was		
	Too little	**About right**	**Too much**
a. Depth of knowledge in the subject fields in which you specialized	[ ]	[ ]	[ ]
b. General education—some knowledge in many fields	[ ]	[ ]	[ ]
c. Psychology of learning and teaching	[ ]	[ ]	[ ]
d. Human growth and development	[ ]	[ ]	[ ]
e. Teaching methods	[ ]	[ ]	[ ]
f. Classroom management, routines, discipline	[ ]	[ ]	[ ]
g. History and philosophy of education	[ ]	[ ]	[ ]
h. Use of audio-visual equipment and materials	[ ]	[ ]	[ ]

PART II:

	Quality of preparation was			
	No preparation	**Satisfactory**	**Excellent**	**Poor**
a. Depth of knowledge in the subject fields in which you specialized	[ ]	[ ]	[ ]	[ ]
b. General education—some knowledge in many fields	[ ]	[ ]	[ ]	[ ]
c. Psychology of learning and teaching	[ ]	[ ]	[ ]	[ ]
d. Human growth and development	[ ]	[ ]	[ ]	[ ]
e. Teaching methods	[ ]	[ ]	[ ]	[ ]
f. Classroom management, routines, discipline	[ ]	[ ]	[ ]	[ ]
g. History and philosophy of education	[ ]	[ ]	[ ]	[ ]
h. Use of audio-visual equipment and material	[ ]	[ ]	[ ]	[ ]

B. Your Teaching Experience

5. In what calendar year did you *begin* your first full-time teaching position?

   _____ year

6. How many years of full-time teaching experience have you completed, including the current year?

   _____ total years of experience

   _____ total years in present school system

7. Since you began teaching, in how many *different* public school systems have you taught full time? Count your present system as one.

   _____ system(s)

8. Has there been a break of as much as one year in your full-time teaching service? If so, how many such breaks? Disregard breaks of less than one full school year.

   _____ breaks in teaching service

9. If there has been a break of more than one full school year in your teaching service, what was your *primary reason* for temporarily leaving teaching? If there has been more than one break, answer for the most recent one. Check ONE.

   [   ] Marriage or full-time homemaking
   [   ] Maternity or child rearing
   [   ] Spouse's work took us to another community
   [   ] Further study
   [   ] Employment in a position out of education
   [   ] Employment in another educational position
   [   ] Military service
   [   ] Ill health
   [   ] Tired of teaching and wanted a rest
   [   ] Dismissal or forced resignation from teaching
   [   ] Other: (please write in) _____

   _____

C. Your Present Teaching Assignment

10. How many classroom teachers are there in your school? (Include yourself and all full-time persons, half or more of whose work loads is classroom teaching.)

    _____ teachers

11. What grades are you teaching this year? Include any prekindergarten assignment under "PK." Circle *all* grades taught this year.

    PK   5   6   7   8   9

12. How is your present teaching assignment classified? Check ONE.
    [   ] Elementary teacher
    [   ] Junior high teacher
    [   ] Middle school—junior high teacher
    [   ] Middle junior—Senior high teacher
    [   ] Combination elementary-secondary teacher
    [   ] Other: (please explain)_____

---

13. What percent of your total teaching time each week is spent in teaching grades or subjects that are *different from your major field of college preparation?* Check ONE.

    [   ] None   [   ] 50–59%
    [   ] Some but less than 10%   [   ] 60–69%
    [   ] 10–19%   [   ] 70–79%
    [   ] 20–29%   [   ] 80–89%
    [   ] 30–39%   [   ] 90–99%
    [   ] 40–49%   [   ] 100%

14. Enrollment and contact time
    a. In what field (English, mathematics, etc.) are you currently teaching the *largest portion* of your time?

       _____

    b. What is the total number of *class periods* you teach per week? (Exclude study halls and homeroom periods.)
       _____ class periods per week
    c. What is the average number of *pupils* you teach *per day?* (Exclude study halls and homeroom periods.)
       _____ pupils
    d. What is the average *length of the class periods* in your school? (Include passing time.)
       _____ minutes
    e. How many unassigned (so-called "free" or planning) periods do you have in your own schedule each week?
       _____ unassigned periods per week
    f. How much time per day, on the average, are you *required* to be with pupils? (Include study halls, homeroom periods, scheduled conference periods, lunch periods if applicable.)
       _____ hours and _____ minutes

15. What is the *exact length* of your required school day? (e.g., if you are required to be on duty by 8:15 A.M. and permitted to leave school at 3:30 P.M., the exact length of your required school days is 7 hours and 15 minutes.)
    _____ hours and _____ minutes

16. On the average how many *hours per week* do you spend on noncompensated school-related activities, such as lesson preparation, grading papers, making reports, extracurricular activities, meetings, etc.? _____ hours and _____ minutes.

17. How many *days* will there be in your *school year* in 1984–1985?
    _____ days of classroom teaching
    _____ days of nonteaching duties before, during, or after the school year for pupils

18. Lunch period:
    a. What is the average length of your lunch period?
       _____ minutes
    b. Do you usually eat lunch with your pupils (i.e., supervise their lunch period)?
       [   ] Yes, all the time
       [   ] Yes, on a rotating basis
       [   ] No
    c. If you answered Yes to "b" above, what is the reason?
       [   ] My own preference
       [   ] It is customary in my school
       [   ] It is required in my school

19. How would you describe your *present teaching load?* Check ONE.
    [   ] Reasonable
    [   ] Heavy
    [   ] Extremely heavy

20. How would you describe your feelings of *strain* or *tension* in your work? Check ONE.
    [   ] Little or no strain
    [   ] Moderate strain
    [   ] Considerable strain

D. Your Professional Growth Activities

21. Below are listed several types of *professional growth* activities. For those in which you have participated during the *past three years,* please check the extent to which you believe each activity contributed to improving the quality of your work in the classroom. Check ALL that apply.

Activity	Extent of contribution to professional growth		
	Great	**Some**	**Little or no**
Sabbatical leave: full-time college work	[ ]	[ ]	[ ]

Sabbatical leave: travel	[ ]	[ ]	[ ]
Other educational travel	[ ]	[ ]	[ ]
School system-sponsored workshops during regular school year	[ ]	[ ]	[ ]
School system-sponsored workshops during the summer	[ ]	[ ]	[ ]
Work on curriculum committee	[ ]	[ ]	[ ]
Committee work or special assignment *other than* curriculum	[ ]	[ ]	[ ]
Faculty meetings	[ ]	[ ]	[ ]
University extension courses	[ ]	[ ]	[ ]
College courses *in education* during regular school year	[ ]	[ ]	[ ]
College courses in subject-matter fields *other than education* during regular school year	[ ]	[ ]	[ ]
College courses *in education* during the summer	[ ]	[ ]	[ ]
College courses in subject-matter fields *other than education* during the summer			
Professional growth activities sponsored by professional associations	[ ]	[ ]	[ ]
Professional reading done on my initiative	[ ]	[ ]	[ ]
Educational television programs	[ ]	[ ]	[ ]
Exchange teaching, domestic	[ ]	[ ]	[ ]
Exchange teaching, foreign	[ ]	[ ]	[ ]
Peace Corps	[ ]	[ ]	[ ]
Other (please specify)			
_____	[ ]	[ ]	[ ]
_____			

What single course, workshop, or other professional growth experience during the past three years *contributed most* to improving the quality of your work in the classroom?

_____

_____

22. Beginning with the summer of 1984 and ending with the close of the present school year in May or June 1984, *how much money* do you estimate that you will have spent from your own funds for *all professional growth activities* enumerated in Question 21? (Please EXCLUDE scholarship funds.)

Educational travel $ _____

All other activities $ _____

E. Your Economic Status

23. What is your *salary* as a classroom teacher for the school year 1984–85? (EXCLUDE any extra pay received for additional school duties.)
$ _____ for year

24. *Additional income.* Below are listed several possible sources of additional income for the full year *beginning with your summer vacation in 1984 and ending* with the last school month in May or June 1985. For each item that applies please indicate the *type of position held* and the *total amount of income received.* Check ALL items that apply.

a. Employment during summer 1984
   [ ] *School work* (e.g., summer-school teaching curriculum work, school repair jobs, etc.) in your school system
   Type of work _____
   Total amount $ _____
   [ ] *Outside work* (e.g., salesman, recreation director, camp counselor, teaching outside your own school system, etc.)
   Type of work _____
   Total amount $ _____
   [ ] *Federal program* (e.g., NDEA or NSF institute or fellowship, project Head-Start, Cooperative Research Grant, etc.)
   Type of work _____
   Total amount $ _____

b. Employment during school year 1984–85
   [ ] *Extra pay for extra duties* (e.g., coaching, music, drama, counseling, publications work, etc., in your own school system)
   Type of work _____
   Total amount $ _____
   [ ] *School work other than extra pay for extra duties* (e.g., evening school, driving school bus, etc., in your own school system)
   Type of work _____
   Total amount $ _____
   [ ] *Outside work* (e.g., salesperson, cab driver, tutoring, local college teaching, etc., outside your own school system)
   Type of work _____
   Total amount $ _____

c. Summer 1984 and school year 1984–1985
   Dividends, rents, interest, royalties, retirement annuity, other than current earnings
   $ _____

25. How many persons, *excluding* yourself, your spouse, and your children, *depend* upon you for support, either wholly or partly? Include dependents living with you and those living elsewhere.
Number dependents _____

26. Do you or your spouse own
    a. Your own home?   [ ] Yes   [ ] No
    b. A car?   [ ] Yes   [ ] No
       How many cars?   [ ] One   [ ] Two   [ ] Three or more

27. Have you taken a *vacation trip of at least two weeks* during the past three years (e.g., travel, camping, trip to lake or seashore)? Check ONE.
    [ ] No
    [ ] Yes, in one of the three years
    [ ] Yes, in two of the three years
    [ ] Yes, in all three years

F. You and Your Family

28. What is your *age?*
    _____ years

29. What is your *sex?*
    [ ] Male   [ ] Female

30. What is your *marital status?*
    [ ] Single   [ ] Married
    [ ] Widowed   [ ] Divorced or separated

31. If you are married, is your husband or wife gainfully employed? Check ONE.
    [ ] Yes; employed full time
    [ ] Yes; employed part time
    [ ] No, but draws retirement pay
    [ ] No, but is disabled and draws insurance or disability retirement benefits
    [ ] No, not gainfully employed at present

32. If you are married, and if your husband or wife is employed full time, is the employment in the teaching profession?
    [ ] Yes [ ] No
    If Yes, is the employment in the same school system in which you teach?
    [ ] Yes [ ] No

33. What are the ages of your children? Write in the *number* of children in each age group.
    _____ under 6 years of age
    _____ 6–11 years
    _____ 12–17 years
    _____ 18 years or older
    _____ TOTAL NUMBER OF CHILDREN
    [ ] Have no Children

34. If you have children below school age, who takes care of your children while you are teaching? Check ONE.
    [　] Day care center, kindergarten, or nursery
    [　] Relatives
    [　] Friends
    [　] Someone you hired in your home
    [　] Someone you hired in their home
    [　] Other, please specify

---

35. What was your main consideration in choosing *teaching* as a career? Please check ONE predominant reason.
    [　] Opportunity for rendering important service
    [　] Financial rewards
    [　] Job security
    [　] Stopgap until marriage
    [　] Example set by a favorite teacher
    [　] Unsuccessful in another line of work
    [　] Easiest preparation program in college
    [　] A tradition in my family
    [　] Desire to work with your people
    [　] Interest in subject-matter field
    [　] Other: (please specify)

---

36. Have you ever served on *active duty* as a member of one of the Armed Forces of the United States?
    [　] Yes　　　　[　] No

G. You and the Community

37. Please check to indicate your *sense of identity* with the community (town, city, or other unit of population) where you live during the school year. Check ONE.
    [　] I am living in my home community where I have lived since childhood.
    [　] I came here as an adult and now feel that I belong.
    [　] I have been here for some time, but do not feel that I belong.
    [　] I have been here for too short a time to expect to feel that I belong.

38. Is your *residence* within the boundaries of the local system in which you teach?
    [　] Yes　　　　[　] No

39. Several types of religious, civic, professional, and *social organizations* are listed below. Please enter a number before each type that

corresponds to one of the following statements, selecting the statement that represents your own relationship to the organization.

1   I am a member and very active worker.
2   I am a member and a fairly active worker.
3   I am a member but not an active worker.
4   I am not a member.

Write in— 1, 2, 3, or 4—for each organization:

— Church, or synagogue, or other formal religious group
— Youth-serving group—Y, Scouts, 4-H, etc.
— Women's business, professional, civic-social group—AAUW, B&PW, Quota, etc.
— Men's service club—Rotary, Lions, etc.
— Fraternal or auxiliary group (Knights of Columbus, Elks, Eastern Star, etc.)
— Civil liberties group—ACLU, Urban League, NAACP, CORE, etc.
— Veterans group
— Political party organization
— Parent-Teacher Association
— Hobby club—music, drama, gardening, etc.
— National Education Association
— State education association
— Local educational association
— Subject-matter or professional special-interest association
— American Federation of Teachers

40. How many hours *per month*, on the average, do you give during the school year to work for organizations such as those listed in Question 39? (Do not include time spent in school-assigned activities or at services of religious worship.)
    _____ hours per month

41. To what extent did you participate in the 1984 national elections? Check ALL items that apply.
    [   ] Voted in the primary election
    [   ] Voted in the general election
    [   ] Contributed money to a political party
    [   ] Contributed my services as a worker in behalf of a political party
    [   ] Did not participate in the 1984 national elections

42. While a teacher, have you ever been a *candidate* for election to a public office (local, county, state, or national)?
    [   ] Yes   [   ] No

43. In your opinion, what level of prestige do teachers have in the community in which you teach?

[   ] High prestige
[   ] Medium prestige
[   ] Low prestige
[   ] Undecided

44. Do you feel that the community in which you teach places any personal pressures or restrictions on your activities outside school hours because you are a teacher?
    [   ] No, not in any way
    [   ] Yes, but not seriously
    [   ] Yes, seriously
    [   ] Undecided

H. Retrospect and Prospect

45. Suppose you could back to your college days and start over again; in view of your present knowledge, would you become a teacher? Check ONE.
    [   ] *Certainly would* become a teacher
    [   ] *Probably would* become a teacher
    [   ] *Chances about even* for and against
    [   ] *Probably would not* become a teacher
    [   ] *Certainly would not* become a teacher

46. What were you doing turning the 1984–85 school year (last year) and what do you expect to be doing during the 1985–86 school year (next year)? Please check ONE item in EACH column.

	1984–1985 (last year)	1985–1986 (next year)
a. Teaching full time in this school system	[ ]	[ ]
b. Teaching full time in another school system	[ ]	[ ]
c. Attending a college or university full time	[ ]	[ ]
d. In military service	[ ]	[ ]
e. Working in a nonteaching occupation	[ ]	[ ]
f. Homemaking and/or child rearing	[ ]	[ ]
g. Unemployed and seeking work	[ ]	[ ]
h. Retired	[ ]	[ ]
i. Other (please specify)	[ ]	[ ]

_____

_____

I. Your Professional Satisfactions and Problems

47. What elements in your present situation as a teacher *encourage and help you most* to render the best service of which you are capable?

_____

_____

_____

(use additional space on the back if desired)

48. What elements in your present situation as a teacher *discourage or hinder you most* in rendering the best service of which you are capable?

_____

_____

_____

(use additional space on the back if desired)

Appendix H

Sample First Draft of a Proposal

Section F. Review Criteria/Activity Evaluation

1. To the extent applicable, address each of the Review Criteria as specified in the guidelines under the program area for which funds are being requested. Clearly indicate the criteria you are addressing. (NOTE: Planning and Evaluation criteria should be addressed in sections E-1 and F-2 respectively. Civil Rights and Accessibility criteria should be addressed in section G.)

We are housed at   University and are in   County school system. However neither organization have budgeted full time arts instruction for the elementary school. In October 1995 I was hired as the first certified art teacher these students have had in over 25 years! We receive some financial support from our parents and community, but we feel these solicitations would be better received if parents and friends were asked to supplement grant funds. For these reasons we have applied for the Kentucky Arts Council grant to have visiting artists in our school.

Teacher support will be given to this project by our part time art teacher and participating faculty. The art teacher will prepare students for the first week of exploration with cartographer Cynthia Cooke prior to her arrival. The second week will be a continuation of the map making project. Pat Banks will teach students watercolor techniques. The students will continue to benefit from these experiences after the initial project is over through their newly developed skills and by materials purchased by the grant moneys. Classroom teachers will accompany their students during the sessions where they will find ways to include the techniques in future plans.

Through the creation of art, my goals are to teach the child how to look at art, understand its place in culture over time and make judgments about its quality. In support of this the goals of the visiting artist are to explore map making and watercolor techniques in cross curricular application. The students will learn more about artists who live in our community, learn the cultural and artistic evolution of maps from around the world, and introduce the idea of art as a career. Activities meet all KERA Learning Goals in Science and Social Studies, Practical Living (2.29–2.30), Math (2.2–2.11), Arts and Humanities (2.22–2.23, 2.25–2.26); also goals 1.9, 1.11–1.13, 1.16, 2.3, 3, 4, 5.1–5.5 and 6.1–6.3 for a total of 40 goals.

We have formed a planning committee and a schedule has been made that allows both Artists the opportunity to work individually with each student through the development of the project. The success of the visit will be evaluated by the degree with which the students have enjoyed working with the artists, the satisfaction they express in their written personal reflections about the experience, and the continued use of the skills taught as a means of expression across the curriculum. We will celebrate our experience with an art show of the works created to which we will invite our parts and the community.

We look forward to hearing from the Kennedy Arts Council so we can immerse our students in the Arts!

Appendix I

Preferences of Journals in Various Disciplines

TABLE I.1 Characteristics of a Selected Sample of Education Journals

	Number of Readers	Refereed	Research Articles (%)	Themed Issues per Year (%)	Acceptance Rate (%)	Weeks Required for Decision (Avg.)	Months Required for Publication (Avg.)	Preferred Length (in Ms. Pages)	Min./Max. Pages	Number of Additional Copies	Required Style	Electronic Submissions	Send Disk	Prefer Letter (L), Phone Call (P), Either (E)
Action in Teacher Education	3,000	3	20	—	20	16—24	1	20	1-20	2	APA	No	No	P
American Biology Teacher	11,000	3	60	0	55	8	5	16	1-16	2	Other	No	No	L
American Secondary Education	420	2	40	0	25	9	1-2	10-16	—	3	APA	Yes	No	L
Child Development	9,000	3	80	8	20	12	8	25	1-60	4	APA	No	No	E
Clearing House	3,000	3	50	20	20	16	5	—	—	1	Chicago	Yes	No	P
Comparative Education Review	2,400	2	80	—	15	—	10	30	20-40	3	Chicago	Yes	No	—
Contemporary Education	2,200	3	5	80	15	2	2	—	8-12	2	APA	Yes	Yes	L
Creative Child & Adult Quarterly	—	2	30	25	40	4	9-15	10	6-18	2	APA	No	No	L
College Student Journal	450	2	50	0	70	4	6-8	12-18	—	—	APA	Yes	No	L
Current Issues in Middle Education	200	3	50	—	50	4-6	2	—	6-10	2	APA	Yes	No	P
Eastern Education Journal	1,500	3	85	—	80	6	6	10-15	—	4	APA	No	No	E
Education	5,000	1	25	20	35	4	9	8-10	—	1	APA	Yes	No	E
Education Forum	7,000	3	40	80	20	16	6	16	10-20	4	Chicago II	Yes	Yes	L
Educational Horizons	12,000	3	30	95	20	12-52	3-12	15	3-20	2	Chicago	—	—	L
Educational Leadership	200,000	0	20	95	5	4	3-24	8	1-20	1	Chicago	No	No	P
Educational Perspectives	1,000	—	50	100	—	3-4	3-5	10-15	10-12	—	Chicago	Yes	No	L
Educational Record	10,000	3	2	100	15	6-8	3-6	12	5-15	1	Chicago	Yes	Yes	P
Educational Technology	5,600	0	20	—	20	2	6-12	10-12	6-25	1	APA	—	—	—
Elementary School Journal	4,327	3	99	40	9	8-12	18	30-40	—	3	APA	No	No	E
Harvard Educational Review	10,000	0	40	25	5	12-24	3-6	1-45	—	2	APA	No	No	L

Journal														
High School Journal	2,000	3	60	12	25	12	12	12	5-18	2	APA	No	No	P
Journal of At-Risk Students	3,000	3	65	0	30	12	6	20	5-25	3	APA	Yes	Yes	P
Journal of Educational Relations	1,000	3	25	—	50	4	3-6	10	5-25	3	APA	Yes	No	L
Journal of Experimental Education	1,500	3	—	10	30	8-20	5	—	—	2	APA	—	—	P
Journal of Instructional Psychology	400	2	75	0	65	4	6	10-14	—	1	APA	Yes	No	E
Journal of Physical Education, Recreation, and Dance	28,000	3	10	10	30	8	9	10	—	3	APA	—	—	E
Journal of Res. in Science Teaching	3,000	3	80	0	20	16-20	6	40	—	3	APA	Yes	No	L
Journal of Staff Development	8,500	3	10	50	34	10	5	12	5-12	4	APA	Yes	No	P
Journal of Teacher Education	—	3	45	20	10	15-20	2	12-14	1-14	3	APA	Yes	No	E
Kappa Delta Pi Record	62,000	3	40	80	35	16	6	12	6-16	4	Chicago II	Yes	Yes	E
Learning and Leading with Technol.	11,000	3	10	—	49	16	6-12	6	3-9	1	APA	Yes	Yes	E
Middle School Journal	26,000	3	25	60	20	14	15	20	8-30	4	APA	No	No	P
NASSP Bulletin	42,000	0	40	25	10	2-4	2-24	7-10	—	0	Chicago	Yes	Yes	L
New Teacher Advocate	33,000	2	10	—	40	16	6	3	1-5	4	Chicago II	No	Yes	E
Perceptual and Motor Skills	2,000	1	90	0	33	3-4	1	—	—	9	APA	No	No	L
Phi Delta Kappan	150,000	0	50	50	5	8	9	15	1-25	0	Chicago	No	No	E
Planning & Changing[a]	558	3	80	25	10	5	24	—	1-10	15	APA	—	—	—
Principal	28,000	0	10	25	15	2-10	6	6-8	3-10	1	Chicago	Yes	No	L
Professional Educator	325	3	70	0	17	10	6	—	—	2	APA	No	No	E
Psychological Reports	1,900	1	90	0	33	3-4	1	25	12-30	4	APA	No	No	L
Reading Research Quarterly	11,000	3	90	0	10	8-12	6-9	—	—	6	APA	Yes	Yes	E
Reading Teacher	70,000	3	90	0	8	10-12	12	15-20	—	4	APA	Yes	No	E
Review of Educational Research[a]	17,000	3	100	0	12	8	3-6	40	1-18	2	APA	—	—	—
School Administrator	16,000	0	20	66	25	8	6	6	2-12	0	Assoc. Press	Yes	Yes	E
School Science and Mathematics	3,500	3	40	15	40	8-16	4-12	10-12	5-15	3	APA	Yes	No	P
Social Education[a]	20,000	3	40	60	30	2	20	—	6-20	4	APA	—	—	P
Social Studies	2,800	2	10	5	48	10	4-8	10-15	10-20	1	APA	Yes	No	E
Teacher Educator	1,000	3	70	25	15	10	4	20	—	2	APA	Yes	No	E
Teachers College Record	3,500	3	50	15	10	30	6	35	10-50	4	Chicago	Yes	—	—
Teaching & Learning[a]	250	2	50	0	40	6-8	3-4	20	6-30	—	Any Style	—	—	L
Techniques	40,000	0	10	0	5-10	6-16	—	—	—	0	Assoc. Press	Yes	No	L
Theory Into Practice	2,500	2	—	100	5-25	4-12	6-8	15	10-18	2-4	APA	Yes	No	E
Training and Development	40,000	3	5	0	10	4-6	6	15	10-25	1	Chicago	No	Yes	P
Vitae Scholasticae[a]	200	2	100	—	80	8	3-6	15-30	5-100	1	Chicago	—	—	L

[a]Data received from previous survey or after computation of figures reported in text had been completed.

TABLE I.2 *Characteristics of a Selected Sample of Other Journals*

	Number of Readers	Contributors Who Are University Personnel (%)	Refereed	Research Articles (%)	Themed Issues per Year (%)	Acceptance Rate (%)	Days to Answer Queries (Avg.)	Days to Acknowledge Receipt of Ms. (Avg.)	Weeks Required for Decision (Avg.)	Months Required for Publication (Avg.)	Preferred Length (in Ms. Pages)	Min./Max. Pages	Number of Additional Copies	Required Style	Effect of Photos on Acceptance (N = None, P = Possibly, D = Definitely, L = Likely)	Welcome Query Letters	Welcome Phone Calls	Prefer Letter (L), Phone Call (P), Either (E)
HEALTH & NURSING																		
Adapted Physical Activity Quarterly	800	80	3	70	—	40	—	10	13	6	20–25	—	3	APA	N	Y	Y	E
American Journal of Physiology	1,500	99	2	99	—	60	7	3	8	4	6–8	3–12	3	APS	L	Y	Y	L
Journal of Allied Health		100	3	95	—	25	5	8	7	5	12	—	1	AMA	N	Y	Y	L
Journal of American College Health	3,000	99	3	60	20	25	7	3	14	5	20	4–35	1	AMA	N	Y	Y	L
Journal of Applied Communication Research	2,000	95	3	90	20	20	2	2	8	12	25	—	2	APA	N	Y	Y	N
Journal of Health Education	10,000	75	3	75	30	20	18	14	8	11	10	1–12	3	APA	P	Y	Y	L

LIBRARIANSHIP/INFORMATION SCIENCE

Journal																		
Journal of Education for Library and Information Science	1,600	95	3	95	25	—	11	11	9	16	—	—	2	Chicago	N	—	—	—
Library and Information Science Research	1,500	80	3	80	—	60	4	2	5	2	20	—	3	MLA	N	Y	Y	L
Library Quarterly	2,000	90	3	85	20	30	3	3	8	6	8–10	—	2	—	N	Y	Y	L
Wilson Library Bulletin	12,000	25	0	—	—	20	10	10	8	5	—	3–12	1	Chicago	P	Y	Y	L

SOCIAL AND BEHAVIORAL SCIENCES

Journal																		
The Counseling Psychologist	2,300	60	3	10	100	—	0	0	6	—	—	—	3	APA	N	Y	Y	L
Economics and Business Education	3,500	11	3	—	—	—	14	14	12	5	—	—	2	—	N	Y	N	L
International Journal of Social Education	1,000	35	3	90	95	18	4	4	—	—	20–25	—	2	Chicago	P	Y	—	—
Journal for Specialists in Group Work	9,000	40	3	30	25	50	14	14	12	12	20	10–40	2	APA	N	Y	N	L
Journal of Child Psychology and Psychiatry	4,000	—	2	90	—	20	10	2	6	6	—	—	3	—	—	—	—	—
Journal of Counseling Psychology	4,000	—	3	90	—	25	7	7	6	6	20–30	—	4	APA	N	Y	Y	P
Journal of Humanistic Psychology	4,000	60	2	10	—	10	14	10	8	12	20	10–40	1	APA	N	N	N	L
Journal of Pediatric Psychology	1,000	—	3	95	15	20	3	2	6	9	25	—	3	APA	P	Y	Y	P
Journal of Youth and Adolescence	2,000	95	1	90	—	30	7	7	25	9	—	15–30	2	APA	N	Y	Y	L
Merrill-Palmer Quarterly	1,400	90	2	83	15	21	7	1	10	11	28	1–40	3	APA	—	Y	Y	L
Psychological Review	2,000	—	3	100	0	15	90	2	90	6	—	—	3	APA	N	N	N	N
Psychotherapy: Theory, Research, and Practice	7,000	—	3	98	—	20	7	7	14	11	15–20	1–20	3	APA	N	Y	Y	—
Social Education	26,000	10	3	10	15	18	3	3	9	7	3–8	3–20	4	Chicago	P	Y	Y	L
Social Science Quarterly	3,600	—	3	—	—	14	0	0	8	9	23	1–30	3	Chicago	P	Y	Y	L
The Social Studies	3,000	60	2	10	30	48	10	2	13	10	—	10–25	1	Chicago	P	Y	Y	L
Sociology of Education	2,500	90	3	100	25	10	7	2	12	9	30	1–50	3	ASA	N	N	Y	—
Theory and Research in Social Education	1,000	95	3	—	10	15	2	1	8	6	20	12+	4	APA	N	Y	Y	L

TABLE I.3   *Characteristics of a Selected Sample of Business Journals*

BUSINESS	Acceptance Rate (%)	Refereed	Number of Subscribers	% of University Contributors	Prefer Query Letters	Welcome Phone Calls	Days to Answer Query Letters	Days to Acknowledge Ms. Receipt	Months Required for Publication
Academy of Management Journal	11	yes	8,900	95	no	yes	1	1	15
Academy of Management Review	12	yes	9,500	99	yes	yes	7	1	8
California Management Review	15	yes	5,500	85	no	no	7	1	8
Journal of Applied Behavioral Science	10	yes	3,000	80	yes	yes	7	7	11
Journal of Human Resource	15	yes	3,000	90	no	yes	14	7	12
Journal of Instructional Development	35	yes	1,500	83	yes	yes	14	3	4
Journal of Management	3	yes	1,300	95	no	yes	5	1	12
Journal of Management Development	35	yes	1,000	70	yes	yes	10	10	4
Organizational Dynamics	12	yes	9,500	99	yes	yes	7	1	8
Personnel Administrator	15	yes	5,500	85	no	no	7	1	6
Personnel Journal	10	yes	3,000	80	yes	yes	7	7	11
Psychology Today	15	yes	3,000	90	no	yes	14	7	12
Training & Development Journal	35	yes	1,500	83	yes	yes	14	3	4
Training	3	yes	1,300	95	no	yes	5	1	12

Key: Descriptive: D   Action: A   Causal-Comparative: CC   Quasi-Experimental: Q   Developmental: V   Theoretical Model Building: T   Historical: H   Correlational: C   Experimental: E

Preferred Length of Mss. (# Pages)	Minimum/Maximum Pages	Theme Issues per Year (%)	Articles Reporting Research (%)	Types of Research (see key)	Number of Photocopies	Accept Letter-Quality Printouts	Accept Dot-Matrix Printouts	Effect of Photos on Acceptance
30	10/50	0	100	D, H, A, CC, Q, C, E	5	yes	yes	no
25	1/25	0	100	T	2	yes	no	—
25	15/30	20	50	D, H, CC, C, E, T	3	yes	yes	Psbl 8 × 10
20	10/30	25	95	D, H, A, CC, Q, V, C, E, T	5	yes	no	no
25	—	—	99	E, T, econ, emprcl	5	yes	yes	no
25	15/30	25	25	D, Q, V, T	4	yes	no	no
23	15/25	0	90	D, H, CC Q, C, E, T	3	yes	yes	Psbl 5 × 7
—	—	50	50	D, H, A, V, T	—	yes	—	no
23	—	0	33	D, H, A, CC V, T	2	yes	no	no
10	5/15	100	30	CC, V, C, T	3	yes	no	Lky 5 × 7
12	8/25	0	1	—	1	yes	yes	no
10	—	25	75	E	0	yes	yes	no
15	10/20	0	8	A, Q, E, T	1	yes	yes	no
10	1/5	0	6	D, A, CC, E, T	1	yes	no	Lky 5 × 7

TABLE I.4 Characteristics of Journals of Special Interest to Texas Educators

Name of Publication	Number of Readers	Publication Refereed	Theme Issues	Acceptance Rate (%)	Issues Published per Year	Articles Published per Year	Preferred Length (pages)	Min.-Max. Length	Theme Issues per Year (%)	Welcome Query Letters	Welcome Phone Calls	Disks Acceptable	Weeks Required for Decision	Months Required before Publication	Will Photos Enhance Chances?	Will Tables Enhance Chances?
Centering Teacher Education	750	Yes	Yes	50	1 or 2	8	10	4, 20	75	Yes	Yes	ASCII	12	5	Yes	Yes
The Delta Kappa Gamma Bulletin	162,000	Yes	Yes	15	4	32–40	7–10	—	100	No	No	—	12	4–6	Maybe	Maybe
The Journal of Humanistic Education and Development	2,500	Yes	Yes	34	4	—	12–14	12,24	—	Yes	—	IBM	8–12	8–12	No	No
Record in Educational Leadership	4,000	Yes	Yes	75	2	40	5	No	50	Yes	Yes	IBM, Mac, Apple	12	3–12	Yes	Yes
SRATE Journal	260	Yes	Yes	50	2	8–10	Up to 15	—, 15	50	Yes	Yes	IBM	5	2–3	No	Yes
Teacher Education and Practice	1,000	Yes	No	80	2	10–12	10	—	—	Yes	No	—	6	1.5–6	No	Yes
Teacher Magazine	100,000	No	No	10	10	20–30	3–5	—	—	—	—	All	2–8	2–3	No	No
Teaching K–8	160,000	—	Yes	20	8	80	—	—	75	No	No	Mac	3	6–24	No	No
Teaching Tolerance	300,000	No	No	10	2	14	8–12	—,16	—	Yes	No	Apple	12	3–6	No	—
Texas Lone Star	13,500	—	Rarely	10–15	10	35–40	6–7	2,12	10	Yes	No	Mac	6–8	2.5–4	Yes	No
Texas Study of Secondary Education	4,300	—	Yes	50	2	30–32	6	3, 8	100	Yes	Yes	Mac	Varies	1	No	No

Subject Matter

Name of Publication	Number of Readers	Publication Refereed	Theme Issues	Acceptance Rate (%)	Issues Published per Year	Articles Published per Year	Preferred Length (pages)	Min.-Max. Length	Theme Issues per Year (%)	Welcome Query Letters	Welcome Phone Calls	Disks Acceptable	Weeks Required for Decision	Months Required before Publication	Will Photos Enhance Chances?	Will Tables Enhance Chances?
College English	18,000	Yes	No	12	8	36	20	20 -,40	—	Yes	Yes	All	8	4	No	No
Dance Magazine	65,000	—	Yes	20	12	Many	7	—	10	Yes	Yes	IBM, Mac, Apple	4	Varies	Yes	Yes
Dialog	28,000	No	Yes	90	8	12–16	5	—	10	Yes	No	Mac	8	4–24	Yes	No
East Texas Historical Journal	550	Yes	Yes	50–60	2	5–7	25	—	—	Yes	Yes	Mac	4	6–18	No	No
Entrepreneurship Theory and Practice	1,600	Yes	Yes	15	4	20–30	20–30	—	50	Yes	Yes	—	6–8	6–9	No	Yes
Image	1,200	Yes	Yes	5	4	—	1	—	25	Yes	No	Mac	Varies	Varies	Yes	No
Journal of Educational Issues of Language Minority Students	4,000	Yes	Yes	25–35	3	45	15–20	5, 25	33	Yes	Yes	—	10–12	10–14	No	Yes
Journal of the History of Philosophy	1,600	Yes	Yes	15	4	20	30	—	—	Yes	No	—	12	12	No	No
The Journal of Nutrition	4,500–4,700	Yes	No	50	12	220	—	—	—	Yes	Yes	IBM	12	4	Yes	Yes
Journal of Social Issues	5,700	Yes	Yes	—	4	8–11	—	—	100	Yes	Yes	—	104	5–6	No	Yes
Lamar Journal of the Humanities	400	Yes	No	33	2	8–10	10–20	—	—	Yes	—	IBM	6–8	12–18	No	No
Language and Speech	1,000	Yes	Yes	40	4	16	—	—	10	Yes	Yes	IBM, Mac, Apple	Varies	4–6	No	No

Continued

TABLE I.4 *Continued*

Name of Publication	Number of Readers	Publication Refereed	Theme Issues	Acceptance Rate (%)	Issues Published per Year	Articles Published per Year	Preferred Length (pages)	Min.-Max. Length	Theme Issues per Year (%)	Welcome Query Letters	Welcome Phone Calls	Disks Acceptable	Weeks Required for Decision	Months Required before Publication	Will Photos Enhance Chances?	Will Tables Enhance Chances?
									Subject Matter (continued)							
The Medallion	2,000	No	No	—	6	—	—	—	—	Yes	—	IBM, Mac, Apple	Immediately	2	Yes	No
NATS Journal	6,000	Yes	No	33	5	20	6–15	—, 30	—	Yes	Yes	—	12–24	1–12	No	Varies
Southwestern Historical Quarterly	3,500	Yes	Yes	15	4	16	40	15, 40	25	Yes	Yes	IBM, Mac, Apple	8	3–9	No	No
Southwestern Musician/ Texas Music Educator	9,530	Yes	No	50	10	12–14	3–4	None	—	Yes	Yes	Other	8–12	1–6	No	No
Teaching Sociology	2,000	Yes	Yes	25–50	4	24–32	12–30	—	50	Yes	Yes	IBM, Mac, Apple	7–8	2–6	No	No

TESOL Journal	14,000	Yes	Yes	—	4	20	4–12	4, 12	25	Yes	Yes	IBM	12	Varies	Yes	Yes
TESOL Quarterly	17,000	Yes	Yes	15	4	6	25	—, 35	25	Yes	Yes	IBM, Mac, Apple	12–16	3–6	No	No
Texas Child Care	30,000	Yes	No	50	4	28–32	9–15	—, 18	—	Yes	Yes	IBM, Mac	4–6	6	No	Yes
Texas Coach	12,900	—	No	99	9	250	4	—	—	Yes	Yes	IBM	1	1–5	Yes	Yes
Texas Journal of Political Studies	150	Yes	Yes	25	2	12	20	—	25	Yes	Yes	—	8	1–4	—	Yes
The Texas Journal of Science	900	Yes	No	70	4	60	8–10	—	0	Yes	Yes	—	12	3–6	No	No
Texas Review	750	Yes	No	0.5–1	2	4–5	—	—, 30	—	Yes	Yes	IBM	8	12	No	No
Texas Studies of Literature and Language	840	Yes	Yes	15	4	20	—	17, Varies	25	Yes	Yes	Mac	3–12	1.5–12	No	No
Writing Teacher	4,000	Yes	Yes	20	5	30–40	10–12	—	100	Yes	Yes	IBM, Mac	8–12	2–18	No	No

Key: — = No response.

TABLE I.5 Characteristics of Selected HPERD Journals

Journals	Issues per Year	Total Circulation	Unsolicited Manuscripts Received Annually	Manuscripts Published Annually	Acceptance Rate (%)	% of Mss. Not Requiring Revisions	% of Revised Mss. Accepted	Status as Refereed Journal	Double-Blind Review of Ms.	Average Decision Time, Submission to Author Notification in Weeks	Average Time, Acceptance to Publication in Months	Preferred Length in Ms. Pages	Abstract Required	Letters of Inquiry Encouraged	Required Style
Adapted Physical Activity Quarterly	4	—	90	Varies	50	0	100	Yes	Yes	—	—	—	Yes	Yes	APA
Aethlon: The Journal of Sport Literature	2	550	75	10	15	0	75	Yes	Yes	16	12	—	No	Yes	PMLA
American Journal of Health Promotion	4	6,600	90	22	—	0	80	Yes	Yes	6	3	15–25	Yes	Yes	Chicago
American Journal of Public Health	12	35,000	1,000	150–200	15–20	0	20	Yes	Yes	6–8	6	15	Yes	No	AMA
Canadian AHPER Journal	6	1,800	30–40	36	55–60	65	90	Yes	Yes	8–12	6–12	8–10	No	Yes	APA
Canadian Journal of History of Sport	2	500	30	8	25	20	50	Yes	Yes	16	6	—	Yes	Yes	—
Clinical Kinesiology	4	1,500	40–48	16–20	65–70	10	85	Yes	Yes	20	9–12	—	Yes	No	APA
Health Education	6	9,000	350	70–80	20	60	80	Yes	Yes	6	8	8–10	Yes	Yes	APA
Health Education Journal	4	5,000	200	50	25	15	75	Yes	Yes	4	3	10	Yes	Yes	Harvard
Health Education Quarterly	4	2,500	—	—	—	—	—	Yes	Yes	12	8	20	Yes	No	AMA
Health Values: Achieving High Level Wellness	6	1,400	110	48	45	10	75–90	Yes	Yes	8	6	12–20	Yes	Yes	AMA
Hygie: Intl. Journal of Health Education	4	4,000	40	20	50	5	80	Yes	Yes	24	12	15	Yes	Yes	Similar to AMA
International Journal of Sport Biomechanics	4	850	60–70	32	49	12	60	Yes	Yes	8	2–3	20	No	Yes	APA
International Journal of Sport Psychology	4	1,000	60	26	30–40	7	30	Yes	Yes	24–32	2	15	Yes	Yes	APA
International Journal of Sports Medicine	6	1,200	150–200	80	55	5	50	Yes	Yes	4–8	5–12	9–15	Yes	Yes	Scientific English

Journal														
Journal of American College Health	6	2,575	100	60	60	0	35–45	Yes	Yes	16	12	10–15	Yes	Yes	AMA
Journal of Applied Research in Coaching & Athletics	4	—	100	20	20	2	90	Yes	Yes	48	6	50	Yes	Yes	Chicago
Journal of Applied Sports Science Research	4	5,500	80–100	16–20	30–35	10	25	Yes	Yes	8	1–2	—	Yes	No	APA
Journal of Leisure Research	4	1,800	50+	20–25	20	0	90	Yes	Yes	14	10	20	Yes	No	APA
Journal of Motor Behavior	4	1,200	50–60	20	40	10	90–95	Yes	No	14	6	20–25	Yes	No	APA
Journal of Park and Recreation Administration	4	850	49	24	60	0	50	Yes	Yes	8	6	10	Yes	No	APA
Journal of Physical Education, Recreation & Dance	9	28,000	235	153	25	10	90	Yes	Yes	16	12	7–12	No	Yes	APA
Journal of School Health	10	8,000	200	75	30	25	90	Yes	Yes	8–12	4–6	10–12	Yes	No	AMA
Journal of Sport and Exercise Psychology	4	2,042	120	27	25	1	80	Yes	Yes	9	6	25	Yes	No	APA
Journal of Sport Behavior	4	600	100	20–25	28	5	90	Yes	Yes	8	9	12	Yes	Yes	APA
Journal of Sport History	3	850	35	10	29	10	50	Yes	Yes	6–8	9	26	No	Yes	Chicago
Journal of Sport and Social Issues	2	425	39	8–10	18	50	80	Yes	Yes	12	10	20	Yes	Yes	APA
Journal of Sport Management	2	550	25–30	10–12	40–50	0	95	Yes	No	10–12	Varies	30	Yes	No	APA
Journal of Sport Sciences	3	600	100	20	25	1	80	Yes	Yes	10	4	5–40	Yes	No	Harvard
Journal of Swimming Research	4	3,000	75	16	20	0	100	Yes	Yes	4	1	4	Yes	No	APA
Journal of Teaching in Physical Education	4	700+	80+	20	20	0	60	Yes	Yes	12	6	30	Yes	Yes	APA
Journal of the International Council for HPER	4	2,000	—	—	—	—	—	Yes	Yes	6–8	—	6–20	No	Yes	No Set Style
Journal of the Philosophy of Sport	1	550	35	12	30	20	80	Yes	No	8	Varies	10–14	No	Yes	Chicago
Palaestra: The Forum of Sport, Physical Education and Recreation for the Disabled	4	5,000	50–60	45	60–70	5	85	Yes	—	4–12	3–12	6–8	Yes	Yes	APA
Parks and Recreation	12	22,000	36–50	60–65	55	1–5	85	No	No	8–24	3–8	8–12	No	No	Chicago
Perceptual and Motor Skills	6	2,000	1,500	350–400	25	2–5	30	Yes	No	3–4	2	—	Yes	Yes	APA
Physical Education Review	2	440	20–25	12–16	60	50	90	Yes	No	8–12	12	20–25	Yes	Yes	No Set Style
Play and Culture	4	300	40	30	56	0	92	Yes	Yes	8	5	20–30	Yes	Yes	APA
Quest	3	700	50	20–30	30–40	0	30–40	Yes	Yes	24–28	3	25–30	Yes	No	APA
Research Quarterly for Exercise and Sport	4	9,000+	300	40–60	25	0	25	Yes	Yes	2–12	8–11	24	Yes	Yes	APA
Sociology of Sport Journal	4	750+	110	24–28	20–25	1–3	20–25	Yes	Yes	6–8	6–9	16–30	Yes	Yes	APA
Strategies: A Journal for Sport and Physical Educators	6	6,000	100	48	50	—	—	Yes	Yes	8	3	10	No	Yes	No Set Style
The Physical Educator	4	5,000	80–85	40–44	50	75–80	75	Yes	Yes	6–8	10–12	10–18	Yes	Yes	APA
The Sport Psychologist	4	675	70	20–25	30	0	80	Yes	Yes	16	6	15–20	Yes	No	APA

TABLE I.6 *Publishing Requirements in Educational Communications, Technology, and Library Science Journals and Magazines*

	Issues a Year	Theme Issues	Articles a Year	Theme Announced	% Research Based	Readership	Refereed
AI Magazine	4	1	16	Winter	80	17,000	L
Artificial Intelligence	12	2	50	1 Yr	98	5000	Na
Byte	12	12	150	6–12 M		500,000	N
Classroom Computer Learning	8		30–35	June		83,000	N
Collegiate Microcomputer	4		50–70		50	1500	Na
Communication Research	6	2	35	1–1½ Yr	85–90	2000	Na
Compute	12		70–80	1 Yr	80	110,000	In
Computers and Education: An International Journal	6	1	24–36	Selected from CAL Conference	100	1700	Na/In
Computers in the Schools	4	1	40	3 M		2000	Na
Distance Education	2	1 in 4	10	18 M	60	100,000	In
EDUCOM Bulletin Review	4	1–2	30	Not announced	25	15,000	Y
Education and Computing	4	V	40–50	Not announced	50		In
Educational and Training Technology International	4		10–12	1 Yr	30–50	2500	L
Educational Horizons	4	4	50	Every two years		15,000	Y
Educational Leadership	8	8	150	Mar., Apr., May	15	135,000	Na
Educational Researcher	9	1	25–30	On occasion	10	16,000	Na
Educational Technology	12	V	100	On occasion	V	50,000	N
Educational Technology Research and Development	4		40		50	4000	Na
Electronic Learning	8		80		10	85,000	N
IBM Journal of Research and Development	6	4	64	1½ Yr	80	50,000	Na
InCider	12		36			200,000	N
Information Technology and Libraries	4		12		60	7000	Na
Journal of Academic Librarianship	6		36		40	12,000	Na
Journal of Artificial Intelligence in Education	4		48		38	5000	Y
Journal of Broadcasting and Electronic Media	4	V	27	1 Yr	80	2500	Na
Journal of Communication	4	2–3	30–35	1 Yr	100	4000	Na
Journal of Computer Assisted Learning	4	V	20		80	1000	Na
Journal of Computer Based Instruction	4	V	20–25	Not announced	70	2300	Na/In
Journal of Computers in Mathematics and Science Teaching	4		48		38	5000	Y
Journal of Computing in Childhood Education	4		48		38	5000	Y
Journal of Education for Library and Information Science	5	V	16	Not announced	16	1800	Na
Journal of Educational Psychology	4					4300	Y
Journal of Educational Research	6		48		100	3500	Na
Journal of Educational Techniques and Technologies	4	1	6+	Winter	10–15	1000	In

Refereed	Anonymous	Rating Scale	Query Letter	Query Phone	Publication Style	Page Length**	Copies to Submit	Receipt of Paper	% Accepted	Decision Time	Publication Time
Y	N		Y	Y		10–15	1	1–2 W	25	1–10 M	6 M
Y	Y		N	N	House	30	3	1 M	30	6 M	6 M
			Y	N	House	3000 Wds	1	2 W	1–2	6–8 W	2–6 M
			Y	Y	House	1000–3000 Wds	1	6 W	50	6 W	V
Y	N		Y	Y	House	None	3	1 W	60	12–14 W	3–6 M
*	Y	Y	Y	Y	APA	25–30	3	2 W	10	8 W	5–6 M
Y	Y	Y	Y	Y	Chicago	25–35	8	2 W	20	2–3 M	3–6 M
Y	Y		Y	Y	House	None	3	2 W	25–50	3–4 M	6 M
Y	Y		N	N	APA	15–20	3	3 W	30	3 M	12 M
Y	Y			Y	APA	10,000 Wds	2	1 M	50	9 M	3 M
Y	Y	Y	Y	Y	Chicago	3000 Wds	1	1–9 W	20	1–9 M	4–6 M
Y	Y		N	Y	House	10	4	S		2–3 M	3–6 M
Y	N		Y	Y		300 Wds	2	1–3 W	50	2–3 M	2–6 M
Y	Y	Y	Y	Y	Chicago	10	3	1 W	5	3–6 M	3–18 M
Y	Y		N	Y	Chicago	8–10	2	1 W	15	2 W–mths	6 M
Y	Y		N	Y	APA	15–20	4	1–2 W	10–15	6 W	2 M
N	N		N	Y	House	10–15	2	1 W	33	2 W	3–6 M
Y	Y		N	Y	APA	10–25	4	1 W	20	2–4 M	3–4 M
			Y	Y	House	5–6	2	1–2 M	5	1–2 M	1–3 M
Y	Y					V	2	S	50	1–2 M	5 M
			Y	Y	AP	10	1	1 W	10	1–3 M	6 M
Y	N		Y	Y	Chicago	20	2	1 W	60	6 W	3 M
Y	N		Y	Y	Chicago	12–25	2	1 W	35	1–3 M	2–12 M
Y	Y		N	Y	Chicago	10–25	3	2 W	20	2 M	8–12 M
Y	N		N	Y	APA	25–30	4	5 D	10–15	3 M	3–6 M
Y	N		N	N	Chicago	25–30	3	2 W	15	3–6 M	6 M
Y	Y		N	Y		3000 Wds	2	S	40	2 M	6 M
*	Y		N	Y	House	21	4	None	18	8 W	9 M
Y	Y		N	Y	Chicago	10–15	3	2 W	20	2 M	8–12 W
Y	Y		N	Y	Chicago	10–15	3	2 W	20	2 M	8–12 M
Y	Y		N	Y	Chicago	20	3	1 D	60	2–4 M	1½ Y
Y					APA	6	4		24	7 M	5–6 M
N	Y			Y	APA		2	2 W	33	2–3 M	2–6 M
Y	Y		N	Y	APA	12–15	3	2 D	10–15	1–2 M	1–2 M

Continued

TABLE I.6 *Continued*

	Issues a Year	Theme Issues	Articles a Year	Theme Announced	% Research Based	Readership	Refereed
Journal of Film and Video	4	V	12–18	V	90–10	2000	Na
Journal of Information Science	6		36		75	3500	In
Journal of Photographic Science	6		50+		100	2000	Na
Journal of Special Education Technology	4					1800	Na
Library and Information Science Research	4		20		95	514	Na/In
Library Resources and Technical Services	4		20+		16+	9000	Na
Mathematics and Computer Education	3		30		None	3000	Na
Media and Methods	5	2	40	6 M	None	41,000	N
New Directions for Continuing Education	4	4	35–40	Invited	20		N
Online Magazine	6		130		75	5800	N
Online Review	6	V	24		50		In
Optical Information Systems	6	3	60	Middle of year	50	2500	L
Performance and Instruction	10		120		10	6000	Na
Personal Computing	12	1	60	Not announced	100	525,000	
Phi Delta Kappan	10		150		75	150,000	N
Research in Science and Technology Education	2		18		100		Na/In
School Library Media Activities Monthly	10		30–40		20	8000	N
School Library Media Quarterly	4	V	12–16	Invited	50	8000	Na
Simulation and Games	4	V	25	6–12 M	75	1500+	Na/In
TechTrends for Leaders in Education and Training	6	6	40–45	April	10	10,000	Na
Technology and Culture	4		12–16		100	3000	Na/In
The American Journal of Distance Education	3	1–3	15–18	3–6M	50	1000	Na
The Computing Teacher	9	4–5	100+	Fall	50	12,000	In
The Library Quarterly	4		12–15		75	3000	Na
Training and Development Journal	12		120		20	30,000	Na

Key:
D = Day	N = No	V = Varies	Y = Yes	** = Double spaced pages
In = International	Na = National	w = Week(s)	Yr = Year(s)	
M = Month(s)	S = Sent same day	Wds = Words	* = Upon request	

Refereed Anonymous	Rating Scale	Query Letter	Query Phone	Publication Style	Page Length**	Copies to Submit	Receipt of Paper	% Accepted	Decision Time	Publication Time
Y	N	Y	Y	MLA	None	3	V		V	2–5 M
Y	Y	Y	N	House	25	3	5D	50–60	1 M	4–6M
N	N	N	Y			3	2–3D	98	2 W–6 M	2 M
Y	Y			APA		4			3.5–4.5 M	
Y	N	N	Y	APA	None	3	1 W	70	5–7 W	3–6 M
Y	Y	N	Y	Chicago	10–15	3	1 W	50	2 M	V
Y	N	N	N	House	2–10	6	Several W	30	6–8 M	3 M
		Y	Y		4–5	1	2 M	5		2 M
		Y	Y	House	12–25	2				
		Y	Y	House	5–10	3	1 W	85	2–3 W	3 M
Y	Y	N	Y	House		3	2 W	35–45	3–4 M	6 M
Y	N	Y	Y	APA	15–20	2	1–2 W	75	2 W	3 M
N	N	N	Y	APA	10	3	2–4 W	60	2–3 M	3–6 M
		Y	N		2500 W	1	1–3 W	5	1–3 W	4 M
		N	Y	Chicago	15	1	3 D	5	8 W	1–12 M
Y	Y	Y	Y		11–12	2	1 D	50	2–3 M	6–12 M
		N	Y	Chicago		2	1–4 W	0	1–6 W	2–8 M
Y	Y	Y	N	House	12–20	2	2 W	20	2–3 M	2–6 M
Y	Y	Y	Y	House	30	3	2 W	40	6–8 W	6 M
Y	N	Y	Y		5–20	3	2 W	25	2–3 M	4–6 M
Y	Y	N	Y	Chicago	40	3	1 W	30	6 M	15 M
Y		Y	Y	Chicago	8	3	1–2 W	50	3–6 M	3–6 M
Y	Y	Y	Y	APA	1200 W	2	1–3 W	45–50	3–6 M	1–3 M
Y	Y	N	Y	Chicago	40	3	2 W	25	6–8 W	7–10 M
Y	Y	Y	Y	Chicago	10–20	2	1 W	20	2 M	3–6 M

TABLE I.7   *Fields of Interest and Publishers' Suggestions*

Journals	Fields of Interest	Publishers' Suggestions
AI Magazine	Artificial Intelligence	*R
Artificial Intelligence	Artificial Intelligence	
Byte	Personal computers, hardware, software, and new technology	*R, *G
Classroom Computer Learning	Technology in K–12 education	Keep in mind that *Classroom Computer Learning* is for K–12 teachers and administrators who are already quite familiar and comfortable using technology.
Collegiate Microcomputer	Use of microcomputers in all areas of higher education	*R
Communication Research	Communication processes across all human social systems, including political, international, mass, organization, family, interpersonal and other communication systems	Acceptance Criteria: 1. Contribution to theory, 2. Research tests theory, 3. New development in method, 4. Quality of writing
Computer	Computer science and engineering	*R
Computers and Education: An International Journal	Use of computers in all levels of education	*G
Computers in the Schools	Educational computing K–12, Higher education	*I
Distance Education	Distance education, external studies, independent learning, adult education, correspondence education, and off-campus education	Present manuscript in journal style. Show evidence of wide knowledge of literature and comparative experience with other institutions and cultures. Voluminous citations are not necessarily evidence of the above qualities.
EDUCOM Bulletin Review	Computing policy making and planning, telecommunication	*C
Education and Computing	Education; computing	*C
Educational and Training Technology International	Educational technology; learning; new technologies	*C
Educational Horizons	Education	Read journal. Write to practicing teachers. Use only as many citations as really necessary, no more than 25.
Educational Leadership	Curriculum, supervision, instruction, and leadership	
Educational Researcher	Educational research	*R
Educational Technology	The complete field of educational technology	*R
Educational Technology Research and Development	Instructional development, effective instruction, computer applications, IAV, media selection and utilization	
Electronic Learning	K–12, college, all curriculum areas	*C, We do not accept many unsolicited articles, but please try anyway—you never know! Jon Goodspeed, Editor, (212) 505-3051

Journals	Fields of Interest	Publishers' Suggestions
IBM Journal of Research and Development	Math, engineering, physics, computers	*G
InCider	Apple II computers	*C
Information Technology and Libraries	Library automation; advanced technology in libraries	Try to take a research orientation.
Journal of Academic Librarianship		Double-space manuscripts and follow the Chicago format for references.
Journal of Artificial Intelligence in Education	Computing educators in general	
Journal of Broadcasting and Electronic Media	Mass communication; broadcasting	
Journal of Communication	Communication media; new technologies	*R
Journal of Computer Assisted Learning	Research; evaluation; use of computers to support learning	Do not make unjustified claims.
Journal of Computer Based Instruction	Computer use for direct instruction in all areas of education, and subject areas	*G, send self-addressed stamped envelope.
Journal of Computers in Mathematics and Science Teaching	Science and math educators	
Journal of Computing in Childhood Education	Childhood education	
Journal of Education for Library and Information Science	Library and information science education	All manuscripts are to be sent to the editor: Rosemary Ruhig DuMont, School of Library Science, Kent State University, Kent, OH, 44242.
Journal of Educational Psychology	Learning and cognition; psychological development relationships and individual related to instruction	
Journal of Educational Research	Research in elementary and secondary schools	Follow APA style; focus on variables that can be manipulated in educational settings.
Journal of Educational Techniques and Technologies	Native, foreign, second language teaching and learning; technology in language teaching and learning	Please use the APA style manual or Pergamon Press's Manuscript Manager—APA software.
Journal of Film and Video	Film and video media	
Journal of Information Science	Information science	
Journal of Photographic Science	Imaging, science, physics, chemistry, photography	*R
Journal of Special Education Technology	Research and theory, applied technology, product reports, and brief reports of technology projects	*G
Library and Information Science Research	Citation analysis, research in public, academic schools, and special libraries	
Library Resources and Technical Services	Cataloging, preservation, collection development, and reproduction of library materials	*I, Write clearly and directly; acknowledge the work of others appropriately; be original.

Continued

TABLE I.7 *Continued*

Journals	Fields of Interest	Publishers' Suggestions
Mathematics and Computer Education	Mathematics and computer education in colleges	
Media and Methods	Technology in education	We are an application oriented magazine. No academic articles; straightforward journalistic style
New Directions for Continuing Education	This is a sourcebook. Current trends and innovative practices in the broad field of adult and continuing education	Chapters are commissioned, not accepted.
Online Magazine	Online database searching	*C
Online Review	Information science, information retrieval, library science	
Optical Information Systems	CD-I, interactive videodisc, CD-Rom, WORM and rewritable disks, R & D, applications and integration	Prefer thoughtful essays as related to various optical technologies rather than an article which offers no insight into efforts.
Performance and Instruction	Performance technology and instructional technology	*R, *G, send self-addressed stamped envelope; write well. Good, readable prose impresses us all out of proportion to its importance.
Personal Computing	Using PCs as a tool in the business environment	
Phi Delta Kappan	Policy issues, research findings, trends in U.S. education, K–12 and postsecondary	*R
Research in Science and Technology Education	Science education; science teaching curriculum evaluation; technological education	Articles must be of an empirical nature. We will consider both quantitative and ethnographic types of research.
School Library Media Activities Monthly	School library media, K–8, curriculum and instruction	
School Library Media Quarterly	School library media programs, information skills	*G, 1. Writing should be lively and readable. 2. If research based, the research should be solid and it should be written up so that it is understandable to nonresearchers as well as other researchers. 3. Articles are welcomed which are theory, issue, or research based, but which demonstrate how to put the ideas into practice in a school library media program.
Simulation and Games	Academic and applied issues in simulation, computerized simulation, gaming, modeling, role-playing, etc.	*G, New ideas and interdisciplinary endeavors are particularly welcome.
TechTrends for Leaders in Education and Training	Educational applications of the newest technologies to the learning process	Write in clear, conversational style about practical things you are thinking and doing. TechTrends features articles of popular interest.
Technology and Culture	History of technology as it relates to politics, economics, labor, business, the environment, public policy, etc.	*I, *G

Journals	Fields of Interest	Publishers' Suggestions
The American Journal of Distance Education	Distance education	*R, *G
The Computing Teacher	Practical ideas a computer using educator can utilize right now for a subject area in the classroom or lab	*G
The Library Quarterly	Research and discussion in library science and related fields including communication, service to children	*I
Training and Development Journal	Current training and human resource practices, new theories and application, controversial issues and business trends affecting HRD	We are a magazine, not an academic journal. Write in an interesting, readable style. Academic research and theories are O.K., but only if described in a compelling way and related to practical, concrete, and specific application in the HRD field. Always keep the reader in mind, and give them information that will help them on the job. No footnotes! If you must use references, incorporate them into the text.

Key: *C = Contact journal first
*G = Send for publishing guide
*I = Publishing criteria in journal
*R = Become familiar with the style of the journal

Appendix J

Sample Journal Article

The last Promising Practice reports on a "teacher-in-residence" program in Alabama that is beneficial for all those involved.

The Teacher-in-Residence
Partnership Program

Introduction

The central theme of the commission reports and task force studies has been that we must improve the quality of education. These reports have not prescribed standardized answers, but they have encouraged entrepreneurship at the state and local levels. Collaborative efforts and programs have been initiated to lubricate the wheels of progress. These include programs between state and federal levels, schools and communities, businesses and schools, and colleges and schools. The focus of this "Promising Practice" is on a partnership program among the Tuscaloosa City School System, the Tuscaloosa County School System, and The University of Alabama's College of Education.

The program, titled "Teacher-in-Residence (TIR) Partnership Program," involves two outstanding classroom teachers selected to serve as regular full-time faculty members in the College of Education's Early Childhood and Elementary Education undergraduate teacher preparation programs.

Planning sessions were held between the two superintendents of the LEA's, the Dean of the College of Education (Dr. Rod Roth), the Head of Curriculum and Instruction, and the Chairperson of Early Childhood and Elementary Education. After approval from the appropriate boards, the following guidelines were instituted.

Fellows

An outstanding primary (1–3) grade teacher would be cooperatively selected from the County school system and an outstanding intermediate (4–6) level teacher would be selected from the City school system. The TIR Fellows would serve as faculty members with the University in a fashion similar to an adjunct or visiting professor.

Qualifications

The following objective requirements were set: current classroom teaching experience at the designated grade levels; tenure in the respective school systems; and a master's degree. Additionally, affective qualifications included the ability to work with university students and faculty, and a positive and enthusiastic manner.

Selection

In June of 1985, teachers in the two participating school systems were sent letters of notification regarding the program. Interested candidates were asked to submit to their Superintendent's Office an application, a one-page statement of educational philosophy, and any additional facts which might favorably influence their selection. The Assistant Superintendents for Personnel (Dr. Nora Price for the City system and Dr. Sydney Poellnitz for the County system) and the Chairpersons of Elementary Education reviewed the applications and selected finalists. The Area Head of Curriculum and Instruction and the Chairperson conducted the final interviews during July. In future cycles of the program the selection process will be conducted during the spring to allow greater transition time.

Duration

The TIR positions are for one academic year and are renewable for a second year upon mutual agreement. Teachers serving two years as a Fellow are guaranteed a return to the same school and grade level from which they left. The two-year time frame was selected as the optimal time length because of the breadth of learning that would be required of the Fellows. A period of time less than two years would reflect more of a novelty approach rather than a sustaining program. The school systems agreed to reverse the primary and intermediate levels of the teachers for the next cycle of the program in 1987.

Salary

The University contracts with the respective school systems for the services of the teachers. The Fellows' salary and benefits will continue in accordance with their permanent positions. Salary checks are issued by the participating school systems. This program was not designed to save money by hiring non-doctoral personnel for the University. The teachers' regular salary exceeds the salaries that would be paid to starting assistant professors on nine-month contracts. If the Fellows choose to teach during summer school, their salaries will be paid directly by the University on a visiting professor basis.

Schedule and Assignments

During the Teacher-in-Residence Program, the Fellows follow the annual and daily University schedule as do regular University faculty members.

Their assignments revolve around a 12 semester-hour core of teaching undergraduate courses. Regular faculty teach 9 semester hours, generally including at least one graduate course, and are assigned 3 semester hours of research and publication time. The Fellows also serve on program committees, advise students, have voting power on departmental issues (excluding promotion and tenure), and generally function in the same manner as regular faculty members. They enjoy having equal status with other full-time faculty members as is reflected in one of the TIRs, Mrs. JoAnn Schweer's, comments: "The opportunity to be chosen as a participant in this program has been a highlight of my teaching career."

Evaluation

Fellows serve as members of the Early Childhood and Elementary Education Program and report directly to the program Chairperson. An annual evaluation of the Fellows will be completed by the Chairperson and shared with the participants, the Area Head of Curriculum and Instruction and the LEA Superintendents. The school systems will meet annually with the Fellows to go over the reports and to assess the quality of the program.

Advantages

The advantages of this program are numerous. The Fellows have the opportunity to experience new, invigorating roles. Mrs. Schweer has observed, "I anticipated the University staff being cautious about my participating; but in reality, I experienced complete cooperation and acceptance." Both Mrs. Schweer and Mrs. Nancy Rogers have expressed their interest in gaining a firsthand understanding of the program philosophy, objectives, and sequencing. Additionally, they have the satisfaction of directly influencing future teachers. Mrs. Rogers observed, "I believe that because of my everyday classroom teaching experiences. I can personalize and bring to life methods and procedures that might otherwise seem only theory."

Upon completion of the program, the school systems gain teachers who have had experiences that will be invaluable in helping them to plan and institutionalize inservice programs. Both school systems employ many University of Alabama graduates. Having their own teachers directly participating in the preparation program significantly increases the sense of joint ownership in the task of preparing new teachers for the profession.

Index